CONTENTS

	Dedications/Acknowledgments	vii
Chapter 1	Shapes	1
Chapter 2	The Body	17
Chapter 3	Color	35
Chapter 4	Lighting	47
Chapter 5	Tech Stuff	59
Chapter 6	Foundations	67
Chapter 7	Beauty and Basics	83
Chapter 8	Design	111
Chapter 9	Hair	133
Chapter 10	Airbrush	155
Chapter 11	Effects	179
Chapter 12	How to Be a Pro	217
	Cosmetics, Tools, Labs, and Effects	247
	The Crew	253
	Glossary	257
	Professional Library	263
	The Pros	265
	Unions	273
	Index	275

FOR ALL MAKEUP ARTISTS, EVERYWHERE

DEDICATIONS

This book is dedicated to my husband John, who has always supported me. To my family, whose artistic abilities never cease to amaze me: Mom, Dad, Son, and Sisters. To my friend and colleague Yvette, who can make me laugh no matter where we are.

And of course who can forget Max?

—Gretchen Davis

ACKNOWLEDGMENTS

This book could not have happened without "The Pros," our amazing friends and colleagues who shared their talents and expertise, their time and valuable contributions to this text. They made this happen though crazy schedules, numerous locations, countries, time zones, and ridiculous work hours to contribute. They are true artists who recognize the need to share our craft.

Tremendous thanks to Darla Albright, Gary Archer, Mary Birchler, Fred Blau, Christine Patterson Ceret, Debra Coleman, Richard Dean, Ken Diaz, Daniela Eschbacher, Kris Evans, Kim Felix-Burke, Dan Gheno, Steven Horak, Don Jusko, Erwin H. Kupitz, Bradley M. Look, Gerd Mairandres, Randy Huston Mercer, Gil Mosko, Matthew Mungle, Kenny Meyers, Dina Ousley, Susan Stone, Joseph N. Tawil, Christien Tinsley, Nancy Tozier, Jenny King Turko, Paul Wheeler, and Patty York.

Unending thanks to S. E. Radich for your undying support, tireless hard work, and flawless organization of this book and its content. You kept it all together, again though several locations, time zones, and countries. Without you, there would be no "input" of text and no coordination of crazy schedules and deadlines! We could not have done it without you.

Thank you Academy of Art University filmmaker and innovator David Oliver Pfeil, who first approached Gretchen about starting a Makeup Program for the school. Without his vision of the importance that Makeup has within the Film Department and as an art form, students would not have had the opportunity to experience and witness what a career as a Makeup Artist could be. Along with David, thank you to Dan Burns and Jack Isgro for their support in the success of the Makeup Program. Jack, your input to the publisher made this book happen. Many thanks to Elisa Stephens who encourages instructors to teach students how it really is in the working world.

Much love and gratitute to our families, friends and mentors who have cheered us on and guided us through this journey, and lastly to all those actors who have allowed us into their world, face to face for countless hours to do "that thing we do". We could not do it with out you.

Thank you.

—Gretchen Davis & Mindy Hall

"Most civilians—people who don't make movies for a living—think makeup men are little more than hovering sprites who powder noses. But they are true artists, often unsung, who imprint film with the soft touch of their brushes and the hard work of their craft.

"The Man Who Aged Me" by Tom Hanks

Article Published in the New York Times, April 27, 2006

This journey started for us when the folks at Focal Press noticed that there was a need for an updated makeup book. Writing about what we do, why we do it, and how we do it, seemed necessary, challenging, and a great way to pass on the artistry and craft of being a freelance Makeup Artist. We were in! Ultimately, the decision was easy. Thinking back, there were too many times when we hired or worked with newcomers who were unprepared for the experience. And in our teaching and lecturing to students we would hear the same misconceptions and questions. We have repeated the same lessons to each newcomer over the years, and were recognizing an emerging pattern in the lack of knowledge and understanding from the students. There was a pattern to earlier books on the subject of makeup, and although they were beautifully photographed and illustrated they did not address all the skills, knowledge, and protocol that is needed for your first day on the job. These books were providing the very basic steps (sometimes outdated) to do makeup, but they were not preparing the student for being on set or working in a makeup trailer. Some of the best lessons come from practical experience working for and with professionals. Getting a job and being asked back is crucial to the extended learning process (or apprenticeship) that every newcomer needs.

We felt a need to illustrate more than one viewpoint and expose the student to variety. Learning from one standpoint puts the student at a disadvantage. There are countless ways to go about creating and applying makeup so we include examples from different artists to help you to develop your instincts and hand. Intentionally there are sections in the book that do not give step-by-step instructions. This gives you the practical experience of working it out on your own and "thinking on your feet." It was also clear that students were lacking in the fundamentals of color theory, color mixing, lighting, anatomy, technical information, and HDTV. We use this knowledge every time we apply a makeup, and found most beginners did not realize the importance of understanding all the elements that affect their work, as well as understanding the working environment.

Lastly, be assured that all product reference, noted Industry Standards, and techniques in the book are real examples of a Makeup Artist's kit and what techniques are used in the field. These lists are a culmination of our more than 25 years of experience, our interviews with Makeup Artists in all mediums, and, without bias or favoritism, we share them with you because of our proven success in using them. We were not paid promotional or endorsement fees by any company or individual. This is an international community; sharing product information and techniques are all part of the lessons learned and communicated with each other through our travels.

SHAPES

I

PROPORTIONS OF THE FACE AND BODY IN ART

An important lesson for Makeup Artists in all areas of makeup is how to correctly determine proportions, shapes, and anatomical structure of the face and body. Makeup Artists are masters at the illusion and manipulation of different shapes and features of the face and the body for makeup designs. Painting and drawing skills will give you the ability to understand and use makeup as an art form. The study of anatomy drawing will teach you, for example, individual skeletal or muscular size, shapes, and functions. "Anatomy is an applied science which underpins fine art, the study of structure is essential for artistic representation. The skeleton, joints and muscular system of a creature determine its proportions and the movement of the body" (Fehér, 7). There are certain fundamental drawing skills that teach you value, form, light, and shadows, as well as how these elements fall onto the surface of the face and body. Proportions play an important role for realism and how a body is drawn so as to appear in motion.

VALUE, SHADOW, AND LIGHT

by Dan Gheno

Includes information presented in a recent article in *Drawing* magazine. The study of values is a complicated subject. When trying to draw in a tonal manner, it helps your ability to see value changes on the model if you learn the terminology of the subject.

Values: Each object, whether simple like a sphere or complex like the human figure, is composed of millions of tonal "value" changes. These range from the brightest

bright (where the object most directly faces the light) to the darkest dark (where the object is turned away from the light source).

Halftones: A generic term that refers to all of the value variations within the light side of the model. The halftones are brightest where the form turns most directly toward the light source, and are darkest just before the form falls into complete shadow.

Dark and Light Halftones: To keep things simple, artists should class their halftones into two different categories: "light halftones" and "dark halftones." Things can go wrong if these two types aren't kept separate. Some artists make all of their halftones equally dark, creating muddy-looking drawings, while others insist on making their halftones equally bright, creating washed-out drawings. Notice in the Watcher picture (Figure 1.1) that the halftone shapes are distinctly lighter on the side of the forehead most directly facing

FIGURE 1-1: THE WATCHER, WOMAN

the light source, while they arc dramatically darker near the shadow shapes on the forehead. Try squinting to test the validity of the value renditions. When you squint, the light halftones should fade away and disappear into the overall light shape, while the dark halftones should visually melt into the adjacent, general shadow shapes.

Shadow: As the form of the model turns completely away from the light source, the dark halftone shapes get darker and darker, until the light completely terminates and the big shadow shape begins. Literally called the "terminator" by those who deal with light as a science, this shadow edge can look abrupt and contrasty at times, or soft and fused at other times. It all depends upon the amount of reflected light bouncing into the shadow side of the model.

Reflected Light: Shadows are simply the absence of light. The only reason anything can be seen within the shadow shape is because of reflected light. The light source illuminates not just the model, but also the surrounding environment. The light bounces off the walls, floor, and ceiling, ricocheting into the shadows, and lighting (or filling) the dark side of the model. Indeed, even various body parts reflect light onto the other shadowed parts of the model. One very important rule to know: no reflected light in the shadow shape can be as bright as the direct light hitting the model.

Core Shadow: When the dark side of the face turns away from any source of reflected light, the shadow gradually darkens until the darkest part of the shadow, called the "core shadow," is reached. This term refers to an area of the form that gets no direct light and

very little reflected light. Even when drawn subtly or in a barely visible manner, the core shadow creates a cornering effect that helps to magnify the plane changes of the model.

PRO TIP

Makeup Artists are often asked to match a likeness from a real person to an actor, or from one actor to another actor (photo double), or from actor to stunt person. These are some examples of many different situations for a Makeup Artist where shadow shapes and their placement on the face is important.

Movement of the Head: To determine the correct proportions of facial features when the head has moved in different angles, use the vertical and horizontal axes. The centerline is the vertical axis. This line determines the movements determires made by the face from side to side. The horizontal axis defines the brow line.

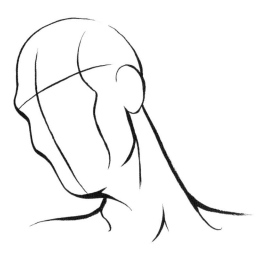

FIGURE 1-2: THE HORIZONTAL AND VERTICAL AXES

3

If the human head is turned in any direction, the main vertical and horizontal axes become elliptical curves.

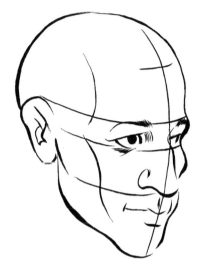

FIGURE 1-3: ELLIPTICAL CURVES

If you were to turn in any direction, the parallel horizontal lines become parallel elliptical curves.

Body and face measurements help the artist correctly achieve the right proportions. Artist Leonardo da Vinci calculated the parts of the body that could be used as units, and was the first to adapt the head for units of measurement. He used the length of the face, but not the length of the whole head. His methods are still in use today.

PROPORTIONS FOR THE FACE AND BODY

by Don Jusko

The skull is the basic division of the human body. To draw the head, start with an oval (3×4). Divide the head into three parts:

1. Top of the skull
2. Pupils are the middle.
3. Bottom of the nose to the bottom of the chin

Add the lips a third of the way down, below the nose. Add the chin crease below the nose.

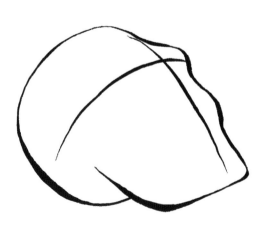

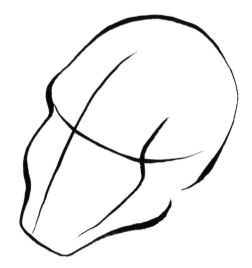

FIGURE 1-4: PARALLEL ELLIPTICAL CURVES

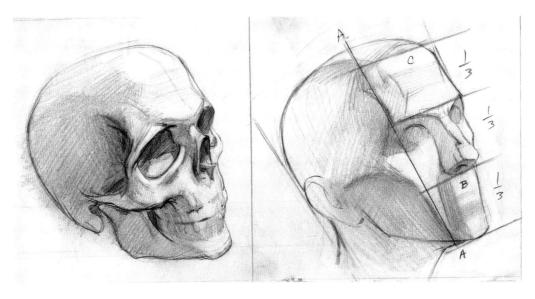

FIGURE 1-5: FRONT VIEW OF DIVISION OF THE HEAD

Profile View: The height of the side head is one head length. The width equals one head length. The top of the ears are in line with the eyebrows. The ear hole is in line with the bottom of the nose and the occipital bone (the hindmost bone of the skull, which forms the back of the skull above the nap). The bottom of the earlobe always varies with each individual.

The face triangle is from the center of each pupil, through the nostrils, to the point between the top front teeth. This is an important trait, as every person's triangle is different.

A smiling mouth lines up under the pupils. The two irises usually equal the maximum smiling width of the mouth. The space between the eyes is an average of $2\frac{1}{2}$ inches. One eye width equals the space between the eyes.

FIGURE 1-7: ILLUSTRATION OF THE PUPILS WITH THE CORRECT SPACE BETWEEN THE EYES

FIGURE 1-6: THE FACE TRIANGLE

The Body: A perfect body is eight heads high. The neck is a quarter of one head length, starting under the chin with the top of the head. The second head starts at the neck mark.

The shoulder-line mark is a quarter of one head down. This leaves space for the chest above the clavicle and for the neck-support muscles.

The Torso Triangle: The shoulder line is two head lengths (not widths) wide, and is the top line of the torso triangle that extends down to the space between the legs. The chin-to-shoulder line is a half of one head length. The nipple line equals one head length, the top of the third head trunk. The belly button to the space between the legs is one head, the bottom of the third trunk head.

The leg space is four and a quarter heads down from the top, including the quarter neck space. The center head overlaps by a quarter of a head. The width of the waist at

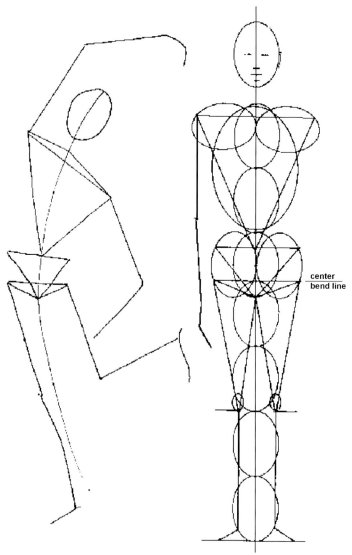

center
bend line

FIGURE 1-8: THE TORSO TRIANGLE

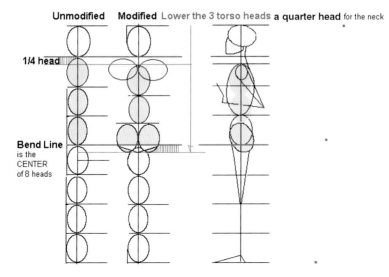

Unmodified   **Modified** Lower the 3 torso heads **a quarter head** for the neck

1/4 head

Bend Line
is the
CENTER
of 8 heads

The bend line remains the center of the body, 4 heads up.

FIGURE 1-9: FULL BODY WITH BEND LINE

the belly button is one head length. From the top line of the hip or trunk triangle to the space between the legs is three quarters of one head high, and is two head widths wide. You get the idea!

The center of the body is the bend line, and can also be measured as four heads up from the base.

BODIES IN MOTION

In art and anatomy, the center of gravity is the point of the body that dictates where the weight is distributed. An imaginary axis used by artists determines where the weight of the body changes. When sitting, the upper body trunk and head rest on the pelvis. When someone is standing, the body is supported by the feet. In movement, such as walking, the center of gravity is pushed forward by the foot and then supported once again. Walking has several movements. Up-and-down movement of the body takes place

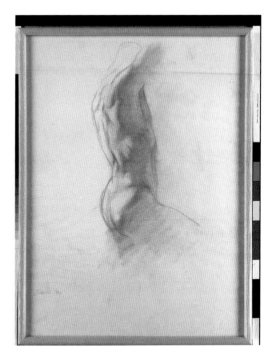

FIGURE 1-10: ARTIST BODY COLOR REDDISH

with each step. Swinging is caused by the center of gravity being shifted from one leg to another. Twisting movements are caused by the shoulders and hips. When a person walks downhill, his or her center of gravity descends with each step. Makeup Artists interpret these movements on paper, by sculpting, or through other artistic media.

DRAWING THE BODY IN MOTION

by Dan Gheno

Begin to draw with a scribble-like gesture, moving randomly back and forth across the page, rapidly drawing the model from head to toe and from one side of the figure to the other side. Once you have a feeling for where the figure drawing is headed, start to toss in lines of action, sweeping angles that crisscross through the figure. Begin to gauge the positive and negative shapes.

FIGURE 1-12: DRAWING BODY IN MOTION

FIGURE 1-11: DRAWING BODY IN MOTION

Angles: Continue to let your hand amble, drawing seemly random, angled lines throughout the figure, trying to find the forms that line up with or contrast with each other. In this case, for instance, notice how the line of the model's right inner ankle lines up with the outside of her right hip. Observe how the complex angles of the right side of the torso contrast with the figure's simpler, flatter left side. Don't limit your use of angles to the inside of the figure. Let them broadly enwrap the outside of the figure. Collectively, the outside angles are called the envelope. Use them to judge the negative space between the limbs and the torso, as well as the general relationship of the ground plane.

Positive and Negative Space: Utilize negative and positive space to help you analyze the forms of the figure. Look at the so-called empty space, or negative space, between the legs, as well as between the left arm and the head. Also look at the space between the right arm and the body. Ask yourself: How big or small are these shapes? Are they long and narrow or short and broad? Do the same for the positive shapes or body forms. For example, how wide are the model's calves compared to her ankles? To keep the relative sizes of your positive shapes under control, gauge each body part against some other basic unit of measurement (see the section "Proportions for the Face and Body" by Don Jusko). For instance, how many head units does a leg measure?

The Line of Action: Look for the internal, directional movement of the forms that you are drawing. You can set them up with lines of action such as the ones drawn in the diagram. Don't be surprised if your initial sketch looks like a stick figure. Sculptors block in their figures in a similar fashion by using what is called an armature—a framework of metallic rods that will govern the thrust of their sculpted clay forms. Whether you are drawing or sculpting, you can use these very simple lines of thrust as a foundation for the outside curves and to orient the overall gesture of the figure.

9

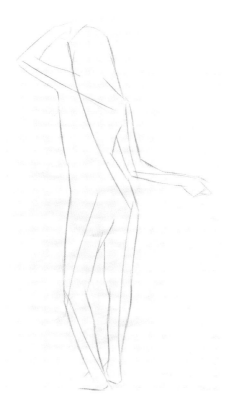

FIGURE 1-13: DRAWING BODY IN MOTION

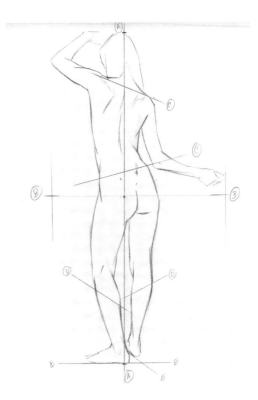

FIGURE 1-14: DRAWING BODY IN MOTION

1. On the paper, put a mark where you want to place the top, midpoint, and bottom of the figure. Try to stay within these boundaries when sketching the figure. Observe the center of gravity, which is represented by this vertical line that falls downward from the pit of the neck. Also observe all of the contrasting, shifting subforms of the figure. The head, neck, chest, hips, and legs are balanced back and forth over this line, one on top of the other.

2. You will usually find the midpoint of the standing figure at the hip bone.

3. The hip usually tips upward above the supporting, weight-bearing leg. Notice that the shoulders usually slant in the opposite direction of the hips.

4. Where is the crescendo, or peak, of the curve? It is almost never in the middle of the curve.

5. It's important to find the ground plane of the floor under the feet.

In conclusion, there are as many ways to start a drawing of the human figure from life as there are artists. The brief outline above is a personal approach to illustrations. It was prepared for students, and has been adapted from an article in *American Artist* magazine (Gheno).

Understanding the portions of the face and body will lead you to the Art of Makeup. Mastering the proportions of the face will enable you to create and design any look.

In the well known Muller-Lyer Illusion, a straight line with flanges pointed outward seems longer than the one with them turned inward. The one tugs the attention beyond the line and seems to lengthen it, the other pulls it center and shortens it. Makeup Artists exploit this effect. For instance, by daubing shadow above the outer ends of the eyes, they draw them further apart. By applying it above the inner corners, they narrow them. (McNeill, 297)

A Makeup Artist will use this principle to compose features that are necessary for the character or beauty makeup. In all areas of makeup, you need to trick the mind as to what is being seen.

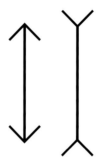

FIGURE 1-15: THE MULLER-LYER ILLUSION

Everyone has their own unique facial features and characteristics. As in drawing, where you place a shadow or highlight represents what you are visually saying about your makeup. In anatomy, the placement of the skeletal and muscle systems in each individual highlights those unique features. Theatre is one of the strongest examples of changing shapes to create characters, although these techniques can be used in all areas of makeup application.

FACE SHAPES

There are five basic face shapes that are used the most often. Many people have a combination of face shapes. Face shapes can be used as a guide, but would also determine where to place shadows and highlights according to what makeup look you are creating. (See Chapter 8: Design.)

The following are the five basic face shapes for you to identify and understand the differences:

Square Face: Large face, straight hairline, square chin, and the cheekbones are not particularly prominent.

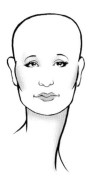

FIGURE 1-16: SQUARE FACE SHAPE

Diamond Face: Smaller in the chin and forehead.

FIGURE 1-17: DIAMOND FACE SHAPE

Heart Face: Larger on the forehead and smaller at the chin.

FIGURE 1-18: HEART FACE SHAPE

Oval Face: Evenly spaced.

FIGURE 1-19: OVAL FACE SHAPE

Round Face: No strong angle, widest at the cheekbones.

FIGURE 1-20: ROUND FACE SHAPE

EYE SHAPES

Eyes can be broken down into six basic shapes:

Even-Set, or Balanced, Eyes: Equals one eye length apart. This is the eye shape that is considered the "perfect" one aesthetically. You can do almost anything with the even-set eye, and not be as concerned with corrective makeup.

FIGURE 1-21: EVEN/BALANCED EYE

Wide-Set Eyes: Are spaced farther apart than the length of the eye. To bring the eyes closer together, place a dark color on the inside inner corner of the eye.

FIGURE 1-22: WIDE SET WITH DARK COLOR APPLIED

Deep-Set Eyes: Are recessed farther into the eye socket. To bring them out, place a lighter-color shadow on the upper lids. Use medium colors in the eye crease, and not

dark colors in the crease. Less is more with this eye shape.

FIGURE 1-23: DEEP SET WITH LIGHT COLOR APPLIED

Large Eyes: Will in some cases need to look smaller. A large eye conveys surprise and/or shock, which we will cover later in our discussion of expressions. To make the eye appear smaller, use dark colors on the eyelid and eye crease.

FIGURE 1-24: LARGE EYE WITH AN EXAMPLE OF MAKING IT SMALLER

Round Eyes: Can handle most colors. It is the eyeliner that will need to be adjusted if you have to make the eye look more almond. Place your eye-shadow color on the eyelid, blending up at the outside corners. You can also place a dark color on the outer top corner.

FIGURE 1-25: ROUND EYE WITH COLOR

FIGURE 1-27: FULL LIPS MADE SMALLER

Small Eyes: Need light-color shadow to open them up. Dark colors will only make them smaller. To give the illusion of a larger eye, use a light color on the eyelid, and medium color in the eye crease. Again, less is more.

Thin lips can be made larger by applying lip pencil to just outside the natural lip line. The farther out you place the line, the larger the lip, but take care to check the symmetry of your work. This is an area in which, if things are not done properly, the illusion does not work. Choose a lip pencil that corresponds to the lipstick color or slightly darker. Powder the lip pencil before and after the application of lipstick. This will set the "new" lip line, as well as help keep the makeup from bleeding. Lipstick colors in light to medium tones are used to create larger lips, as well as all-red tones.

13

FIGURE 1-26: SMALL EYE WITH COLOR

LIP SHAPES

Full lips are considered the perfect aesthetic. There are situations where you will have to create the illusion of smaller lips. To do this, apply lip liner just inside the natural lip line.

Choose a liner that is close in tone to the lip tone, or match to the lipstick. Lipstick colors should be medium to dark.

FIGURE 1-28: THIN LIPS MADE LARGER

To create an even lip shape on someone with a thin upper lip, apply lip pencil on or just above the top lip line. Then line the bottom lip at the lip line. Use powder to set, then apply lip color.

FIGURE 1-29: TO CORRECT THIN UPPER LIP

To balance a thin bottom lip with the top lip, do the reverse. Line the top lip at the natural lip line. Line the bottom lip past the natural lip line to create balance and symmetry. Again powder to set your "new" lines.

FIGURE 1-30: TO CORRECT THIN BOTTOM LIP

What if you do not need or want to change the lip shape? In this case, apply lip liner right at the natural lip line and fill in with lip color. You do not need to powder, because you have not changed the natural line. However, if it is a kissing scene you should powder the lips to set the makeup, or use a lip stain.

DRAWING LESSONS

The more often you practice drawing skills, the better you'll translate that into makeup applications. Learn to see faces as planes, edges, and shadows or a living sculpture. The first lesson is a basic exercise in observation and letting go—two skills a Makeup Artist will use often. Lessons Three and Four will train your mind to see faces and objects as shapes. For all the lessons, you never want to erase.

Lesson One: Contour Drawing

This lesson should be repeated using a different part of the body each time (hand, torso, arms, and so on).

1. Choose a face or figure. (Use a live model.)

2. While staring at the model, put your pencil down onto the drawing paper at the point where you want to start.

3. Follow the edge of the form with your pencil (without lifting the pencil) onto your paper without looking down at what you are drawing.

4. After moving around the edges of the object, move your pencil inside the object. Draw the contours and planes of the inside features without lifting your pencil.

5. Now look down at your work. Add any shadows or highlights to your drawing.

Lesson Two: Contour Drawing

1. Choose several (three or four) photos of faces from a magazine.

2. Repeating the steps in Lesson One, do a contour drawing of each photo.

3. Using carbon paper, transfer each drawing that you finish onto a clean sheet of paper, overlaying each drawing

on top of the other, creating your own design.

4. When you are done with step 3, above, fill in any shadows, highlights, or textures around and inside the drawings.

Lesson Three: Shadows

This lesson will enable you to see faces and objects in different shapes created by light and dark.

1. Find a photo of an interesting face with a lot of contrast.

2. On a clean sheet of paper, re-create the face in the photo using only the shapes of the shadows and highlights. Try not to use any lines. If this is difficult, you can work on one area of the face at a time (nose, eyes, lips, chin, and so on).

Lesson Four: Shadows

1. Take a cloth of some sort—for example, a light-colored sheet.

2. Bunch the sheet up into peaks and valleys.

3. Set a simple light source over the sheet.

4. Observe how the cloth looks under the light. Where do the shadows fall with each crease?

5. With a pencil, draw the sheet using simple outlines and only shadows, taking up the whole artist paper. Your design should go off the edges of the paper. At the end, your material can have a look of fluid movement or even resemble a mountaintop.

REFERENCES

Barcsay, Jenö. 2006. "Anatomy for the Artist" from *The Center of Gravity*. New York: Sterling Publishing Co. Inc.

Fehér, György. 2006. *Cyclopedia Anatomicae*. New York: Black Dog and Leventhal Publishers.

Gheno, Dan. www.dangheno.net (adapted from Starting a Figure Drawing From Life. *American Artist,* 17).

Jusko, Don. Human Proportions and Painting. www.realcolorwheel.com.

McNeil, Daniel. 1998. *Constellation of Desire, The Skin Code*. Boston: Little Brown and Company.

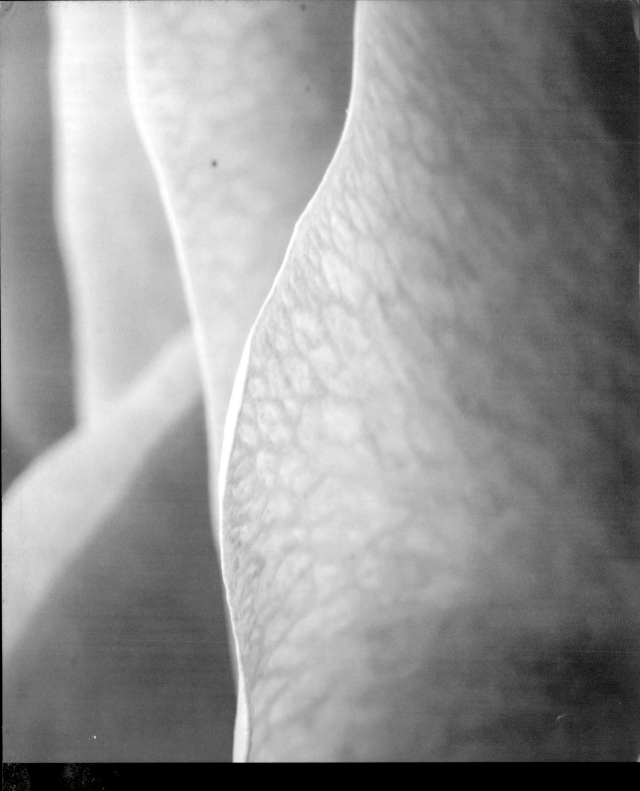

THE BODY | 2

Anatomy is important for the Makeup Artist. Makeup Artists who are asked to create anything that is directly related to the human body will study the vascular, muscular, and skeletal systems to correctly interpret how the makeup or appliance will be executed. The muscles that help form facial expressions, support the skeletal system, and protect internal organs are just as important to the Makeup Artist as how the body moves and the center of gravity. Understanding the vascular system adds to our knowledge of how to achieve realistic trauma. There are countless books on the subject, and we highly recommend owning a collection of anatomy books as well as medical reference books.

Anatomy is the study of the human body. The skeletal system is the physical foundation of the body, with 206 bones of different sizes and shapes. The skeleton is for the most part moved by muscles acting as levers. Bones can be classified as long, short, or flat. Joints are two or more bones that fit together. One of the functions for facial bones is determining the high and low planes of the face—characteristics that make us all different from each other. The primary function of the skeletal system is to support the body, protect internal organs, serve as attachments for muscles, produce white and red blood cells, and store calcium. The skeletal system is divided into two different areas: the axial and the appendicular. The axial makes up the skull, vertebral column, sternum, and ribs. The appendicular is made up of the upper and lower extremities.

The skull of the skeleton is also divided into two parts: the cranium, which protects the brain and has eight bones, and the facial skeleton, which is made up of 14 bones.

Figures 2.1 and 2.2 show the surface anatomy of the face and Figure 2.3 the skeleton system.

THE BONES OF THE CRANIUM

Occipital: The hindmost bone of the skull. Forms the back of the head above the nape.

Parietal: Two bones that form the sides and crown of the cranium.

Frontal: Forms the forehead.

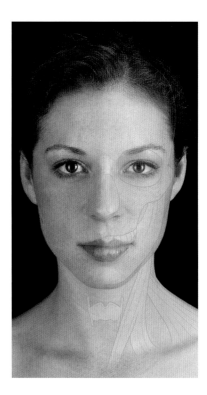

FIGURE 2-1: FACE SURFACE ANATOMY
Photographer Darrell Peterson remain in his sole copyright. 2005, Elsevier LTD All Rights Reserved

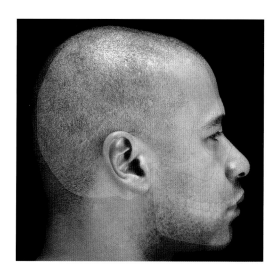

Temporal: Two bones that form the sides of the head by the ears.

Ethmoid: Between the eye sockets. Forms part of the nasal cavities.

Sphenoid: Joins all the cranium bones together.

THE BONES OF THE FACE

Nasal: Two bones that form the bridge of the nose.

Lacrimal: These two bones make up the eye sockets.

Zygomatic (or Malar): The two cheekbones.

Maxillae: Two bones that form the upper jaw.

Mandible: The lower jaw, the largest and strongest facial bone.

THE MUSCULAR SYSTEM

There are over 600 muscles in the muscular system (Figure 2.4). Muscles are divided into three classes: cardiac, striated (skeletal), and nonstriated (smooth). We deal only with the striated or skeleton muscles that are attached to bones and controlled by will.

Ligaments (which hold the bones together) and tendons (which are connectors between the bones and the muscles) help aid muscles to execute movement. Origin is where the muscle is attached to bones that do not move. Insertion is a muscle attached to a movable bone.

VASCULAR SYSTEM

The vascular system (Figure 2.5) is a set of complex veins that transport blood to and from the heart, transport oxygenated blood from the lungs to the heart, and drain blood from the intestines and the supporting organs. The cardiovascular system is made of heart and blood vessels, arteries, veins, and capillaries called the circulatory system. The pulmonary circulation sends blood on a path from the heart to the lungs and back again, and the systemic circulation sends blood from the heart to other parts of the body and back again.

FACIAL MUSCLES AND EXPRESSION

Facial expressions are universal. The six basic facials codes are enjoyment, anger, fear, surprise, disgust, and sadness. Makeup Artists are often asked to reproduce these emotions with the use of makeup. The facial muscles come into play by forming these

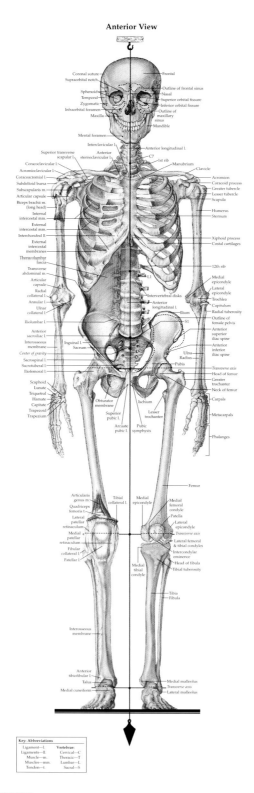

Anterior View

FIGURE 2-3: THE SKELETON SYSTEM

© 2007 Wolters Kluwer Health/Lippincott Williams and Wilkins.

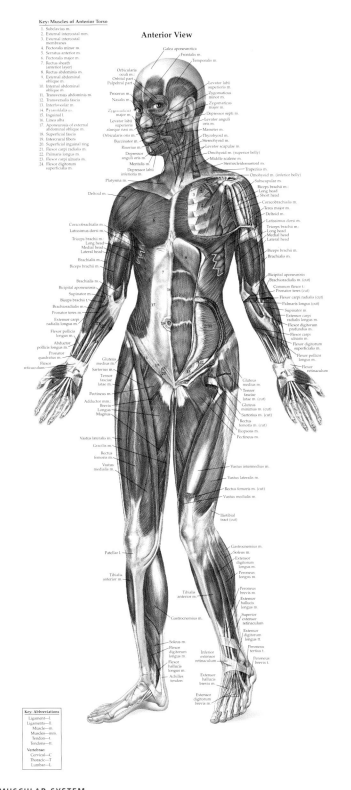

FIGURE 2-4: THE MUSCULAR SYSTEM

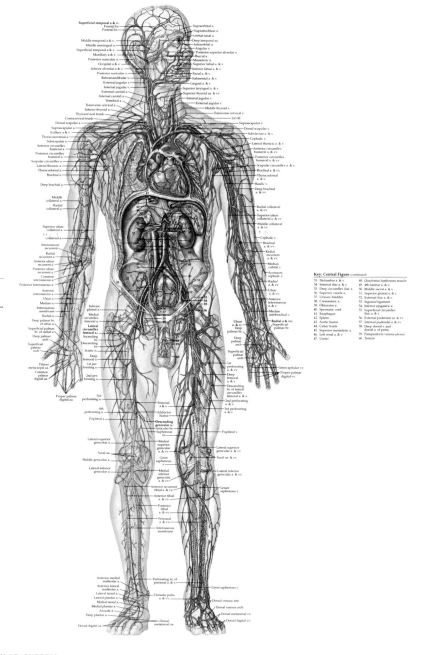

Key: Central Figure

1. Parietal pleura
2. Right internal thoracic a. & v.
3. Right brachiocephalic trunk
4. Brachiocephalic trunk
5. Left common carotid a.
6. Superior vena cava
7. Pericardium
8. Ascending aorta
9. Pulmonary trunk
10. Left pulmonary a.
11. Right lung
12. Right atrium and auricle
13. Left auricle
14. Left pulmonary a.
15. Right coronary a.
16. Anterior interventricular a.

17. Diaphragm
18. Hepatic vv.
19. Inferior vena cava
20. Inferior phrenic aa.
21. Superior suprarenal aa.
22. Right suprarenal gland
23. Middle and inferior suprarenal aa.
24. Right kidney
25. Testicular aa. & vv.
26. 10th rib
27. Abdominal aorta
28. Inferior mesenteric a.
29. Ascending lumbar v.
30. Common iliac aa. & vv.
31. Anterior superior iliac spine
32. Iliacus muscle

Key: Central Figure (continued)

33. Iliolumbar a. & v.
34. Internal iliac a. & v.
35. Deep circumflex iliac a.
36. Superior vesicle a.
37. Urinary bladder
38. Cremasteric a.
39. Obturator a.
40. Spermatic cord
41. Esophagus
42. Spleen
43. Aortic hiatus
44. Celiac trunk
45. Superior mesenteric a.
46. Left renal a. & v.
47. Ureter

48. Quadratus lumborum muscle
49. 4th lumbar a. & v.
50. Middle sacral a. & v.
51. Superior gluteal a. & v.
52. External iliac a. & v.
53. Inguinal ligament
54. Inferior epigastric a.
55. Superficial circumflex iliac a. & v.
56. External pudendal aa. & vv.
57. Internal pudendal a. & v.
58. Deep dorsal v. and dorsal a. of penis
59. Pampiniform venous plexus
60. Testicle

FIGURE 2-5: THE VASCULAR SYSTEM

expressions. Changing or reshaping the eyebrow, adding a highlighter or shadow in the right place, can give off different emotional signals.

Facial muscles are formed in four different groups: scalp and facial muscles, eye and eye socket muscles, mouth muscles, and jaw muscles.

SIX FACIAL CODES

Enjoyment (Figure 2.6): A smile employs two muscles. The zygomatic major curves the mouth, and the orbicularis oculi raises the cheeks. The cheeks, in turn, press the skin toward the eye, causing a squint. Eyes appear brighter.

Anger (Figure 2.7): The person looks in deep concentration. Eyebrows appear downward, and the lips look pursed (orbicularis oris muscle). When angry, the blood can rush to the face. A flushing of redness can occur.

Fear (Figure 2.8): Eyes are wide and eyebrows lifted toward each other. Lips pull back (buccinator muscle) and even tremble.

Lips can be dry. In terror, nostrils dilate, pupils widen, and perspiration appears on the forehead.

Surprise (Figure 2.9): Surprise is a lot like fear except that, for the seconds before fear takes over, the eyes and mouth open (temporalis muscle working with the masseter muscle), and the eyebrows arch (frontalis muscle). Surprise in nature began as a protective measure. We humans raise our eyebrows.

Disgust (Figure 2.10): The mouth can open slightly. The nose can turn up slightly and

FIGURE 2-7: ANGER

FIGURE 2-6: ENJOYMENT

FIGURE 2-8: FEAR

FIGURE 2-9: SURPRISE

FIGURE 2-10: DISGUST

wrinkle (procerus muscle), as if to acknowledge something foul.

Sadness (Figure 2.11): The face seems to sag. Wrinkles on the mid-forehead, eyebrows droop, and the corners of the mouth go down (triangularis muscle).

From *The Face, The Skin Code* by Daniel McNeill.

SKIN

The skin (Figure 2.12) on our bodies is the largest organ we have, weighing in around six pounds. The skin is made up of several layers. The outer layer is the epidermis, which protects us from disease and

FIGURE 2-11: SADNESS

dehydration. The next layer is the dermis, which contains blood vessels, nerve endings, and glands. Beneath all of that, let's not forget the subcutaneous, which has connective tissues and fat, maintaining our body heat and storing energy.

Wounds and diseases also play a big part for the Makeup Artist. It becomes clear why it is important to study the human body. Having medical books of all kinds is a valuable tool for research. Not only should you know the medical explanation of wounds or diseases, but also the scene or environment that caused the wound or disease in the first place. With that knowledge, you can then decide what products you will use and how to execute a realistic makeup. The following touches on only a few examples of wounds and diseases that involve anatomy and the Makeup Artist.

Shock: A term used for tissue and organ failure. There are three forms of shock. All have three stages. Stage One symptoms include cold, pale skin, and rapid heartbeat. Stage Two symptoms include weak pulse and cold, clammy skin. Stage Three is unconsciousness, shallow breathing, and rapid falling of blood pressure.

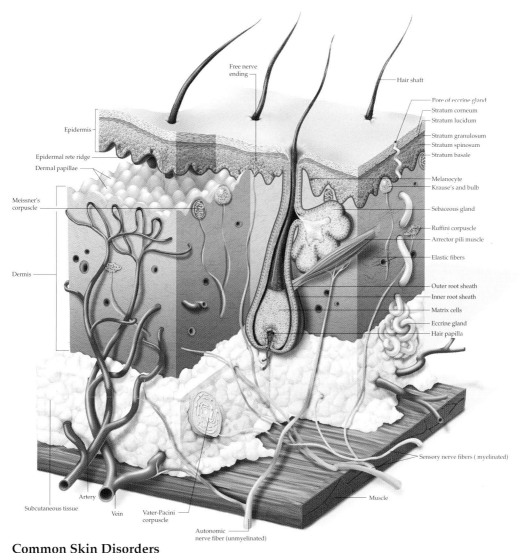

Free nerve
ending

Hair shaft

Pore of eccrine gland
Stratum corneum
Stratum lucidum

Epidermis

Stratum granulosum
Stratum spinosum
Stratum basale

Epidermal rete ridge
Dermal papillae

Melanocyte
Krause's and bulb

Meissner's
corpuscle

Sebaceous gland

Ruffini corpuscle
Arrector pili muscle

Elastic fibers

Dermis

Outer root sheath
Inner root sheath
Matrix cells
Eccrine gland
Hair papilla

Sensory nerve fibers (myelinated)

Artery
Muscle

Subcutaneous tissue
Vein
Vater-Pacini
corpuscle

Autonomic
nerve fiber (unmyelinated)

Common Skin Disorders

FIGURE 2-12: SKIN CHART FOR MORE DETAILS AND SKIN DISORDERS.

© 2007 Wolters Kluwer Health/Lippincott Williams and Wilkins.

Disease: Can be caused by a number of things: age, gender, infection, smoking, drugs, to name a few. There are times that a disease has no known cause. When you have a change of metabolism or cell changes, symptoms can occur that, in turn, make a person aware that a disease is present. Most often a disease goes through stages. Those stages start with exposure to a disease and end with remission or full recovery.

Allergies: Can be caused by airborne irritants. Symptoms can include sneezing, watery eyes, itchy throat, headaches, sore red eyes, runny nose, and dark circles under the eyes.

Anthrax: A bacterial infection. Inhalation anthrax symptoms are fever and nausea with flu-like symptoms. Breathing can be difficult. Intestinal anthrax symptoms are fever, nausea, decreased appetite, and abdominal pain. Cutaneous anthrax is characterized by small, elevated, itchy lesions.

FACIAL SKIN DISORDERS

As a Makeup Artist, you'll need to recognize skin disorders and what is the best method for correcting or camouflaging the surface of the skin. Using an airbrush works well for many of the following situations because you will have less contact with the surface of the skin. It also reduces the amount of rubbing and blending that can irritate already sensitive skin. Skin disorders that cause the skin's surface to be dry and flaky will also benefit from less rubbing when using an airbrush. Bradley Look will explain how to address the following skin disorders:

Port-Wine Stain (Nevus Flammeus): Flat, irregular red to purple patches. Starts out as a smooth surface, but can become an uneven, bumpy texture. Most often will darken with age.

> **Bradley Look:** To camouflage port-wine stains, mix a mint green adjuster into a base color. Lightly haze the area, letting the edge trail off. Let this dry before covering the affected area and the surrounding skin with foundation. If there is still some bleeding through of the port-wine stain, use Michael Davy's Airbrush Grade Prosthetic Cosmetic 2, which has double the amount of pigmentation.

Psoriasis: An ongoing disease with periods of remission. Dry, flaky scales or thickened skin around lesions can be itchy and painful.

> **Bradley Look:** To camouflage psoriasis, stipple a light layer of rubber mask grease over the affected area. Lightly powder to set. Using an airbrush, lightly cover the area with several light passes of airbrush product. Since psoriasis is notably seen only on the elbows and knees, additional body makeup might be required using the same technique if the condition is visible elsewhere on the talent.

Rosacea: Common among people with a Celtic background. Rosacea has a butterfly-like redness over the nose and cheek area. People most often mistake rosacea for acne.

> **Bradley Look:** To camouflage rosacea, use a similar technique to the one outlined for port-wine stain.

Scars: Usually thick and pink with a smooth texture. Over time, scars should fade to a very pale white. Scars are broken down into two types: indented or protruding.

> **Bradley Look:** For the indented scar, using a tattoo palette, apply a highlight (slightly paler than the skin tone) around the edge of the scar. Next, around the area of highlight, apply slightly darker tone than the skin color. By the creative use of highlights and shadow, you are attempting to make the scar appear less indented. Afterward, spray over with appropriate

foundation color. For a protruding scar, apply tattoo palette colors in the exact opposite order as listed above. Shadow is applied to the edge of the scar and blended outward. Foundation is then airbrushed over the entire area. Note: A hypertrophy scar can be toned down using makeup; the 3-D dimension is still quite visible if not properly lit.

Vitiligo: Complete loss of pigment over time. There is often a splotchy look to the skin. In fair skin, you might not notice it as much, but it is disfiguring to darker skin tones.

> **Bradley Look:** To camouflage vitiligo, airbrush a medium flesh tone over the area. Next, lightly airbrush the foundation color over the affected area and the rest of the face.

VIRAL, BACTERIAL, AND OTHER DISORDERS

Conjunctivitis: Bacterial infection of the eyes. Symptoms are pain, tearing, and redness with fluid discharge of the eyes.

Meningitis: Bacterial infection of the meninges, which are the delicate membranes that cover the brain and spinal cord. Symptoms can include fever, severe headache, stiff neck and shoulders, a dark red or purplish rash anywhere on the body, mental confusion, vomiting, and sensitivity to bright light.

Tuberculosis: Bacterial infection in which bacilli are deposited into the lungs. Symptoms are fatigue, weight loss, night sweats, and weakness. A cough can also be present.

Tetanus: Bacterial infection caused by open cuts and wounds having contact with infected soils, dust, and other agents that cause local infection at the site of the wound. Unchecked, the infection will enter the bloodstream, causing painful, deep-muscle spasms.

Pneumonia: Bacterial infection. Pneumonia is the most dangerous to the very young or the elderly. Coughing, fever, chills, deep chest pain, wheezing, and fatigue are some of the most common symptoms you would expect to see.

Herpes Zoster: Viral infection. Symptoms are small, painful red skin lesions that develop along the nerve path.

HIV (Human Immunodeficiency Virus): Virus is passed by blood-to-blood contact and sexual contact.

Mumps: Viral disease characterized by swelling and tender parotid gland and salivary glands.

Leukemia: Blood disorder. No one knows the cause of this disease, although genetics, environment, or the immune system might play a part. Symptoms include paleness, high fever, abnormal bleeding, and weight loss. As the disease progresses, the symptoms become more severe, including infections, organ enlargement, and tender bones.

Rubella: Viral disease. A rash forms on the face, then quickly spreads to the rest of the body.

Smallpox: Viral disease. A rash forms on the face, spreading to the trunk of the body. Lesions form inside the mouth and nose.

Chicken Pox: Viral disease. A small rash forms that turns into papules.

ENVIRONMENTAL CONDITIONS

Frostbite: Freezing of body parts, mostly nose, fingers, and toes. Frostbite has three different stages. First stage is pain with itching, maybe swelling. Second stage has blisters that can turn black. In the third stage, you'll observe redness, deep colors of purple, severe blisters, and sometimes a loss of extremities in the affected area.

Heat Exhaustion: Occurs when someone has been exposed to heat for long lengths of time. There is also a loss of fluids. Symptoms include being tired, nausea with vomiting, sweating, and headache.

Heatstroke: Elevated body temperature. Symptoms include red skin, no sweating, elevated body temperature, difficulty breathing, confusion, seizure, and possible coma.

ANATOMY TERMS

Anatomy is a complex field, but we'll concentrate on the areas Makeup Artists most likely will use as reference. The following terms outline only a few of the examples found in the skeletal, muscular, and circulatory systems.

The Skeletal System

The skeleton is divided into two different areas. The axial is made up of the skull, vertebral column, sternum, and ribs. The appendicular skeleton is made up of the upper and lower extremities. The skull is divided into cranial bones. These bones form the cranial cavity. The cranial cavity houses the brain and facial bones, which, in turn, form the face.

The Skull

Frontal Bone: Bone located at the forehead. Helps define the orbits of the eye.

Mandible: The lower jawbone.

Maxillae: The upper jawbones.

Nasal Bones: There are two nasal bones. The vomer bone separates the nasal cavities.

Occipital Bone: Large bone that makes up the base of the cranium.

Zygomatic Arch: Bone that defines the cheekbone.

Spinal Column

The spinal column is made up of 26 bones. The bones protect the spinal cord. The spinal cord is strong and flexible—allowing movement, supporting the head, and serving as the attachment for the ribs and muscles.

Upper Body

Clavicle: Collarbone.

Scapula: Along with the humerus, helps to form the shoulder joint.

Ribs: Curved bones connected to the thoracic vertebrae.

Sternum: Breastbone.

Humerus: Upper arm bone.

Radius: One of two lower arm bones. The radius is narrow at the end that connects with the humerus, and wider at the joints it forms with the wrist bones.

Ulna: One of two lower arm bones opposite in shape to the radius.

Carpal Bones: Wrist bones.

Metacarpals: Hand bones.

Phalanges: Finger bones.

Lower Body

Pelvic Bone: Attaches the lower body to the axial skeleton.

Femur: Thighbone. It is the strongest bone in the body.

Patella: Kneecap.

Tibia: The larger of the two bones that form the lower leg bone.

Fibula: The smaller of the two bones that form the lower leg bone.

Tarsals: Anklebones.

Metatarsals: Foot bones.

Phalanges: Toes.

Joints: Where two or more bones come together to either aid movement and/or keep the skeleton together.

The Muscular System

Muscles are described by size, shape, origin, and function. There are over 700 known muscles in the body.

Facial Muscles
Jaw Muscles
Masseter: Raises the jaw and clenches the teeth.

Temporalis: Helps the masseter muscle to raise the jaw and clench the teeth.

Mouth Muscles

Buccinator: Draws the corners of the mouth backward, flattens and tightens the lips.

Caninus: Raises the corner of the mouth.

Mentalis: Raises and tightens the chin, thrusts the lower lip up and outward.

Orbicularis Oris: Circles the mouth and purses the lips.

Risorius: Pulls the corner of the mouth sideward and outward.

Triangularis: Pulls the corner of the mouth downward.

Zygomaticus Major and Minor: Muscles that raise the mouth upward and outward.

Eye Muscles
Corrugator: Assists the orbicularis muscles in compressing skin between the eyebrows. Vertical wrinkles form.

Orbicularis Oculi: Closes the eyelids and compresses the opening of the eye from above and below.

Procerus: Tightens the inner eye by wrinkling the skin on the nose.

Face Muscle
Frontalis (Frontal Part): Draws the scalp to the front, wrinkles the forehead, and pulls the eyebrows upward.

Platysma: Neck muscle that draws the lower lip downward and upward.

Circulatory System and Veins
The circulatory system is made up of two different systems. In the pulmonary system, the right side of the heart receives deoxygenated blood from the rest of the body and pumps it to the lungs. In the systemic system, the left side of the heart receives oxygenated blood from the lungs and sends it to the rest of the body. Arteries carry blood from the heart to the tissues and organs. Veins return the blood to the heart.

Arteries
Aorta: Largest artery in the body.

Coronary Arteries: Supply blood to the heart.

Brachiocephalic Trunk, Right Carotid Artery, and Right Subclavian Artery: Provide blood to the neck, head, and upper limbs.

Left Carotid and Left Subclavian Arteries: Provide blood to the left side of the head, neck, and upper limbs.

Celiac Trunk, Superior Mesenteric Artery, and Inferior Mesenteric Artery: Supply blood to the abdominal internal organs.

Renal Arteries, Suprarenal Arteries, and Gonadal Arteries: Provide internal organs to the back of the abdominal wall.

Left and Right Common Iliac Arteries: The abdominal aorta divides into left and right common iliac arteries.

Veins
Superior Vena Cava: Receives blood from the upper body by way of the internal jugular, subclavian, and brachiocephalic veins.

Internal Jugular: Receives blood from the head and neck area, including the brain.

Subclavian: Empties blood from the shoulder area.

Brachiocephalic: One of two veins that form the superior vena cava.

Inferior Vena Cava: Receives blood from the pelvis, abdomen, and lower limbs.

Portal System: A set of veins that deplete blood from the intestines and the supporting organs.

Hepatic Portal Vein: Vein that leads from the intestinal veins to the liver.

Splenic Vein: Vein leaving the spleen.

Superior Mesenteric: Blood returns to circulation through this vein by way of the small intestine.

ANATOMY LESSONS

It is hard to constantly memorize and remember every bone and muscle in the body, not even counting the vascular system. But even learning the basics and having those references to remind you of the correct placement of bones and muscles is important. The first two lessons are important because the more often you look at and write down a term, the more you'll start to recognize it.

Lesson One: The Skeletal System

1. Find an unlabeled drawing, photo, or chart of the skeletal system.

2. Make a copy of the unlabeled skeletal system for yourself to write on.

3. List the bones correctly on your copy of the unlabeled chart, checking your answers from the labeled skeletal system chart in Figure 2.3. You need to list only the basic bone structures: skull, neck, shoulders, arms, chest, wrist, fingers, legs, ankles, feet, toes, and so on.

Lesson Two: The Facial Bones

1. Find an unlabeled drawing, photo, or chart of the facial bone structure.

2. Make a copy of the unlabeled facial bone structure for yourself to write on.

3. List the basic facial bone structures on your copy of the unlabeled chart, checking your answers using the labeled facial charts in Figures 2.1 and 2.2.

Lesson Three: Facial Muscles

1. Find three or four photos of interesting faces with lots of different expressions.

2. Make copies of each of the photos.

3. List the correct facial muscle(s) on the photo that is/are causing the expression in the photo (for example: crying, laughing, being scared, and so on).

4. Repeat step 3, above, for each of the different photos.

Lesson Four: Body Wounds

This lesson can be done over time to get what you want. Using a camera, take pictures of several different types of wounds. You can also use several photographs found in magazines or medical books.

1. Observe up close what the shapes, sizes, colors, and textures are for each wound.

2. Write down where the wound is located on the body, using the correct medical terms to describe the location. (For example: The scratches are located on the epidermis in the torso area, and so on.)

The idea of this lesson is for you to start looking at wounds or illnesses in terms of colors, shapes, and textures instead of by what you think you already know. Starting a book for future reference is always a good idea. At the end of one year, review your book. It could include some of the following wounds:

• A bruise (new, a few days old, a week later)

• Scratches (new and old)

• A cut (new and old)

- Scar(s)
- Blister(s)

REFERENCES

(Contributers) Cheryl A. Bean, Peggy Bozarth, Yvette P. Conley, Lillian Craig, Shelba Durston, Ken W. Edmisson, William F. Galvin, Deborah A. Hanes, Joanne Konick-McMahan, Lt Manuel D. Leal, Dawna Martich, E. Ann Myers, Sundaram V. Ramanan, Barbara L. Sauls, Janet Somlyay, Sandra M Waguespack.

Atlas of Pathophysiology. Second Edition. Lippincott, Williams & Wilkins. A. Wolters Kluwer Company, Philadelphia: Anatomical Chart Company, Skokie,Il.

Alcamo, I. Edward. 2003. *Anatomy Coloring Workbook I, second edition.* New York: Princetonreview Inc.

Barcsay, Jenö. 2006. *Anatomy For The Artist.* New York: Sterling Publishing Co.Inc.

DiMaio, Vincent J. M. 1998. *Gun Shot Wounds, Practical Aspects Of Firearms, Ballistics and Forensic Techniques, second edition.* Boca Raton: CRC Press, Boca Raton.

Fehér, György. 2006. *Cyclopedia Anatomicae.* New York: Black Dog and Leventhal Publishers.

Habif, Thomas P. 1996. *Clinical Dermatology, third edition.* St Louis: Mosby Year Book Inc.

Look, Bradley. 2007. *How to Cover Facial Disorders.*

McNeill, Daniel, 1998. *The Face.* Boston: Back Bay Books; Little, Brown & Company.

MedicineNet. 2007. *Frostbite.* www.medicinenet.com/frostbite/page2.html.

———. 2007. *Heat exhaustion.* www.medicinenet.com/heat_exhaustion/article.html.

———. 2007. *Heatstroke.* www.medicinenet.com/heatstroke/article.html.

Moses, Kenneth P., John C. Banks, Pedro B. Nava, and Darrell Peterson, 2005. *Atlas of Clinical Gross Anatomy.* Mosby.

3

COLOR

The basics of color are essential for you, as a professional Makeup Artist, to know and understand. You will use this knowledge in every makeup you do. There will be countless times when color issues come up that you will have to be able to problem solve.

You cannot problem solve unless you understand color and its functions. The wrong color choice can change everything about what you as an artist are trying to say with makeup.

Color understanding is used to create mood, to enhance skin tone and character design, and to correct environmental issues such as lighting and mixing of pigments.

Artists can—and often do—select many palettes, whether in blues or earth colors, for example. But if you are trying to mix colors and get the widest range, you want the three primary colors that allow you to do that. In the subtractive process, those colors are cyan, magenta, and yellow. The purer each of these is in terms of color, the wider the range of colors you can mix. This includes the Makeup Artist who mixes pigments for a variety of surfaces and skin tones. Mixing pigments to create Pax Paint is an example of Makeup Artists using paint color in their work. Pax Paint is a combination of Pros-Aide (adhesive) that is mixed with acrylic paints to be used on a variety of surfaces in which there is a strong bond of color that will not lift or flake off.

All aspects of makeup—foundations color-correcting skin tones, lip tones, concealing tattoos, birthmarks, blemishes or irregularities in the skin, and coloring prosthetics—use color.

Some examples are:

- Will the shades be positive or negative?
- How will colors look under certain lighting conditions?
- How will a color register on film or HDTV?
- How to correct skin tones?
- How to counter color for film or HDTV?

It is always a good idea to study color theory in detail, as it is an interesting and complex field.

Don Jusko founded the Real Color Wheel (RCW, Figure 3.1), which has modernized the way we use and relate to color.

Don's color wheel is one in which every color has an opposite color to be used in mixing neutral darks. Any artist who wishes to mix dark colors without black pigments can use the RCW. You could also use this color wheel to match, darken, or lighten skin tones and to find the complement colors to existing colors—for example, accents to eye shadows and lipstick colors. According to Don, "It is important for an artist to know how colors relate to one another, which opposite colors will darken the existing colors, and which colors are analogous."

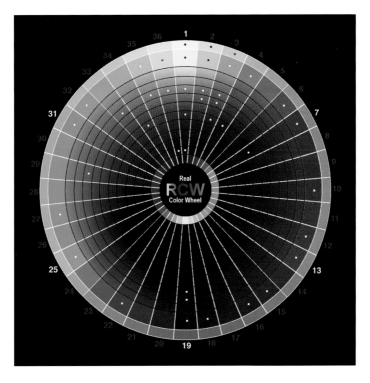

FIGURE 3-1: DON JUSKO'S RCW COLOR WHEEL

In this chapter, we refer to Don Jusko's Real Color Wheel and how it relates to the Makeup Artist.

HOW TO USE THE COLOR WHEEL

A color wheel in this true form gives the artist a tool to create different hues and to shade them to neutral darks. The Makeup Artist would take this one step further by considering what colors also would work under different conditions: lights, color corrections, color grading, and so forth. The following will give you the basic language used to decipher the blending of hues.

To begin to understand how to use the color wheel, it is important to know where to start.

On the RCW, the colors on the outside of the wheel are pure hues. What you can add to alter these colors is a tint with white, a tone with white and the complement color, or a shade with just the complement color. This will determine the final outcome of that color, including the addition of analogous relationships next to each other on the wheel. Always start matching or plotting a pure color from the outside of the color wheel—this is the pure hue. Finding the correct color or area of color, you can decide where to go from there. For example, if you want to find the complement of the color that you have already plotted, go to the opposite side of the color wheel. You will know the color will work. You can then tint, tone, or shade that hue to get the desired effect.

FIGURE 3-2: APPLE PRIMARY COLORS

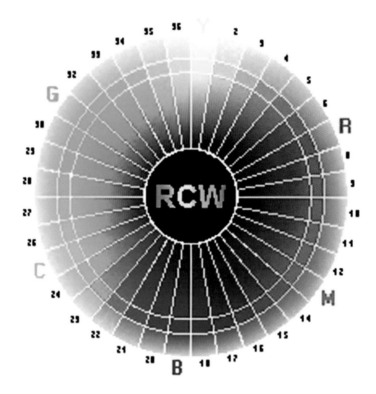

FIGURE 3-3: SECONDARY COLORS AND A WHEEL

TERMS

Hue: Any color.

Primary Color (Figure 3.2): There are three primary colors. They can be mixed together to make all other colors. Transparent Yellow is PY 150 or PY 153. Transparent Magenta is PR 122. Transparent Cyan is PB 15.

Secondary Colors (Figure 3.3): Colors that are made by mixing together two primary colors.

Red: Made by mixing yellow and magenta.

Blue: A combination of magenta and cyan.

FIGURE 3-4: A TINTS COLOR WHEEL

FIGURE 3-5: A BLACK & WHITE SCALE

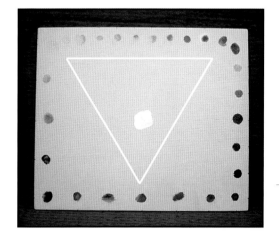

FIGURE 3-6: DOTS OF COLOR

Green: A mixture of cyan and yellow.

Tints (Figure 3.4): Made by adding white to any hue.

Dual Tone: A pigment that changes hue from mass tone to top tone. In other words, a color that changes as it gets lighter—not just in value, but in its actual color. For example, a brown color that changes to a bright yellow color is a dual tone. Purple that changes from a cool dark to a warm light is a dual tone.

Top Tone: Adding white to a color.

Mass Tone: Color right out of the tube or pure powder pigment.

Undertone: Adding clear media

Transparent: Dyes are clear—you can see through transparent dyes.

Translucent: Milk is translucent—it can never be transparent by adding a clear medium.

Opaque: Dense, like a small rock—it cannot be seen through.

Classic color schemes will help you to decipher which way to plot a color on the color wheel.

Monochromatic (Figure 3.5): Any one color mixed with white.

Analogous (Figure 3.6): Colors next to each other on the color wheel—for example, orange and red or yellow, orange and red, or cyan and green.

Complementary (Figure 3.7): Any colors 180 degrees apart on a 360-degree wheel.

Triadic: Any three colors that are 120 degrees apart on the wheel, usually primary colors.

Split complementary colors are formed like a Y on the color wheel—one color on each side of a complementary color.

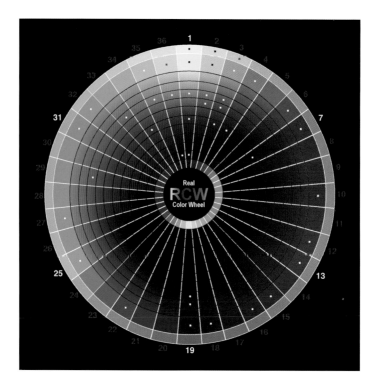

FIGURE 3-7: RCW WHEEL

Opposition, or complementary, pigments make neutral darks. If you mix two opposite pigments, the color will result in a darker hue. This enables the Makeup Artist to work with darker pigments without using black. It is also a great way to mix pre-existing makeup when you want to form a darker shade. Because the pigments complement each other, there will be a natural look to your work. The darker pigments will not clash against the skin tone of the person you are working on.

The following outlines the six opposition colors and the neutral darks they will generate.

- Cadmium Yellow Light and Cadmium Yellow Medium are opposite Ultramarine

FIGURE 3-8: CADMIUM YELLOW LIGHT, CADMIUM YELLOW MEDIUM, ULTRAMARINE BLUE

Blue (Figure 3.8). Notice that yellow darkens to brown. Brown and ultramarine make the neutral dark.

- Cadmium Orange is opposite Cobalt Blue (Figure 3.9).

- Burnt Sienna (Figure 3.10), which is a dark orange, is opposite Cobalt Blue.

- Opaque Cadmium Red Light and Red Dark are opposite Cyan (Figure 3.11). Cyan is also called Thalo Blue.

- Quinacridone Magenta Transparent PR122 is opposite Thalo Green (Figure 3.12).

- Purple is opposite Yellow Green (Figure 3.13). Green Oxide Opaque is a dark yellow green to be used as the opposition color.

The chart in Figure 3.14 illustrates how you can combine pigments to produce browns.

The chart will also show you how to mix pigments that will give you cool browns or warm browns. Brown neutral tones in

FIGURE 3-9: CADMIUM ORANGE AND COBALT BLUE

FIGURE 3-10: BURNT SIENNA

FIGURE 3-11: OPAQUE CADMIUM RED LIGHT, CADMIUM RED DARK AND THALO BLUE

FIGURE 3-12: QUINACRIDONE MAGENTA TRANS. PR:122 AND THALO GREEN

FIGURE 3-13: PURPLE OPPOSITE YELLOW GREEN

FIGURE 3-14: BROWN PIGMENT CHART WITH YELLOW TO BROWN NATURAL OXIDES, BOTH RAW AND BURNT

makeup are generally complementary to most skin tones, and especially with eye shadow for a more natural look. For natural-looking makeup, a variety of neutral browns flatters and registers well for the camera. Highlighting and contouring with neutral browns has a less harsh effect. In situations where browns register darker on film, staying with neutral browns avoids having your brown registering too dark and unflattering. Remember that what you decide to use is the outcome of the problem solving for the makeup situation you have at the time. What is the skin tone? What is the lighting situation? Is this a makeup special effect? What medium is it? Are you working in theatre, film, television, HDTV, or print? Whatever the situation, knowing what pigments make brown is a plus.

MIXING PIGMENT FOR FLESH TONES

by Don Jusko

Every skin tone is unique. All the colors and ranges of colors from #1 yellow to #7 red are colors used to get skin tones. Colors from yellow to red all darken to brown, either by adding brown or by mixing brown. All skin colors have a range of 10 tints and 10 darks for each of the seven colors. To make a skin tone lighter, you will take the color already plotted and lighten it with white or yellow. To make a skin tone darker, you will take the color already plotted and darken with browns and the complement color. The Makeup Artist can also change existing foundations or mix your own by using the color wheel.

COLOR FUNCTION

Usages and combinations of color greatly affect your final makeup application (Figure 3.15).

You will also need to address the undertones in the skin, eyes, and lips. Color can balance, conceal, correct, or show emotion. Example: If there is too much red in the face, you can apply a green or yellow under or over the foundation to neutralize the red.

FIGURE 3-15: TUBE PIGMENTS FOR COLOR FUNCTIONS

You need to understand how colors function in relation to makeup artistry.

Red is one of the secondary colors. Magenta is a primary color. The complementary color to red is cyan. Red is made by mixing yellow and magenta. A cool cherry red (RCW #12.6.5) will bring life into a darker cool skin tone, but only if the skin tone is cool as well. Orange red will give a healthy glow to golden skin. Red is also used in makeup effects to show sun damage, alcohol abuse, windburn, crying, skin lesions and rashes, bruising and trauma to the skin, and to neutralize any gray undertones in appliances, and tattoo cover-up.

Blue is a secondary color. The complement to blue is yellow. Cyan is a primary color. Blue is a combination of magenta and cyan. Blue will work with most skin tones. Blue and shades of blue should not be used for bluescreen work—it will disappear. Blue can be used in makeup to portray illness, death, cold, and freezing, as well as bruising of the skin.

Yellow is a primary color. The complementary color to yellow is blue. Yellow is used to add warmth to other colors. Yellow browns (gold) in eye shadows, blushers, and lipsticks flatter golden skin tones. In makeup, yellow can be use to portray illness, weakness, rotting, and bruising.

Green is a secondary color. Green is a combination of cyan and yellow. The complement color to green is magenta. Green can be cool (blue green) or warm (yellow green). In makeup, green is used to neutralize reds (for example, to tone down ruddy skin tone or broken capillaries in the face). Warm greens (with yellow added) look good on golden tones, or golden skin tones. Cool greens (with cyan or blue added) look good on cool tones, or skin with cool undertones. Green is also used in bruising and to portray illness, cold, or rotting. Green is also used to cover tattoos. Green or shades of green should not be used in greenscreen work—anything green becomes invisible.

Orange is a warm color that is between yellow and red on the RCW. The complementary color to orange is halfway between cyan and blue, called Cobalt Blue (RCW #22). Orange is a vibrant color that can be used as a highlighter on warm and dark skin tones. Orange is a good color to use for masking out blue, as in beard stubble and covering tattoos. Orange also will neutralize blue undertones (or blue lighting) in dark skin tones.

Violet (RCW #14) is the color between purple and magenta. Violet is a cool color. The complementary color to violet is chartreuse. Violet is used to correct too much yellow or shallowness in skin tone. Most cool skin tones look good in the color violet. In makeup, violet and combinations of violet are used for bruising, wounds, freezing, and death.

Pink is red with tint (white) added. There is a warm pink, which is a light red, and a cool pink, which is magenta. Pink is flattering to most skin tones. Magenta pink is good on cool skin tones. Warm pink (with golden tones added) looks good on warm skin tones. In makeup, pink is used in eye shadows, lipsticks, and blushers to show good health.

Black is often used to darken another color and make a shade of that color. Shading colors can also be made by mixing opposite colors together. Black mixed with white makes a neutral gray. Cool, darker skin tones tend to look good in black. In makeup, black is used in eye shadows, eyeliners, brow color, and mascara. Black can be used to add drama or depth to existing colors.

White is added to other colors to make tints. In makeup, white or off-white can be used as highlighters, or to make darker colors stand out. Cool, darker skin tones tend to look good in white.

COLOR LESSONS

Color is one of the most important things to have a good understanding about. The more you use what you read, the easier using color becomes. Whether you use a traditional color wheel or the Real Color Wheel is up to you. The lessons address using the different primary colors, but the knowledge can also be used for more-traditional ways of color mixing. Just think of these color lessons as a way to mix to get even more color choices.

Lesson One: The Color Wheel
1. Using artist paper and a pencil, draw a Real Color Wheel. Be sure to use the correct dimensions and straight edges. Use the RCW in Figure 3.1 for reference.

2. Paint in the correct colors on your wheel.

3. After you are done painting, number and name the wheel.

Lesson Two: Complementary Pigments Make Neutral Darks
1. Draw three simple contour drawings of an object or face.

2. Pick three of the opposition colors in Figure 3.7 to use as details, shadows, or highlights (for example, Cadmium Orange and Cobalt Blue are opposition colors).

3. Use the colors separately and mixed together to create neutral darks.

Lesson Three: Complementary Pigments Make Neutral Darks
1. Use the example from Lesson Two, but instead follow the brown pigment chart (Figure 3.14) for reference.

Lesson Four: Creating Several Skin Tones
1. On artist paper, create several skin tones by using pigments that have been tinted or darkened accordingly. Remember to use all the ranges of color from #1 yellow to #7 red.

2. Darken these colors to brown by mixing your browns.

3. When you come up with skin tones you like, write down, next to the color, the exact combination you used. This is a way to keep records for future use.

REFERENCES

Jusko, Don. www.realcolorwheel.com.

———. www.realcolorwheel.com/complementsneutral.htm.

———. www.realcolorwheel/pigmentrcwmap.htm.

———. www.realcolorwheel/tubecolors.htm.

4

LIGHTING

Lighting can be one of the most important tools for a Makeup Artist. It is always a good idea to know what type of lights are being applied and the kind of gels or filters that will be used in front of the lights or the camera lens. Makeup is often adjusted to meet those demands. Most often, if you have designed your makeup with the lighting in mind, your artistry will be enhanced by it. If you ignore the effects that lighting and color have on your makeup application, the mistakes will be obvious for all to see. It all works together and takes years to really learn, but you will get invaluable practical experience with each job. Eventually, you will recognize what colors work with the lighting situations you are in, and the more information you know about lighting, filters, and gels, the better the outcome.

Before a shoot starts, ask questions of the Director, the Cinematographer (also known as the DP, Director of Photography), or the Gaffer (Lighting Designer). If they are not available, sometimes the First AD (Assistant Director) can help. Of course in some jobs, you will not get the chance to ask any questions. Be observant, watch the lighting crew and camera, and ask questions when they are not busy. Most people are very happy to explain their job or situation to you. Is it a film, video, HDTV, or stage production? You should know whether you are filming indoors or outside, day or night, and what lights, filters, and gels are planned. There are so many factors, and the more you know, the better off you are. Remember, this is not a perfect world— there will be many, many times that information is not available. So know your

stuff, and be ready to work out of your kit and think on your feet.

Joseph N. Tawil, President of GAMPRODUCTS, Inc., is an expert in light and color mixing. He suggests: "Often I recommend that lights be set up in the makeup room in which you can put colored gels to simulate the lighting on stage or for camera."

This is a perfect working condition, but you cannot count on it. On some productions, this will be accommodated, but it depends on the project, prep time, and—very important—the money. Lighting packages can be expensive, and so are those lightbulbs.

COLOR DESCRIPTION TERMS FOR LIGHT

by Joseph N. Tawil, President, GAMPRODUCTS, Inc.

Hue, value, and chroma are terms from the Munsell system of color notation (published in 1905). It is a system designed for explaining color in ink and paint rather than color in light. However, the three descriptive terms are used to define the color of light, contributing more to the confusion than to the clarity of the subject. The vocabulary of color is a minefield of contradictions and confused meanings. Colorimetry is another system for describing color, and is of particular interest because it relates well to colored light. In colorimetry, the following terms are used to describe the color of light:

Dominate Wavelength (DWL): The apparent color of the light. Similar to the term hue, meaning the apparent color (e.g., red).

Brightness: The percentage of transmission of the full spectrum of energy (similar to value). Often described as intensity.

Purity: The purity of color is similar to chroma. It describes the mixture of color of the DWL with white or the color of the source. If there is only color of the DWL, it is 100 percent pure; but if there is very little DWL in the mixture, as in a tint, the color could be as low as, say, 5 percent pure.

White: The presence of all colors in the light.

Black: Absence of all colors.

Texture: The surface properties of a color, as in shiny or matte, reflective or diffusing.

THE LANGUAGE OF ADDITIVE AND SUBTRACTIVE COLOR MIXING

by Joseph N. Tawil, President, GAMPRODUCTS, Inc.

Color mixing with lights is called additive color mixing (Figure 4.1). This tricolor mixing theory was proposed by Sir Thomas Young in the early 1800s, and it is the basis for all film and video color systems today. Young discovered that by mixing red, blue, and green light, he could make the most of the colors in the visible spectrum. Young determined that red, green, and blue were the ideal primary colors of light because they allow for the widest variety and create a reasonable white. Red, green, and blue are three colors that are widely separated from each other. Because of this, they will combine to make many other colors, including, in the right circumstances, white.

Combining two primary colors creates a secondary color that is a complement of

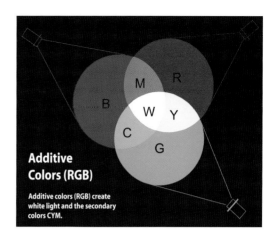

FIGURE 4-1: ADDITIVE COLORS

the third primary (complement, as in completes). For example, by combining red and blue, you get magenta and other colors in the violet and pink range. Combining blue and green generates cyan (blue green) colors. Combing red and green creates yellow and other colors in the orange range.

Complementary colors are also called secondary colors. Violets and pinks are complementary to the primary color green because they contain red and blue. Oranges and yellows are complementary to the primary color blue because they contain red and green.

Tricolor mixing is illustrated in Figure 4.1. It is interesting to note that the complementary colors (or secondary colors) created in the additive color-mixing process—cyan, yellow, and magenta—are the primary colors of the subtractive color-mixing system. Obviously, this in not an accident, and the two theories do tie together.

Subtractive Color: Subtractive color filtering (Figure 4.2) is something all of us

Subtractive Color Mixing

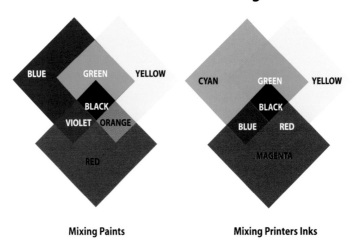

Mixing Paints

Mixing Printers Inks

FIGURE 4-2: SUBTRACTIVE COLOR CHART

have experienced in elementary school, where we have mixed paints to make a variety of colors. Later, we will. It's possible to read art books where painters talked about mixing primaries to make different colors. The primaries are often described in these art books as red, yellow, and blue. Filmmakers, however, see the subtractive color-mixing primaries described as yellow, cyan, and magenta. Using the same language to describe primary colors in both the subtractive and additive color-mixing processes causes a great deal of confusion. Printers and filmmakers define the subtractive primary colors more accurately as cyan, yellow, and magenta (CYM), separating them from the additive color process. In subtractive color mixing, as we mix the primary colors of paints, inks, or filter emulsion layers, the resulting color gets darker and darker, and eventually black.

Subtractive color mixing is what we do when mixing makeup pigments, as opposed to the Lighting Department, which will use the additive process for color mixing. In other words:

Additive Color: In the additive color-mixing process, we are adding primary colors to come to white light. In the subtractive color-mixing process, we are mixing the primary colors to come to black.

When the artist knows that the word "additive" means mixing light to get a color, and the word "subtractive" is mixing pigments (makeup), all the mystery about a light source is better understood.

Correction Filters: The primary function for correction filters is to balance to a given light source. The two points of balance most often used are 3200K (or tungsten), and daylight (usually 5600K). Most film and television is divided between the two. For example, if you are shooting in an office with sunlight coming through the window, you will want to correct for one or the other. You either warm the sunlight toward tungsten, or you raise the apparent color temperature of the incandescent to daylight. The Makeup Artist needs to understand that the light itself does not affect the makeup, but how the lights are manipulated by additive color mixing with the use of gels and filters in front of the light source does.

Fluorescent Light: This type of light is problematic because of the green spikes attributed to it. Manufacturers make two kinds of fluorescents: warm and cool. The warm leans toward tungsten, and the cool leans toward daylight. Other problems with fluorescents are inconsistent lamp manufacturing, aging lamps that are still being used, and the fact that certain colors are always missing from the spectrum. If you find yourself on a shoot with fluorescents as a light source, and you need to match or create a specific color (let's say lipstick), take a test photo before the shoot begins.

Video Lights: Video often uses softer lights (soft boxes) for indoor interviews. Film and video usually work with HMI (hydrargyrum medium-arc iodide) if shooting outside in the daylight or with incandescent in the studio. Be prepared to make adjustments to the makeup if the actor is being moved from an interior shot to an exterior shot. There is a big difference in the visual perception of the colors when incandescent lights are used inside to do your makeup, and then you go outside and shoot in daylight or with HMI lights.

Stage Lighting: Stage lighting uses light for different reasons. There are a wide range of colors used theatrically. When you're working in the theatre, the lighting designer is there during the technical/rehearsal period, and their color design can be discussed then.

The theatre usually uses an incandescent source unless you're looking at a xenon follow spot or HMI follow spot, which is very close to daylight, and much bluer in its energy. The makeup is decided by how bright the light will be, how large is the stage being lit, what color gels or filters are being used to light the actors or objects onstage, and how the light is used around the stage.

Photography: Photography uses light to create greater dimension, to highlight different areas, and to reduce or magnify details. Natural light is often used to create moods. Artificial lights are used to control different shooting situations. Tungsten or incandescent lighting is most often used.

GEL FILTERS

Gel filters (Figure 4.3) are used in front of the light source to change what the light is putting out. Lighting designers use gel filters for many different reasons. Gel filters are made of transparent plastic that is heat resistant, and they come in different translucent colors. They should not absorb heat, and are usually made of polyester or polycarbonate. You usually buy them in sheets or rolls. Film people tend toward rolls, theater people toward sheets. Why gels and filters are used and what color is chosen can affect your makeup. There are also digital equivalents of lighting gels and filters created by companies such as GAMPRODUCTS, Inc. with Digital Film Tools. The following explains the color of the gels for photo cameras, film cameras,

video, theatre, and digital add-ins, and what each color is most often used for, as well as how to adjust your makeup to work under these conditions.

General Breakdown of Colored Gel Filters for Light Sources

No-Color Blue: Top light for theatrical daytime. Top light in theatre tends to pale the skin tone. Areas of the face such as the eyes tend to sink or cast a shadow.

Blue Gels: Used most often to match daylight or to suggest nighttime. Can be used to make a light source bluer, and also used with other gels to achieve specific color temperature. If used with + or − green, will help correct some fluorescent or discharge sources. Used on lights and

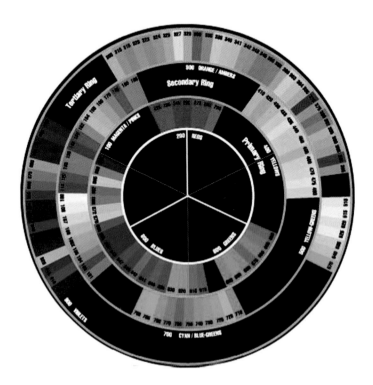

FIGURE 4-3: FILTER COLOR WHEEL

windows. Blue gels, depending on what is being shot, can have a cooling effect on the skin tone and over all the makeup. Reds look like hues of violets and pinks (tints). Blues and blue greens tend to fade. Lipsticks appear darker.

Grey Gels: Used on lights where color temperature and sharp shadow or patterns must be maintained. Works as a neutralizer and will also neutralize your makeup colors.

Orange Gels: If used with appropriate amount of + or − green, will help correct some fluorescent of discharge sources, and can also be used to simulate sunlight. Use on light or windows. Makeup colors stay the same, but try not to layer with too many warm tones, which could create an orange face. If the person has a ruddy skin tone, add green to your makeup.

Yellow Gels: Fills for sunlight and to warm a room. Makeup stays the same, but if the person has sallow skin, use violet to add life.

Yellow Gold Gel: Warm tones, enhances skin tones. Makeup stays the same. If you have golden undertones in the skin, all the warm colors will work. If you have cool undertones, blue greens and red violets look nice.

Peach Gel: Can be used to make a light source more orange. Will enhance skin tone. Makeup stays the same. A flattering color for all skin types. Used most often for video or close-up beauty shots.

Red Gels: Used for sunsets, sunrises, fires, and to add contrast. Red fades most of your makeup. Lips appear much lighter. Greens will look darker, and violets will look black. Good to create contrast. Used most often for theatre or specialty film.

Green Gels: Used to match the green spike in fluorescent lights or discharge. Also can be used with other gels for color effect. Used on lights, windows, and to contrast. All green colors will fade. Blushers all but disappear. Lips look dark, so a lighter and brighter lipstick works. The warm tones in red orange, orange, and yellow orange look good. Blues will take on a blue green tone.

CAMERA FILTERS

by Paul Wheeler, Digital Cinematography

Camera filters are used to alter the temperature of lights, change an image, or enhance colors. The following filters can also be used with digital shooting situations:

Color-Compensating Filters (CC Filters): Come in primary colors and are used in front of the camera lens to correct light.

Color-Correction Filters: Used to correct a daylight scene when shooting with tungsten-balanced film.

Skin-Tone Warmers: Filters that will warm up skin tones that would appear cold otherwise.

Sepia, Coral, and Others: Filters that lend a variety of tints to a scene.

Graduated Filters: Usually come in colored or neutral density filters. These filters are used to darken or color one area of a scene without affecting the rest of the scene.

Natural-Density Filters: Used to open up the aperture at which you will shoot the scene.

Low-Contrast Filters: Reduce the overall contrast in a scene.

Ultra-Contrast Filters: Like the low contrast filters, but work with the incident, ambient light. Ultra contrast filters work beautifully with bringing up shadow details.

Fog Filters: Try to emulate fog. Images will have less definition and contrast.

Double Fog Filters: Objects near to the camera will appear less affected than those far away.

Pro Mist Filters: Give a glow around intense sources of light. Highlights become "pearlized."

Net Filters: Nets will affect the scene differently depending on the color used. A white net will diffuse highlights into shadows. Dark nets will often bleed shadows into highlights. A brown net will add richness and overall warmth.

Enhancing Filters: Bring out one color at a time without affecting any of the others. These filters affect the red and orange portions of a scene.

Fluorescent-Light Correction: The FLB filter corrects fluorescent light to type B film or tungsten-balanced video camera. The FLD filter corrects fluorescent light to daylight camera.

Polar Screens: Screens that are used to darken the blue portion of a sky in color photography as well as reducing reflections in parts of a scene.

FIGURE 4-4: THE EFFECT OF INFRARED LIGHT ON SKIN TONE

BLACK-AND-WHITE PHOTOGRAPHY

Black-and-white photography with the use of light registers color in variations of gray. Seen this way, more attention should be given to composition and the levels of tone a color will be. Tones are used with light in black-and-white photography to portray emotions, through the lightness or darkness of shadows. The direction of light is important to the Makeup Artist. Front lighting will reduce the textures and depth of the photo. Backlighting will highlight the image and reduce the detail. If the image is lit from the side, it will have a greater dimension. When shooting outdoors in direct light, shadows will appear darker, with contrasting lights and darks. Cloudy or misty days will soften shadows. But this said, how the sun reacts during a shooting day will greatly influence your decisions. Full sun will create a harder light, with stronger shadows and highlights. Cloudy or partial sun has a softer look. Your makeup could look one way in the morning light, and another way at noon when the sun is strongest. Be aware of this throughout the day.

Artificial lights are used to control the brightness of the image and for different lighting effects. Usually tungsten or incandescent lighting is used. These light sources can also be used in color photography. Digital black-and-white photography works by switching the modes within the camera from a color LCD to grayscale. Pictures are taken with color signals that are recorded by CCD, but the image is later processed to remove all color. Filters are also used in all forms of black-and-white photography. Many photographers feel that if you have experience and expert knowledge in black-and-white photography, you will thrive in color photography. That is because of the natural instincts you will develop by working in gray tones. That theory works for the Makeup Artist as well.

Filters Used in Black-and-White Photography

Black-and-white photography uses filters to alter shades of gray. The following filters and their functions will allow the Makeup Artist to adjust makeup according to what filters are used, whether for art's sake or for natural makeup, when adjustments are necessary.

Red Filters: Red filters are used to add dramatic contrast in black-and-white photography. In color photography, red reduces blue and green. Red filters will enhance any red.

Yellow Filters: Will darken blues and lighten green, yellow, orange, and red colors.

Orange Filters: Work the same way as red filters and yellow filters, except with less intensity than red but more intensity than yellow.

Green Filters: Will lighten green colors.

Blue Filters: Will lighten blues and darken yellow, orange, and red. Works well to enhance fog mist or haziness.

Diffusion Filters: Are used for a soft-focus effect (as in softening wrinkles on the face).

Optical Effect Filters: Are multiimage filters such as star filters. These filters can bring a soft, diffused look to the image.

Polarizing Filters: Are used in color and in black-and-white photography. Reflected sunlight is reduced, haze can be penetrated, and overall skies are darkened. Color saturation is increased. Reflections are reduced or eliminated.

Today, there is, more than ever, a growing field of technology in the world of entertainment. What a production chooses to shoot and edit with can be wide open. This technology has opened the door to new and wonderful tools to work with. One of those tools is being able to edit digitally and create the same effect that gels and filters give when used on a light source. Digital Film Lab is a unique plug-in from Digital Film Tools meant to simulate a variety of color or black-and-white photographic looks, diffusion and Color-Grad camera filters, light gels, film stock, and optical lab processes. You would still apply the same principles (filter gels) on what colors to choose for makeup to better fit the digital color process it would go

FIGURE 4-5: DIGITAL PLUG FILTER ORIGINAL

FIGURE 4-7: DAY FOR NIGHT

FIGURE 4-6: DIGITAL PLUG FILTER ANTIQUE

FIGURE 4-8: COOL

through later. Figures 4.5 through 4.11 show Digital Film Tools simulated color gels and filters from Digital Film Labs.

LIGHTING LESSONS

Lighting, like color, is complex. A simple lesson in light and gels will remind the Makeup Artist why these things can affect his or her work.

FIGURE 4-9: BLEACH

FIGURE 4-10: HALO

FIGURE 4-11: INGRY
Photography by Larry Stanley

Lesson One: Gel Filters

1. Take a digital camera and hold a colored gel filter up against the lens. Take a close-up picture of an object under a simple light source (for example: a plant, flower, lips, animal, or whole face).

2. Using that same object and same light source, continue to take pictures, one at a time, with the following colored gels: blue, gray, orange, yellow, red, and green.

3. Observe each picture.

4. Write down the differences that the gel filters make to the same object.

This lesson is extreme. You'll rarely have an actor pure blue or pure green because of filters. However, it does show you how your makeup should be adjusted when gel filters are being used.

REFERENCES

Tawil, Joseph N. *Color Description Terms For Light.* www.gamonline.com/catalog/colortheory/language.php.

—— *The Language of Additive and Subtractive Color Mixing.* www.gamonline.com/catalog/colortheory/language.php.

Wheeler, Paul. 2001. *Digital Cinematography.* Jordon Hill: Focal Press, imprint of Elsevier.

Zolenski, Vicki. 2007. *Black and White Photography.* www.blackboardarts.com.

Internet Resources
Digital Film Tools. www.digitalfilmtools.com.

GAMPRODUCTS, Inc. www.gamonline.com.

Ilford Photo. www.ilfordphoto.com.

Robin Kanta Photographic Supply. www.photofilter.com.

www.montanaphotographer.com

5

TECH STUFF

Makeup Artists should be aware of what medium is being used to film, and should apply the makeup to reflect that. What are the meanings of some of the words "digital" and "HD"? What is "bluescreen" or "greenscreen"? What is a monitor? The following outline describes media that you will often encounter while working as a Makeup Artist.

WHAT HD LOOKS LIKE
by Paul Wheeler

High-definition (HD) images are very sharp, with long tonal ranges. Colors are lifelike and true. Whether seen on a monitor or digitally projected, there is no dirt on the pictures, no scratching, and no picture instability. Adjustments can be made with filters or within the camera menus.

With HD (Figure 5.1), one of the most obvious changes when you watch a projection by a state-of-the-art HD projector is the total lack of grain usually associated with film. However, grain can be added with filters if so desired. Images on set can be checked by real-time monitors to evaluate what your makeup looks like

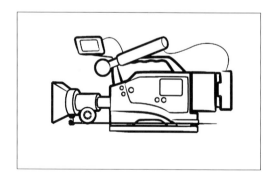

FIGURE 5-1: A DIGITAL HI-DEF CAMERA

before the shot. A 24-inch high-definition monitor works best.

MAKEUP DEPARTMENT AND HD
by Paul Wheeler

The relationship between a Director of Photography (DP) and the Makeup Designer and their team, I believe, has to be one of close cooperation—especially if there are prosthetics on set or, as so often happens in period pieces, wigs. The closeness between the join for a prosthetic or hairpiece needs to be reflected in the closeness in cooperation between these two crafts.

Working on HD or film is very similar. If the HD camera utilizes $^2/_3$-inch chips, then the DP will be restricted in the amount of diffusion that can be deployed in front of the lens in a very similar way to a Super 16 mm camera. Any form of diffusion on a $^2/_3$-inch HD camera has to be very light. This is because diffusion has a greater effect in HD, and this makes it very difficult for the DP to find that subtle level of diffusion where the lace will disappear, but the rest of the scene will not look false. If the camera utilizes a single chip similar in size than a normal 35 mm film frame, then the ability than deploy diffusion to help with the makeup will, again, be similar—but this time the help can be greater than with the smaller image formats.

Basically, if the Makeup and Hair teams are familiar with working in the 35 mm film theatrical environment, then they should have no trouble whatsoever with the HD environment. That said, a few things are easier in HD, and just a couple of things need more-careful watching.

If the production is using an HD monitor of decent quality and size on set, then the DP and Makeup Supervisor have a much easier task. On a well-set-up 14-inch (or, better still, 24-inch) HD monitor, most problems can be more quickly and effectively dealt with. It's that adage of "what you see is what you get"—whereas peering down an optical viewfinder on a film camera will not tell you as much. Remember, though, neither will be quite as devastatingly critical of your work as when the image is blown up to a cinema screen. But the same has always been true of film.

Note that each frame of film has the little silver grains in slightly different places. Each pixel on an HD image is in exactly the same place on an HD image. Usually, as far as the Makeup Artist is concerned, that is not a problem—but, just occasionally, it needs watching. If the camera or the artist is moving, you can usually forget about this—but if both are static, then something like the pattern of a wig net can, very occasionally, line up with the pixel array, and the net will look awful. If spotted early on, no problem. Just a slight change in camera angle will usually put the aligned lines out of alignment, and all will be well.

MEDIA EXPLANATIONS

Motion Pictures in Digital: Motion pictures that are shot digitally are films in which their images are captured on digital formats. These images can be taken with any media that can use digital technology. Digital cinematography is a term usually used to describe when film is being substituted for digital. Cinematography

digital cameras are usually progressive high-definition formats. Cameras for digital motion pictures are becoming more and more advanced and easier to use with already-existing camera lenses for film.

Resolution in Digital: This is a little more complex than what you would assume. Each pixel of the image is partial toward red, green, or blue. The color image is taken from this pattern of colors. Film stock has a certain amount of grain to the image, which some people feel is lacking with digital pictures. However, a high-end DP knows how to light and use the correct filters to get the same images and textures of film. Color grading is often created digitally instead of using a photochemical process.

High-Definition Television: HDTV is a television broadcast using higher-resolution formats. When considering resolution, the screen and how the image is transmitted come into play. HDTV has a least twice the resolution of standard television. The picture on HDTV is clearer, with better color spectrum.

Digital Television: DTV is a telecommunication system for broadcasting. Pictures and sound are received by digital signals. Digital television systems can carry both standard-definition and high-definition formats. Digital television can be received in different ways: aerial, pay-TV, digital cable, digital satellite, and DTV monitor.

Digital Photography: Images are captured with electronic devices that record the images on binary data. Digital photography image quality is expressed by pixel counts and the way the camera can turn data into the correct color balance.

Photographic Film: Can be polyester, nitrocellulose, or cellulose acetate. The film is coated by silver halide salts that are suspended by gelatin. When exposed to light, it forms an image. The film is put through a chemical process to expose that image.

Black-and-White Film: There is one layer of silver salts. When grains are developed, the salts are converted into metallic silver. This blocks the light and will be exposed as the black part of the negative.

Color Film: Uses three layers. Dyes are added to the silver salts, which in turn become more sensitive to color. The layers are usually blue, green, and then red. When the film is being processed, the salts turn into metallic silver, which reacts by forming colored dyes.

Print Film: Print film when processed turns into a negative. The negative can be color or black and white. Print film must be viewed by being printed on photographic paper or observed through a lens.

Bluescreen (Figure 5.2): Is used often for shooting people. Skin tones (reds, yellows, and greens) are opposite of the blue background. Bluescreen works by photographing or filming an actor in front of a blue background. Shades of blue should not be used while shooting bluescreen. The blue makeup might cause a spill format in the background to appear on the surface of the face. With incorrect colors, the face can almost start to look transparent. Warm colors work best. When

FIGURE 5-2: BLUESCREEN
Photo by: www.eefx.com – chroma key screens and supplies

shooting for bluescreen, lights and gels are often used to cast off yellow, orange, and warm tones. This is all to keep the actor separated from the background.

Greenscreen (Figure 5.3): Is often used in the same way as bluescreen. Greenscreen has a stronger luminance than blue and shows more detail. Because of this clarity, greenscreen is used often for special effects. Special effects can also include people in the shot. The same principle applies as far as makeup. Leave out colors that will blend with the background to avoid makeup that could cause spills and transparency to your work.

Example: Superman flying through Manhattan.

FIGURE 5-3: GREENSCREEN
Photo contributed by Bob Kertesz, www.bluescreen.com

FIGURE 5-4: MONITORS
Photo contributed by: www.Marshallelectronics.net

Whitescreen: Is used for a variety of reasons. The background is white, which adds to the contrast between screen, clothes, makeup, and hair. There are no wrong or right choices except to watch colors that are pale, clothes that are pastels or white. These colors might blend into the background.

Monitors (Figure 5.4) help the Makeup Artist to judge how the makeup looks under the lighting conditions on the set. Paul Wheeler:

Monitors are set up for the director and DP first. Where they are set up and how will keep the AC (Assistant Camera) busy. The practice I like is for the Second AC to cable from a single primary source on the camera a feed for the monitor the Director and DP will be using. When this is done, a second feed, totally independent from the first feed, is supplied for everyone else to tap into. The Second AC can rig a single monitor for the Script Supervisor, Makeup, Hair, and Costume. That is, if the DP allows it.

In some situations, there will be different areas for viewing, as Paul Wheeler describes. It not only depends on the DP, it also depends on the Director. The Director and the DP will decide where and how many setups of monitors there will be. One monitor for just the Director and the DP allows them to work in a quiet environment, without the distraction of others, or to work in private. It is very common to have two setups for monitors. There can also be a third setup for monitors for the clients, visiting guests, studio executives, and so on. If a monitor is not provided for you, and you need to check your work, ask the First AD if a monitor can be set up for you. Remember, every set is different. Some jobs will have monitors available for you, and some will not.

Here are a few examples of monitors to look for:

Cathode Ray Tube: CRT monitors are also available in true progressive-scan monitors.

High-Definition Monitor: A good monitor for the Makeup Artist to view. You will get a real image of what to expect, and the details will enhance any flaws. Talented DPs will actually use this monitor to light the set.

Liquid Crystal Display: LCD monitors usually found attached to the camera or on a flexible arm that allows the Focus Puller (First AC) to see the action being shot.

This monitor is lightweight and nice to look at, but is not the right monitor to check for colors and lights and how they affect your makeup.

Plasma Screens: Available in larger screens, often between 42 and 61 inches. They have a little less quality than the CRT monitors.

PRO TIP

In filming situations, if you need to check your makeup, ask the DP or Camera Operator for permission to look through the lens. This way, you are seeing the image with gels, filters, and the lighting in place. Sometimes in film, using the monitor is not the best way when checking or correcting your makeup.

SCRIPT BREAKDOWN

Script breakdown is the process of analyzing your script. Breaking down a script is not a suggestion—it is essential toward your process of analyzing, developing, and designing makeup. All departments do a breakdown of the script, starting with the

Producers, who need to budget and schedule, based on the information in the script. An understanding of the script is necessary for answering the many questions that will come up during prep and filming. This allows the Makeup Artist to effectively deal with the changing conditions and concerns of a shoot. You will build lists of characters, scripted notes on the characters (how they look and dress), makeup effects, location or environments that will affect you, and any written descriptions affecting makeup. This information will influence the design and needs of the Makeup Department, including budgeting. Script breakdown is your chance to understand how the story moves, to get an understanding of everything that has to happen to the characters, how many "script days," which scenes are day, which scenes are night, and if there are any environmental factors (such as rain). Script breakdown will help you make decisions on how to achieve and maintain the makeup looks. There are computer programs available for script breakdown. It is recommended that you use both manual and computer breakdowns for makeup.

1. Start by reading through the script without taking notes.

2. Read through a second time, making notes on what "day" or "night" it is, per scene.

Your days/nights will need to be checked against the Script Supervisor's breakdown. Always defer to the Script Supervisor's breakdown—this is given to all departments, and is the definitive breakdown of the script.

3. Read through a third time, making character notes, and start an effects list.

4. List all characters, along with any script descriptions of their looks.

5. List all makeup effects or looks that need to play in continuous scenes. Make notes on how long an effect or look works. This is your makeup continuity.

Example: Fred is hit in SC 3. His cheek is bruised.

Question: How many scenes does the bruise work, and what is the progression or age of the bruising? When is the last time you see the bruise?

Example: Mary and Joe leave the diner. It starts to rain. They run two blocks to the car.

Question: Where do they drive to? How long do you maintain the "wet look"?

Your effects list will also help you in budgeting for the department. The better you know and understand the script, the better prepared you are for conversations with the Director, Producers, and other department heads.

REFERENCES

Wheeler, Paul. 2001 *Digital Cinematography*. Linacre House: Focal Press, an imprint of Elsevier

—— 2003. *High Definition and 24 P Cinematography*. Linacre House: Focal Press, an imprint of Elsevier.

Internet Resources
Digital photography. http://en.wikipedia.org/wiki/Digital_photography.

Digital television. http://en.wikipedia.org/wiki/digital_television.

EEFX. www.eefx.com.

HDTV. http://en.wikipedia.org/wiki/HDTV.

www.bluescreen.com

UNDATIONS

For every person that sits down in your chair—whether you are working on a film, designing elaborate characters for theatre, creating an image for a photo shoot, or skillfully applying a beauty makeup for television—you will need to know that person's skin tone. If you do not get this part right, your makeup will appear dull, gray, and lifeless. One of the things you'll learn as a Makeup Artist is how to be quick and to think on your feet. In many cases, we do not have the luxury of time to work on a person—everyone from the Director to the crew is waiting on you. Train yourself on the steps to analyzing skin tones, and you will be a better Makeup Artist. This would also include makeup effects. Makeup effects deal in great length in the art of skin tones and color layering.

The primary function of the skin is to protect, and to regulate heat. Differences in skin color are due to the amount of melanin activated in the skin and the way it is distributed. Melanin is the pigment of the skin. Melanin protects the skin cells from ultraviolet rays by absorbing and blocking UV rays through tanning, which is a reaction to sun exposure. UV rays have the greatest impact on how skin ages. Approximately 80 to 85 percent of our aging is caused by the sun. Melanin in the skin is nature's sunblock, and the more melanin in the skin, the darker the skin tone. Scientists have estimated that people of African decent have some 35 different hues or shades of skin. Undertones that tend to dominate dark skin tones are yellow, orange, red, olive, and blue. You

have to learn and really understand how to deal with all the different undertones in the skin. Do not rely on just looking at the surface of the skin—the undertones that are present just under the surface will affect the color you apply to the skin. This takes much practical experience and exposure to the wide variety of skin tones and different combinations, as well as situations you will be with. Ethnicity, environment, and illness all play a part in a person's individual undertones, and in some cases are not easily recognized. Look at what happens to color when applied to the skin. Does the color enhance the skin tone, or is there a gray or dull quality? Unless the part calls for illness, your goal is a healthy tone to the skin.

Nancy Tozier, Director of Education and President of Take up Make-up Cosmetics, says: Learning color theory can help you change a good makeup application into a great one. By understanding color theory, you can take years off a face, make eyes show from across the room, create harmony, and change dull to outrageous, while always knowing exactly what you're doing."

Tozier teaches throughout the United States and internationally. She specializes in teaching the artistry of makeup, color analysis, and skin care. The following outline will show you how to incorporate the color wheel to plot skin tones. You will also learn to custom blend foundations and powders with color to enhance or correct skin tones. Again, this theory in the use of color is a basic knowledge for all Makeup Artists. Nancy will guide us with her knowledge through color theory and mixing foundation.

She explains: "The key to understanding color theory is the artist color wheel." (See Figure 6.1.) Nancy continues:

If you divide the color wheel in half from top to bottom, the colors on your right are the cool colors—blues, and shades of blue (blue green, blue violet, and raspberry). We associate these colors with the cold. The colors to the left are the warm colors. They contain yellow. We associate these colors with fire. The color at the very top of the wheel, red, can be warmed if a little yellow is added, moving toward the orange tones on the left. That very same red can be cooled by the addition of a little violet, moving toward the blue tones on the right. In the same way, green, at the very bottom of the color wheel, can be cool if a bit of blue is added

to it, and can be warmed by adding a bit of yellow. You can see how very similar colors can be warm or cool depending on whether blue or yellow undertones are added.

How does the color wheel apply to custom blending cosmetics?

In Chapter 3, we showed you the Real Color Wheel (RCW) for mixing pigments. Nancy uses the traditional artist color wheel for custom blending of cosmetics. The traditional color wheel primaries are red, blue, and yellow. Makeup foundations have these colors in them. To custom blend a foundation to match the client's skin perfectly, you must begin by determining if the client is warm toned (with golden undertones) or cool toned (with blue undertones). People rarely look blue, so we say cool (or blue) undertones. A variety of brown shades can be made by combining the primary colors.

To intensify a color, you add an additional amount of that same color. To neutralize a color, we look at our color wheel and choose the color directly across from the color we want to lessen. For example, if a foundation is too yellow, if we look at a color wheel, we see the opposite color is violet. We add small amounts of violet until we reach the desired tone.

Here is a guide to determine which colors intensify a color, and which colors neutralize a color.

- If the person needs more gold, add yellow.
- If the person needs less yellow, add violet.

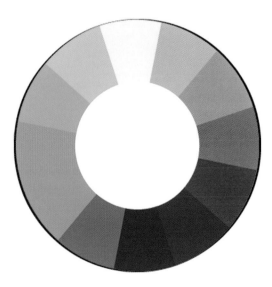

FIGURE 6-1: ARTIST COLOR WHEEL

- If the person needs less pink or has rosacea, add green.

- If the person needs less peach, first add mint, then violet.

This method can be used with translucent powders as well. Most private-label makeup companies offer the tools to custom blend, as well as empty bottles or jars, and larger-sized foundation bottles to work from. Always mix your foundations in a beaker for accurate measurements. With practice, you will learn the exact amounts to add. If you add too much color to neutralize, you can always add back in some of the opposite color. Check your color wheel.

COLOR THEORY AND MIXING FOUNDATIONS

by Nancy Tozier, Director of Education and President, Take up Make-up Cosmetics

To custom blend a foundation that matches the client's skin perfectly, you must begin by determining if the client is warm toned or cool toned. Does the client's skin have golden undertones or cool undertones? (Cool undertones are sometimes referred to as blue undertones, but because people rarely look blue, let's say cool.) Here's what to do:

1. If you have on hand different colors of cosmetic or barber caps or drapes, that would be helpful in determining skin tones.

2. Look closely at the actor's skin tone. Do you see any gold? Don't confuse a beige or brown tone with golden. Many people

with different depths of color can be cool toned.

Make sure that the actor is seated in bright daylight so that you will get the best view of the skin without interference from other sources of color.

3. If you think the actor has a warm skin tone and their skin is fair, then light golden yellow, gold, or adobe would be good colors to place next to the skin.

If you think the actor has a golden skin tone but has darker coloring, burnt orange, avocado green, or deep gold would be good colors next to the skin. What you are looking for is if their skin takes on a healthy look.

PRO TIP

You can use blusher or eye-shadow colors from your makeup kit that are similar to the colors suggested above for checking skin tones.

4. If a color is wrong for a person, their skin will take on a grayish cast. If the color is good for a person, they will look healthy and vibrant. Don't let your preference for a color cloud your vision. You are looking for the effect on the skin, not if you like the color. Learning to see the whole picture takes practice, so don't get discouraged if it isn't easily apparent at first. Use the chart opposite to help you find the colors that bring out the best for clients with different skin tones.

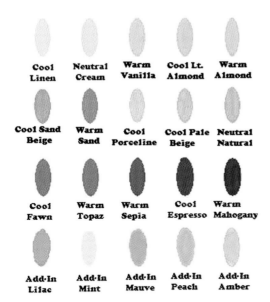

Cool Linen	Neutral Cream	Warm Vanilla	Cool Lt. Almond	Warm Almond
Cool Sand Beige	Warm Sand	Cool Porceline	Cool Pale Beige	Neutral Natural
Cool Fawn	Warm Topaz	Warm Sepia	Cool Espresso	Warm Mahogany
Add-In Lilac	Add-In Mint	Add-In Mauve	Add-In Peach	Add-In Amber

FIGURE 6-2: TAKE UP MAKE-UP COSMETICS' COLOR CHART

FOUNDATION MIXING

by Nancy Tozier, Director of Education and President, Take up Make-up Cosmetics

Once you have determined the shades that are best suited to the person, you will begin the process of mixing foundations to correct or enhance the actor's skin tone.

First, be sure that the client is seated in good daylight, just as you did in the color exercise. You will need to have the following on hand:

1. Several shades of foundation that are close to your client's natural coloring.

2. Several shades of corrector in mint green, pale yellow, violet, and white.

3. A glass beaker to mix your new foundation in.

4. A skin-care spatula for mixing.

5. An empty foundation bottle in which to pour the finished foundation.

6. Clean paper towels for keeping things tidy.

Select a color of foundation similar to the level of lightness or darkness of your client's skin. At this point, you also need to try to match the client's undertones. Does her face look golden, pink, greenish, or peachy? Look for a similar foundation color. Most custom blend foundations come with the following additives: yellow, violet, green, or white. You may have to mix two different foundations if the client's coloring falls between the shades of foundation that you are using. Place a little less than two ounces of foundation in the beaker. Remember that you will be adding some color, and you want the finished amount to fit into the bottle.

Test the color on the client's jawline. You want to match the color of the client's neck. A foundation that matches the client's neck will give the most harmonious appearance. We've all seen too many faces that appear to be a completely different color than the person's neck. A sure sign of unprofessional makeup!

Now determine if the foundation needs correction. If, for example, the client's skin is more golden than your foundation, you would add more gold. This is called intensifying a color. If your client's skin is less golden than your foundation, you want to lessen the amount of gold in the foundation. This is called neutralizing a color. If you add too much color, you can always neutralize it by adding some of the opposite color, easily identified using the color wheel.

- If the client needs less yellow, add violet.
- If the client needs less pink or is covering rosacea, add mint green.
- If the client needs less peach, first add mint, then violet.

This method can be used with translucent powders as well. Most private-label makeup companies offer the tools to custom blend, as well as empty bottles or jars and larger-sized foundation bottles to work from.

So, in review, to intensify a color, add more of the same color; to neutralize, add the opposite.

SPECIAL FOUNDATION NEEDS

Nancy explains that sometimes a person's skin color presents a special problem. For example:

- Someone with rosacea needs help managing redness.
- Someone will naturally have so much golden (yellow) tone that they look sallow.
- Some skin tones have an almost greenish hue that can actually appear unhealthy.

Here are some techniques:

If a person has very red skin, find a foundation that matches the neck (which is usually much less red), and begin by adding mint green to it. The color of the foundation will begin to look dull, but when applied to the face, it neutralizes the unwanted color and gives a calmer, less red appearance.

For someone who is overly yellow, adding violet to a foundation that matches the neck will neutralize the yellow and look

beautiful. In this situation, often the neck is yellow as well, so foundation will need to cover the neck and be well blended at the base of the neck.

Nancy gives us valuable lessons and understanding on skin color analyses and foundation mixing. In today's fast-paced industry, we work with premixed foundations, as well as concealers, tinted primers, and camouflage creams to correct if we are not mixing colors. We also mix these "premixed" foundations together on palettes to get the match needed. You will be mixing and matching on your feet, and working in environments that require you to be time sensitive. You will be doing a practical color analysis of the skin by testing the foundation on the skin at the jawline to see if it matches with the face and the neck. You will be draping your actor with a barber's drape or hairstylist's cape. They come in several colors, but most Makeup Artists use black. If the actor is wearing clothing in a color that is not suitable for the color palette designed for the project or is not good for their skin tone, the drape or cape will help you neutralize this problem and let you see how your color choices are working with the individual's skin tone.

FOUNDATIONS AND PRIMERS

Makeup foundation's cosmetic purpose is to even out skin tone, hide fine lines, and provide a base on which to apply makeup. Foundations also provide added moisture to the skin, protect from the environment, and, with some products, provide a light sunscreen.

Foundation or makeup base comes in a variety of textures and consistencies: tinted moisturizers, liquid, cream, cake, stick, cream to powder, and powder. You can achieve a different level of coverage with each type of foundation. Color, consistency, and coverage will guide you in choosing what foundation to use for different skin types and situations, and if you should or should not use a primer first.

Ingredients are another important factor in choosing what foundation to use on the various different skin types you will encounter. Water-based, emollient-based, and mineral-based products are all Industry Standards and should be part of your kit. In today's industry, skin care has become very important. People pay close attention to the care and condition of their skin and the products that work best for them. You will need to stay up on the latest in skin-care treatments, products, and ingredients.

PRIMERS

Foundation primers even out the texture of the skin, keep the makeup smooth and flawless, add longevity to the makeup, and protect the skin underneath. They also prevent moisture loss. Some Makeup Artists always use a primer to prep the skin before applying foundation. Some use primers only when they decide primers are needed to achieve a certain look or when they need to protect the skin. Silicone-based primers are great for sensitive or allergic skin. The silicone used is nontoxic. These primers actually protect the skin from the makeup foundation by putting a barrier between the foundation and skin. This will lessen the breakouts for sensitive or allergic skin. Silicone primers also fill in enlarged pores, acne scars, fine lines, and wrinkles. Primers come in violet, green, pink and yellow tint. These are great to help even out undertones on skin that does not need heavy concealing. All primers are applied before the foundation with a sponge, brush, or hands.

Some examples of industry primers are: ColorScience, Laura Mercier Foundation Primer, LORAC, Paula Dorf, smashbox, and YSL.

Note: If you apply primers, foundations, blush, and so on with your hands, you must wash your hands thoroughly with soap and water before and after. Hand application is controversial in the film/television world; not so for print. Many Makeup Artists believe it should not be done under any circumstance, that it is unprofessional and not sanitary. Of course, just as many Makeup Artists believe it is a valuable technique, especially when working with

73

liquids. Actors are also split on their preference—some love it; others prefer no contact with the skin except with a sponge or brush. If you are working as an additional Makeup Artist for crowd scenes, hand application is not practical because you have too many people to make up.

FOUNDATIONS

The most popular foundations in the industry are tinted moisturizers, liquids, and cream-based, water-based, emollient-based, and mineral-based foundations. You will need to have all of them in your kit, with a good selection of colors for mixing and matching. This will allow you to handle any skin tone and type. Cake and stick foundations are also used, but not as readily, though they are also found in most makeup kits.

Tinted Moisturizers: Are the sheerest or lightest of coverage, when you do not need a lot of correction. Tinted moisturizers will even out skin tone, and can add just a hint of color if needed. They are great on men, or when you need just a hint of added color on good skin.

Industry Standards: Laura Mercier Tinted Moisturizer, Stila Color Tinted Moisturizer.

Liquid Foundations: Give a sheer overall coverage that looks natural, and are easy to apply with a sponge or brush to get a smooth finish. They are good for all skin types, and are available in water-based, emollient (hydrating), and mineral-based formulas. For oily or sensitive skin, use a water-based foundation. For dry or mature skin, choose a hydrating foundation.

Mineral foundations are good with all skin types. Liquids are widely used in the industry, easy to mix, and do not have to be powdered.

Industry Standards: Armani, Bobbi Brown, Chanel, Clinque, Estée Lauder, Iman, M•A•C, Make Up For Ever, Revlon ColorStay, Visiora.

Mineral Foundations: Are great for sensitive or acne-prone skin. There are fewer ingredients, and because the minerals are inert, they will not support bacteria. They are great for people with allergies and sensitive skin, as well as rosacea. Mineral-based makeup gives long-lasting coverage that does not settle into fine lines or irritate the skin. They should be applied with a sponge or makeup brush. They are available in liquid or powder form. They offer broad-spectrum UVA and UVB protection, and are water resistant, and contain no talc or parabens. They are not tested on animals.

Industry Standards: Bare Escentuals, glominerals, Illuminaré, Jane Iredale, ColorScience.

Cream Foundations: Usually come in a compact or stick (pan stick). They are wonderful on all skin types and provide excellent coverage. Cream foundations are widely use in all media, and are easily applied with a sponge or brush, providing overall coverage with a rich texture and deep tone. You can achieve different finishes with cream foundations: sheer, more coverage, and layering over a liquid for even more coverage. Layering over a liquid gives you a beautiful and flawless finish, but because it is more product, there could be some film and lighting situations that it would be too heavy for. It is good for all skin types, but best on dry skin. It should be set with powder.

Industry Standards: Black Opal, Bobbi Brown, Cinema Secrets, Gerda Spillmann, Iman, M•A•C, RCMA, Visiora.

Powder Foundations: Are great for the two-for-one application. They give a flawless matte finish. Apply with a dry sponge or makeup brush. For more coverage, use a damp sponge to apply. It's not for every skin type, and works best on oily or acne-prone skin, but also works well for normal or combination skin. It's great for quick solutions when there is no time, on set touch-ups, or for fast application of color. It's also good in humid conditions.

Industry Standards: Lancôme Dual Finish, M•A•C Studio Fix.

Cream to Powder Foundations: Are good for most skin types, but great for combination skin. They should be applied with a dry sponge.

Try: Benefit's some kind-a gorgeous, Vincent Longo Water Canvas Creme-to-Powder Foundation.

Cake Makeup: Comes in the form of a "cake" and is usually applied with a damp sponge. It gives a matte finish. The sponge should not be wet, but damp to get a smooth finish. It is used extensively for stage performers for face painting, clown makeup, fantasy, and body makeup.

Industry Standards: KRYOLAN, Mehron.

Fillers and Mattifying Products: Are great to use on bare skin. The fillers are clear or opaque, and fill in fine lines and scars. Fillers can be used on bare skin, under makeup, or over makeup. Mattifiers take down shine, and are great for bare skin, bald heads, and prosthetics.

Industry Standards: Make-Up International Face to Face Supermatte Antishine (comes in Light, Medium, and Dark), Lancôme Pure Focus T-Zone.

Try: Benefit's is dr. feelgood for smoothing and filling in under or over makeup.

CONCEALERS

Concealers even out skin tone, and cover blemishes, scars, bruising, discoloration, and circles under the eyes. They have a thicker composition than foundation, and are available in cream, stick, tube, pots, and liquid. Sometimes a concealer is the only product a Makeup Artist needs to even out someone's skin tone (see "Spot Painting" in Chapter 7). You will also use concealers on the body to cover any unattractive marks, bruises, or scars, or to cover tattoos. For the face and body (not the eye area), concealers with a high pigment are best for camouflaging because they provide complete coverage and last longer. You need to blend the concealer well into the skin so that it disappears, especially if you are not using a makeup foundation on the skin. You can apply concealer under or over makeup foundation.

Note that concealers are designed to be applied over the foundation if you are using a liquid or cream base. If you are using a powder or dry foundation, apply the concealer underneath the base. With the

Foundation Product Comparisons

Colors are classified according to temperature and charted below in descending values (or steps) from light to dark. Graftobian's Hi-Def Creme Foundations are used as the baseline color range for other product comparison matches because of their wide range of selection of accurate skin tone colors in each temperature.

Temperature	Graftobian	RCMA	Cinema Secrets	Visiora	MAC	Shu Uemura Nobara Cream	Black Opal	Revlon ColorStay
Warm	Graceful Swan				C15	983		
Warm	Ingénue		301S-63		NC15			Buff
Warm	Vixen		302S-65		NC35, C3			Sand
Warm	Temptress		304S-32					
Warm	Buttermilk		303S-66					
Warm	Enchantress	Shinto #1	509-62			554		True Beige
Warm	Femme Fatale	LN1						Early Tan
Warm	Desert Sand	Shinto #2				754		Rich Tan
Warm	Winter Wheat	Shinto #3	201S-67			545		Toast
Warm	Golden Sunset				NC60, NW35			
Warm	Deep Xanthe	Shinto #4						
Warm	Ginger	Shinto #5					Nutmeg	
Warm	Midnight Marigold	Shinto #6			NC50, NC65, C7			Caramel
Warm	Burnt Amber	Shinto #7	202S-20					Cappucino
Warm	Sienna						Black Walnut	Mocha
Three shades below are unique medium to medium dark colors in warm temperature.								
Warm	Sunlit Linen						Kalahari Sand	
Warm	Caramel			CN102				
Warm	Pecan	Shinto #8					Hazelnut	
Temperature	Graftobian	RCMA	Cinema Secrets	Visiora	MAC	Shu Uemura Nobara Cream	Black Opal	Revlon ColorStay
Neutral	Bombshell							
Neutral	Prima Donna							Nude
Neutral	Leading Lady							
Neutral	Sweetheart							
Neutral	Glamour Girl					564		
Neutral	Cabaret Kitten							
Neutral	Broadway Star							
Neutral	Show Stopper							
Neutral	Screen Goddess	LN1						Natural Tan
Neutral	Diva				NC45			
Neutral	Chestnut	MB5				334	Au Chocolat	
Neutral	Warm Umber				N4, NW45 & 50		Walnut	
Neutral	Hazelnut							
Neutral	Hidden Magic		204S-27					
Neutral	Nightfall							
Five shades below are unique medium dark to dark colors in neutral temperature:								
Neutral	Evening Mist	S1						
Neutral	Olivia			MV 101	C5, C50			
Neutral	Smoke	KT4						
Neutral	Soft Wisp							
Neutral	Phantom				W55			
Temperature	Graftobian	RCMA	Cinema Secrets	Visiora	MAC	Shu Uemura Nobara Cream	Black Opal	Revlon ColorStay
Cool	Buff		501-11	MV010				
Cool	Sunrise Flush	Ivory		CN001	NC20, NW20	574		Ivory
Cool	Aurora	GENA	598-14	MV001				Tawny
Cool	Cashmere Beige	Olive #1		MV002	N1			Natural Beige
Cool	Morning Glow	Olive #2		CN002	NW25 &3 0, N2	365		Medium Beige
Cool	Afterglow	Olive #3		MV003		354		
Cool	Cedar Spice	Tan Tone		MV004				
Cool	Ceylon Cinnamon	KT2		MV005	N6			
Cool	Henna	KM5		CN005, MV006				
Cool	Auburn	RJ2		CN006				
Cool	Sable					314	Carob	
Cool	Shadow Dance						Ebony	
Three shades below are unique medium to medium dark colors in cool temperature:								
Cool	Bisque	KW4						
Cool	Butterscotch	KM2					Heaven Honey	
Cool	Sandstone	Olive #4						

Original product match collaboration by Suzanne Patterson and Mary Erickson. Chart concept design by Michelle Talley. Revised and expanded format updated with additional category and product matches by Suzanne Patterson.

FIGURE 6-3: FOUNDATION COMPARISON CHART BY MARY ERICKSON AND SUZANNE PATTERSON

FOUNDATIONS

exception of dry foundations, most Makeup Artists do both, under and over, when applying concealer. Your choice will become part of your working technique and style. In difficult camouflage situations, you will need to apply both under and over the foundation to get the coverage needed. Try applying concealer both under and over a foundation for effect.

Industry Standards: KRYOLAN Dermacolor, Ben Nye, Joe Blasco.

Under-eye concealers come in stick, cream, or pot, as well as liquid. Look for concealers that are creamy in texture, with light to medium pigment. Remember that the skin around the eye is delicate, so the products you use to conceal around the eye area should be, too. If the product is too thick or uses a heavy pigment, you will have to work too hard to blend, irritating the thin skin tissue. Choose a concealer one shade lighter than the foundation that you are working with, and one that has moisturizing

FIGURE 6-4: DERMA COLOR PALETTE

properties. A stick concealer offers more coverage but is more difficult to blend, so it can be hard on the skin around the eyes. To avoid irritation and to keep the stick sanitary, do not apply the stick directly to the skin. Do not powder under the eyes.

Industry Standards: Paula Dorf, Iman, Kanebo, LORAC, Touche Éclat (YSL), Valorie.

HIGHLIGHTS AND CONTOURS

Throughout the makeup world, you'll get different opinions on if or when you should apply the theory of highlights and contours. As lighting and film stock have evolved, so has makeup. Back in the day, Makeup Artists would "blank out" the face to start with a blank canvas, and use the tools of highlight and contour to literally paint the preferred features back in. Today, this technique of "blanking out" the face is rarely used, but there will be a moment in your career when you will need to apply it—a drag makeup, for example. Today, Makeup Artists use highlights and contours in a subtle way, without blanking out the features of the face first. We create dimension and highlight features, but with a realistic touch or aesthetic. Sometimes a Makeup Artist is using the technique of highlight and contour without really knowing it. Examples include applying a lighter color under the eyebrow (highlight), or adding a touch of shade under the cheekbone to sculpt out more definition (contour).

What are highlights and contours, or highlights versus shading? Highlights are lighter colors that are applied to any area the Makeup Artist wants to stand out. Contours are darker colors that are applied to any area the Makeup Artist wants to sink or set back. Although the face has shape and depth, there are certain lighting situations that can turn the face flat. The more of a three-dimensional effect that the Makeup Artist can achieve, the better the makeup will be. That said, there is nothing worse than an overdone look when the Director has requested a no-makeup look.

With blending, you can create beautiful, flawless makeup using highlights and contours with no one being able to see the makeup. There are many Makeup Artists who either highlight or contour, but not both. Think about it. If you apply a lighter shade, for example, on the top of the cheekbone, you will automatically create a sink or shadow right below there for your contour. The same can be said of the opposite. If you apply a contour or shade, for example, in the temple area, you will create highlights on the top cheekbone and outer upper brow bone. We'll go into more details with the charts on what colors work well for both highlights and contours. In the long run, it is important for a Makeup Artist to learn facial structure and to recognize the importance of where lights and darks fall on the features of the face.

PRO TIP

Forward planes catch the light. Recessed planes recede.

—Gerd Mairandres, Wigmaster, San Francisco Opera

HIGHLIGHTS

The correct colors to use for highlights are important. If the highlight color is too light or too heavily applied for all media (film, TV, HD, print, and theater), your work will be seen as heavy-handed. Highlights in off-whites, cream, pinks, gold, yellows, or any color that is a few degrees lighter than the skin tone that you are working on will work best—except pure white, which in most situations is too harsh. Remember what you learned in Chapter 3—that white mixed with another color is a tint, so you can be as creative as you want to be.

CONTOURS

Shades of darker makeup from blushers to pigments can be used depending on what type of makeup you are creating. Good colors are brownish pinks, reds, grays, oranges, and again any shade that is a few degrees darker than the skin tone you are working on. You should never use pure black to contour. Remember, if you go back to Chapter 3, you'll see six examples of mixing color to get neutral darks, and color pigments to make browns.

BLENDING

Blending is the art of applying makeup using your tools to achieve a smooth, seamless finish with no visible line or hard edge. A skillful balance of strong or not-so-strong colors can be blended together without seams to create contrasts or dramatic effects.

In painting as well as in theatrical makeup, the technique of chiaroscuro is used to create a bold contrast between light and dark. Chiaroscuro, an Italian term literally meaning "light-dark," originated as a term for a type of Renaissance drawing on colored paper. The artist worked from the base tone toward light and dark. It is also a term used in makeup to refer to blending from light to dark for a three-dimensional, seamless effect. It is very helpful for all applications of makeup to learn chiaroscuro. You use subtle graduations of color in light and dark shades to enhance the delineation of character for dramatic effect. Remember to blend to the end.

Note: Chiaroscuro is also a term used in cinematography to indicate extreme low-key lighting to create distance areas of light and darkness in film, especially black-and-white film.

MORE ABOUT PRODUCTS

Eye Shadow

Cream Shadow: Cream eye shadows are used alone or with other eye shadow products. They can come in tubes, pots, wands, and compacts. Cream eye shadows can have a dewy, glossy, or frosty appearance, depending on the product. Some are formulated to be waterproof or water resistant.

Cream to Powder: Cream eye shadow that dries to a powder finish. Can be worn alone or layered.

Gel: Found most often in pots, gel products are used as eye shadow or eyeliner. They are quick drying, easy-glide application, and long lasting. They can be used in combination with other eye shadow products. Gels also come in glosses that dry to a shine that gives the eye shadow an appearance of being wet.

Liquid: Liquid eye shadow generally comes in a tube, usually with a wand or brush attached.

Loose Powder: Comes in jars. It can be used wet or dry. Products are highly concentrated with color. They can be used alone or layered in combination with other eye products. They are messy—the loose powder tends to "float" everywhere. If using, do the eyes first, foundation last, to prevent shadow from dropping onto the foundation.

Pencils or Pens: Are highly pigmented, frosty or sheer. Some formulas are waterproof or water resistant in small or large pencil form. You will need special sharpeners for these.

Pressed Powder: Are usually in compact or drop-in disks to customize your eye-shadow palette. It can be used wet or dry.

Waterproof Eye Shadow Products: Are usually found in jars, tubes, or pencil form. They contain a polymer ingredient. They are formulated to not crease or fade.

Eyeliner

Cake: Applied with a brush that is damp. Cake eyeliner is great for smudging. Cake products usually come in compacts or jars, and are creams or powder formulas.

Gel: Used like a liquid or cake, but is easier to apply. It is long lasting. Gel is applied with a brush and usually found in jars.

Liquid: Adds drama to your look, and a must for many "period" looks. It is applied with a brush and is quick drying, but needs a very steady hand. "Painters" work well with liquids.

Loose Powder: Highly pigmented powder that can be used wet or dry. Use a sealer on top for longer wear. Loose powder can be messy.

Pencils: Easy application and blending. They can be formulated in waterproof and water-resistant products, and come in frost, kohl, and matte, with either a fine point or thick.

Sealers: Products used to protect any eye shadow or eyeliner from smudging, smearing, or lifting. Sealers are usually found in liquid form, and can be mixed with eye shadow (or product) in the application (think watercolors).

Mascara
Cake: Is applied with an eyelash brush or small fan brush. Cake mascara and a fan brush gives you a thorough coat on the lashes, with no "clumps," and works great to get the base of the lashes, particularly on light or blonde lashes.

Clear: Comes in tubes and is applied like regular mascara. It gives a nice sheen to the lashes, and helps to show off definition and length in the "Natural Look."

Fillers: Are found alone or combined into the mascara formula. They thicken and lengthen. They are usually made out of nylon fibers.

Top Coats: Applied to the eyelashes after mascara, they are used to add sheen and vibrancy to the lashes. They can also be used as a sealer for the mascara.

Primers: Act as moisturizers for the eye, and also prepare the lashes for mascara. They are helpful in creating a longer look and in protecting the eyelashes from mascara. Remember to apply first, before mascara.

Tinted: Colored mascara, usually in tubes.

Waterproof: Smudgeproof, creaseproof, and quick drying. You must have correct mascara remover in order to take off waterproof mascara. Primers can be used first, for ease of removal.

Blushers
Cream Blush: Can be highly pigmented. It can be used alone or with other products. Formulas come in cream to powder finish. Cream blushes come in jars, compacts, sticks, and liquids.

Pressed Powder: Can be used alone or in combination with creams. It comes in a wide range of textures and formulas in compact form. It is great for "on-set" touch-ups because it is pressed and not loose.

Loose Powder: Comes in a wide range of textures and formulas. It can be used alone or in combination.

Tints and Gels: Found in creams, gels, moisturizers, and liquids. Tints and gels are sheer translucent in color. Many are made to be an "all-in-one" product for cheeks and lips. Some are water resistant and oil free. They can be used alone or combined.

Eyebrows

Cake: Powder form, pressed or loose, and come in jars, compacts, and pencil form. They are the easiest and most natural way to define a brow. Cake eyebrow definer is most often used with a stiff eye brush. It can be wet or dry.

Gels: Usually transparent, but are available in tints. Gels can be used alone or after brow color has been applied. They dry quickly, are often waterproof, and hold the brow shape in place.

Pencils: Eyebrow pencils have an extra-hard point for drawing, shaping, and filling in brows. They are very pigmented, and come in assorted colors, and can be used in combination with other brow products.

Thickening: Eyebrow thickeners are like mascaras for the eyebrows. They have hairlike fibers that are suspended in the formula to add volume and coverage to the brows.

Wax: Used to shape, enhance, or fill the brow while holding the brow shape. It comes in different colors and can be combined with other products.

Lipstick

Cream: Contains moisturizing properties and is highly pigmented. Cream lipsticks go on smooth, and some contain sun protection and vitamins. They come in matte, shine, and frost formulas.

Matte: Lipstick that is flat with no shine. It tends to be very pigmented. It is great for creating "period" looks. Matte lipsticks are long wearing because they are so dense.

Frost: Comes in lipsticks, pots, gloss, and tints, with different levels of frost or glitter.

Gloss: Sheer formulas with high gloss or wet look. Gloss lipsticks can be used alone or in combination as a top coat to the lips.

Treatments: Balms, conditioners, and treatment sticks for the lips. They are available with sun protection, natural plant extracts, vitamins, and moisturizing properties. They soothe dry lips and can come in tints. They may be used alone or in combination.

Lip Scrubs: Treatment products to exfoliate the lips (get rid of dry skin).

Lip Plumper: Contains ingredients for plumping the lip area. Sometimes there is a tingling sensation when applied.

Lip Wax: Wax formula used before lipstick application to fill in lines and wrinkles. Lip wax also preps the lips for lipstick.

Lip Liners: Come in pencil, pen, or stick form. They are used to reshape and enhance the lip line before lipstick application, and can be used alone with a lip moisturizer (like a tint) or in combination with all lip products.

Websites and Addresses

Frends Beauty Supply, www.naimies.com

Nancy Tozier, Take Up Cosmetics
www.sephora.com

Suzanne Patterson, www.creativeartistryfx.com

7 | BEAUTY AND BASICS

At one time it was critical because of the nature of lighting and film technology, as well as theatrical custom, to eliminate as much detail of the actor's face as possible and to draw in, often almost cartoonishly, those features meant to be seen. As film stock and lighting became more forgiving, and "reality," rather than "theatricality," became the accepted convention, beauty makeup has, too, evolved to appreciate a more naturalistic aesthetic.

—Richard Dean, Makeup Artist

Your imagination and your knowledge of shapes, the body, color, and lighting enable you to paint with endless possibilities. In this chapter, we will start with the basic skills and makeup applications that a Makeup Artist uses every day. We want you to excel in the basics before moving on to more advanced makeup applications and designs. This is why we started the book with the more technical aspects of makeup. In order to have the background needed to move forward and excel, you need to understand all the elements and aspects that affect your work. To make up the whole, you need all the parts. We will note "Industry Standards" throughout this chapter and the rest of the book for you to know and recognize. These are products that will be found in every makeup kit. Brand and name recognition are important to the industry. Once you know that a product works, photographs well, and does not cause skin irritation, you will rely on that product to always work for you when there is no time for discovery, experimenting, or testing. Industry Standards are trusted and proven—they

work. We will cover the testing of looks in Chapter 8, "Design."

Within one day, a Makeup Artist could do any number of different makeups—for example, a beauty makeup, cover an actor's tattoo, break a nose, apply a tan or sunburn, add 10 years to a character, apply a five o'clock shadow, or give the "homeless extra" the grime needed to sell the look. (An "extra" is a background actor, sometimes referred to as a "background artist"; these actors play a supportive but integral role in filmmaking, and need to have the same attention to detail as a principal actor.)

We have our own slang in the makeup world. Makeup artists often refer to "a makeup" or "the makeup" when speaking or referring to a colleague. They are referring to the specific look that is being done: a character or design of makeup. Example: "The makeup looks muddy." "Muddy" is unclean, not blended well, uneven application (not good), and "the makeup" is the finished application of the artist.

It could also be a day about creating natural looks that seem organic without the assistance of makeup. You need to develop a subtle eye and hand for the realistic looks. Believability to the eye is key. It is requested in all media, for all ages and genders, and is a frequent request by all Directors, Producers, and clients.

Understanding the many different interpretations of makeup is also important.

What is natural to one person is over-made-up to another. In the beginning of your career, this is one of the more frustrating situations: unclear communication about the makeup. It is subjective and at times difficult to communicate what a look should be. With experience comes the ability to assess the situation and decipher what is being requested. There is also time during the prep pause of a job for understanding what is needed. Prep is the period prior to filming, shooting, or staging when you have initial design discussions and even "test the makeup looks" (see Chapter 8: Design).

Take any opportunity to hone your talents and skills for all skin tones and types. The more faces you do, the better you will be. A great opportunity is working "the line," or "bull pen," for a film or opera company. You are one of many Makeup Artists painting for the crowds, and you have little time to do it in. This exposes you to so many faces and corrective situations.

PRO TIP

I take one summer job in NYC each year during my time off from the Met to hone my skills at cranking out full makeups in 10 to 15 minutes, recalling my early days on "the line" at San Francisco Opera, where we were trained to complete a full makeup (on choristers and supers [supers are stage "extras": nonsinging background artists]) in 8 to 10 minutes.

—Steven Horak, Makeup Artist, Metropolitan Opera House, New York City

Retail cosmetic counters also offer a chance to gain experience with a wide variety of skin tones, facial structure, and vanity, but you will experience doing only "symmetrical beauty makeup," which is not always applied in film.

The camera loves irregularity. It photographs well, so we do not necessarily strive for symmetry in film (see Chapter 8: Design).

Makeup Artists use their artistry on the skin to create, but we do provide a service. We care for the person's outer look or character, and in some situations for the person himself or herself, and that person's skin. We care for the looks we create and the person we paint on. Maintaining the look of the character takes place over the length of the film or project, one day or several months. Film and TV have long days: 12-plus hours per day—with 13 to 14 hours per day being normal, and the possibilities of going 18 to 19 hours per day.

Makeup applied in the morning needs to be maintained and many times reapplied thoroughout the day. It can be grueling and exhausting, but, we hope, creatively fulfilling.

With film, there is a beginning, a middle, and an end to the story, with the character's movement (and makeup) throughout. In TV, there is a continuing story line, with the same character movement (and makeup)—just a much longer, and sometimes seemingly unending, story line. Print shoots have a shorter day—8 hours is the norm—creatively driven by the Photographer, Art Director, and the client. On some exterior location shoots, they will split up the day: shooting in the morning sun, take a break from the midday sun, and start shooting again in the late-afternoon sun. Stage productions can have long hours in their rehearsal schedule: 10- to 12-hour days—this is the rehearsal and prep time before opening the show. Once a stage production has "opened," the show calls vary between three and five hours per call (or show), with one day per week as a maintenance day, where you start work earlier to do repairs and maintain the show. Some days have two show calls: matinee and evening performance. Theatrical productions work six days per week. Opera schedules are continuous throughout their season, with every opera house maintaining a different "season." Try all media available to you. It is great experience, and helpful in deciding where your talents, personality, and intuition work best.

THE SKIN

Opinions are divided as to the level of attention Makeup Artists should pay to skin care. There are three types of Makeup Artists when it comes to skin care. There are Makeup Artists who believe that skin care should be left to the individual. These artists believe it is up to the individual and/ or their dermatologist to care for the skin, reasoning that it takes time to correct skin conditions and develop a proper skin-care regime, which needs to be done morning and evening. Some products need to be absorbed completely before applying makeup (so done at home before work), and in some cases, treatment products should be used only at night before bed (retinols). It takes time and money to develop a skin-care routine that works best for the individual. Many times you need several weeks to correct skin conditions—it cannot be done in a day. This group of Makeup Artists will expect the individual to maintain their own daily routine of skin care and cleansing. They will expect them to show up to work ready for makeup application, having already applied their products at home, which gives the proper time for absorption. For this group, the care of the skin is the individual's responsibility and that of their dermatologist.

There is another group of Makeup Artists who are also licensed aestheticians (the study of skin care). This group of Makeup Artists will be more involved in skin care. As the style of filmmaking, technology, and surgical procedures advances and increases, so has the trend for arming oneself with skin care knowledge. This group of Makeup Artists will recommend products and prep the skin before makeup, as well as cleanse and treat the skin at wrap. ("Wrap" is the term called by the First AD—Assistant Director—at completion of the day's filming.) These Makeup Artists believe in being proactive in the care of the skin, and diminishing breakouts as much as possible or correcting dull skin. Acne can be diminished by makeup, lighting, and filters on the camera, but with a 40-foot screen, dimensional imperfections are hard to hide. (If shooting digital, there can be correction in "post" or the final product.) Clear skin is always the optimum, and this type of Makeup Artist has the knowledge and background to work toward the goal of correcting skin problems to achieve smooth, clear skin.

The last group of Makeup Artists falls in between the two other types. This group will have knowledge of skin care and will take the time to be current in products and treatments for the skin, although they may or may not be licensed aestheticians. They will prep, tone, moisturize, sunblock, and sometimes apply masks. They probably will do cleansing at wrap. It has become common to see a professional towel caddie on the counter in makeup trailers (towel caddies keep wet towels warm for cleanup). All the groups of Makeup Artists work with sunblock. We have a responsibility to protect the skin in exterior locations. Your choice of involvement will become your working style, and should be based on your beliefs and education or knowledge of the skin. We do recommend that, regardless, you take the time to keep current with skin-care trends and makeup products throughout your career. If you do choose to make skin care part of your working style, please note that it adds time to your day, and some productions will not want overtime incurred for cleanup at wrap.

PRO TIP

Anything glued or applied to the face, neck, or body by a Makeup Artist that needs a solvent to remove must be removed by the Makeup Department. The time it takes to remove is "on the clock" (official time of payment).

There are actors and individuals who will request and prefer that the makeup is removed at the end of each day. Have a supply of clean white washcloths and a nonirritating cleanser—for example, Cetaphil Gentle Skin Cleanser. Cetaphil is a gentle facial cleanser that does not strip the skin of its natural pH balance; it is an Industry Standard. Using bottled water, if a sink is not available (trailer water is nonpotable, not recommended for the mouth, face, or eyes), wet the washcloth and put it in the microwave for one to two minutes. If the towel is too hot, allow it to cool before using. This is the simplest and safest way to cleanse the skin. Washcloths are a fantastic way to remove makeup and clean the skin without harm. There are also makeup-removal wipes. Choose one without alcohol (alcohol is drying to the skin). Wash your white towels in warm or hot water with bleach for sanitation.

87

PRO TIP

Be careful with alcohol-based toners. The alcohol strips the skin of its natural oils and pH balance, causing the brain to signal the production of more oil to the surface of the skin in an attempt to bring back the balance to a "normal" pH. pH is the relative degree of acidity and alkalinity of a substance. Don't dry the skin out!
—Joel Garson, *Milady's Standard Fundamentals for Estheticians*, 9th ed.

THE SETUP

In order to get started, you need to "set up" your workstation with the proper products and equipment. Every workstation varies with each Makeup Artist, but there are Industry Standards for setting up your station, with station setup and products that will be consistent from one Makeup Artist to another, no matter whose station you are looking at (Figure 7.1).

Having your station set up with the proper tools, equipment, and products, clean and ready to go, instills confidence in the individual who sits in your makeup chair. This is one of the first moments of critique when working with new people. They will look at your station, your products, and how your kit is set up. Your makeup kit should be clean and organized for sanitary reasons and ease of movement during a makeup. Some artists keep their makeup kit on the counter next to them. You will be quickly judged on the condition of your makeup kit. Your products should be current, in good condition, with all batteries fully charged or plugged in. The strength of alcohol must be 99 percent to be effective. Makeup brushes, makeup palette, and tools should be clean and ready. Hand sanitizer (99 percent alcohol) and brush

cleaner should be out and within easy reach.

Note: Alcohol is not an EPA (Environmental Protection Agency)–registered hospital-grade disinfectant.

A typical setup for a makeup station is a clean cotton terry towel (colors vary; many prefer white towels only because you can bleach them) placed on the counter in front of you with a Professional Prep Towel on top of the cotton towel (Kimberly-Clark Professional Set Up Towels are the Industry Standard). This is a sanitary setup to keep your products and brushes off the counter, clean and germ free. Your makeup palette, tools, and brushes would go on top of this two-layer setup. Clean your station, makeup brushes, tools, and hands in between each person. Make sure to have a garbage can or bag close by for disposing of garbage. Also have a cloth drape or barber's cap for protecting clothing or costumes during makeup. Cloth drapes are more comfortable for the individual, but, depending on the makeup you are doing, also have a plastic drape available. Plastic is hotter for the individual.

Sanitizing products: 99 percent alcohol in a spray and dispenser, small bowl or jars for cleaning brushes, hand wipes, gel hand sanitizer, spray water.

Industry Standards: Evian Mineral Water Spray, Glacial Spray Water, La Roche-Posay Thermal Spring Water, Jao Hand Sanitizer.

Canned spray water is a preference. It is a source of clean water for working on the

FIGURE 7-1: DEBRA COLEMAN'S MAKEUP STATION
Photo courtesy of Debra Coleman, Makeup Artist and member of Local 706, Los Angeles.

face and around the eyes. There will be times when you do not have running water, and you will rely on your canned spray water for a clean source of water.

Grooming equipment: shaving powder, Tend Skin (Industry Standard), electric shaver, sideburn trimmer (Industry Standards: Wahl, Panasonic), clippers for beard trimming (Wahl), small hair scissors for trimming, nose-hair trimmers (Panasonic), disposable shavers, shaving cream.

Nail care: nail clippers, cuticle trimmers, nail files and orange sticks (do not share nail files/or orange sticks—buy in bulk and give out), cuticle remover, cuticle cream, hand cream, base coat, top coat, quick-dry spray, various nail polish colors, non-acetone polish remover.

Kleenex facial tissue, cotton facial pads (cotton only, due to possible allergies to synthetics), Q-tips, cosmetics Q-tips (the tips are different, made for applying makeup), your makeup brushes, makeup products, and cosmetics.

Note: this is a very basic setup. Every Makeup Artist personalizes their station, so no two look alike, but they will have some of the same products/equipment or Industry Standard products.

It is time for practical experience with applying makeup. For some of these makeups, you will not be given steps to follow, just text. For others, you will be given steps. Time to think, and paint.

PRO TIP

There are a million ways to do anything. Find the one that works for you.
—Randy Huston Mercer, New York Makeup Artist

CONCEALING AND CORRECTIONS

Mastering the art of concealing for all skin tones and skin types, such a vast variety, will come easier to you now that you have studied color theory and foundations.

You will use color theory to cancel out reds, blue, grays, greens, and any other unwanted color or undertones in the skin, as well as blemishes, scars, birthmarks, and tattoos. Concealing can be done under or over the makeup foundation or base, except for birthmarks, port-wine stains, and tattoos. These require full coverage, and should be done first.

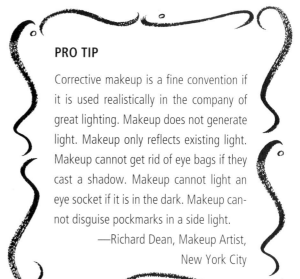

PRO TIP

Corrective makeup is a fine convention if it is used realistically in the company of great lighting. Makeup does not generate light. Makeup only reflects existing light. Makeup cannot get rid of eye bags if they cast a shadow. Makeup cannot light an eye socket if it is in the dark. Makeup cannot disguise pockmarks in a side light.
—Richard Dean, Makeup Artist, New York City

For under-eye concealing, choose a product that is emollient and designed for the eye area. These products are lighter, more emollient, and many have reflective qualities that are great for diffusing fine lines around the eye. They glide smoothly onto the delicate skin around the eye. The least amount of tug and pull or stress from application, the better. Do not set with powder. Avoid using powder under the eyes, which can be drying and may emphasize the correction.

Industry Standards: Kanebo, YSL Touche Éclat, Iman, Laura Mercier, NARS.

For concealing or correction on the face, choose a product that is medium weight. Note that all types of concealers (light, medium, or dense) will work on the facial skin—it depends on what you are covering. Your style and what you have to cover will help you choose the product and application, under base or over base. The severer the discoloration, the more need to use a denser product or 100 percent pigment for camouflaging.

For birthmarks, port-wine stains, and tattoos, you will need a two- to three-layer process for complete coverage. This is done before applying a makeup base. This layering of color allows you to cancel out color completely, without any bleed-through. Sometimes a color will bleed up through the cover-up, usually in a gray undertone. You will use the stipple technique to apply color over each layer. For your first color, use the opposite color on the color wheel to cancel out the discoloration. Your second color is dependent on how much coverage is needed: (a) if just two layers are needed, your second layer is a matching flesh tone, or (b) if three layers are needed, your second layer is a mauve (red) or orange tone to cancel out any gray bleed coming through from the first layer. Many times there will be a gray bleed or tone coming through the correction. You will see it with your eye and in the makeup mirror. In these situations, you need three layers of color. Your second layer will be to neutralize the gray, and your third layer is the flesh tone. This is 100 percent coverage for those situations with intense color (port-wine stain) or ink (tattoo). These products are 100 percent pigment. They are not sheer, and are designed for camouflaging.

Try: Dermacolor by KRYOLAN and Dermablend.

NATURAL MAKEUP

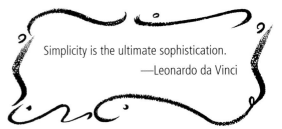

Simplicity is the ultimate sophistication.
—Leonardo da Vinci

When the character needs (or the Director requests) a "natural look" for makeup, you want to show good health and appearance. You will spend most of your time enhancing the skin tone to show good health. Correct any discoloration, cover any scars or blemishes, and make the skin look healthy and vibrant. Remember to strive for realism. A tinted moisturizer works well in this look to even out the skin without looking like makeup (try Laura Mercier Tinted

Moisturizers). This is also a great choice for men and children. An alternative is to mix a small amount of oil-free moisturizer (try All You Need+ from Prescriptives) with your liquid or cream base. This will give you a sheer coverage that does not look overdone. If you need a bit more coverage, use a liquid or cream without mixing moisturizer into it. In situations where the actor's skin is good and does not need a base or foundation, use the "spot paint" technique to balance out the skin tone. Spot painting is the technique of literally painting with makeup or concealer just the area or "spot" that needs it. Do not overapply or bring the makeup too far into the surrounding area of skin. You want to paint just the specific spot. KRYOLAN's Dermacolor (an Industry Standard) works well with spot painting. It is noncomedogenic, and gives you dense, full coverage (camouflage) that you can feather or blend the edges with your makeup brush. Set with just a hint of powder: not too much, or the area will look dry. You can forgo the powder if needed, but you will have to reapply or touch up if you do not set the makeup. Use Face to Face Supermatte Antishine by Make-Up International (an Industry Standard) to take down any shine on the other areas of the face. For more tips on spot painting see "Spot Painting" later in this chapter.

Remember to match the foundation or base to the skin at the jawline. This helps to balance the tone in the neck and face so you are working with as little product as possible—remember, this is the "natural look." The skin on the face is much different in tone and texture from the neck.

Blend down past the jawline under the chin area. You want to avoid any lines of demarcation or "the mask" look to the face.

Once the skin is looking healthy and vibrant, you need to add color to the cheeks, and bring attention to the eyes, lips, and eyebrows. For a natural blushed effect, place cheek color in the apple of the cheeks, either cream or powder. Reds, pinks, and peaches are best.

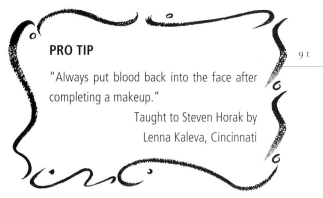

PRO TIP

"Always put blood back into the face after completing a makeup."

Taught to Steven Horak by Lenna Kaleva, Cincinnati

Bringing It "Back to Life" and Keeping Makeup From Looking Too Masklike

"Bring it back to life" is another makeup slang term you will hear to refer to almost all makeup applications. If something is looking dull or lifeless, you will be instructed to "bring it back to life." This can happen with concealing as well.

Next, accentuate the eyes by adding any needed definition without doing a full beauty makeup. Choose soft browns, taupes, or gray to define the lash line using pencil or powder. We do not suggest liquid liner for the "natural look"—your hand needs to be very skilled. Place the line right on the base of the eyelashes. Remember, you are defining the natural line to add definition, not doing eyeliner, so you do not want a thick line.

Trick: use the "dot method" by placing dots of color into the lash line, both top and bottom, instead of drawing a line. By dotting in color, you create the illusion of a greater or stronger lash line without noticing the liner. This technique works excellently on men.

If you decide a bit of eye shadow is needed, use a lighter color all over the lid in creams, beiges, and pinks to even out the lid. Choose soft browns or taupes in the eye crease. Again, a very subtle hand is needed. Curling the eyelashes adds length without too much product (Industry Standard: shu uemura), and use mascara if needed. Clear mascara is also a great choice if the lashes are already long. If a brown or black mascara is needed, apply a thin coat with a mascara fan. Mascara fans are great for this look—you have more control over the application and can really

get beautiful lashes without too much product (We Recommend Brush Up With Barbara). Remember to apply mascara to define the lashes, but not make them look coated.

Bring subtle definition to the eyebrow by grooming the eyebrows and, if needed, adding a touch of color for shape and fill. Care must be take when adding color to the brows in the "natural look." Use short brushstrokes (or pencil strokes) in a 45-degree angle for similar hair growth. Trick: paint the eyebrow hair instead of painting the skin in this look. Using a mascara wand, apply color directly to the hair and not the skin. This is great on men. It will not work on someone's brow that is in need of filling because of lack of hair.

Try: Roux (Tween Time) Stick by Revlon, Stacolor, Reel Color. Taupe and soft browns work well and do not photograph too dark. Medium to dark browns will photograph darker than they appear to the eye. Too much in this look, and your makeup will not look natural.

Keep the mouth looking healthy by using just enough color to blush the lip. Use lip stains, tint with a matte or sheer lipstick, or use a lip pencil with a lip moisturizer to get the color and attention needed without looking too "lipsticky." There should not be too much gloss for this look. Do not use lip gloss or heavy shine on men or children. Keep the focus on giving the individual the appearance of good health. Your technique needs to be subtle and clean without the obvious enhancement of makeup. Again, it's the "natural look."

PRO TIP

Dispense mascara onto artist's wax paper. Using the wand from the tube of mascara, pull off mascara onto the wax paper. This allows you plenty of product to do both eyes by using disposable wands or a mascara fan, and keeps the tube of mascara sanitary.

No double-dipping of the wand into the tube! Disposable wands come by the dozen.

FIGURE 7-2:

FIGURE 7-2A

SPOT PAINTING

If the actor's skin tone and condition are good, then no foundation or makeup base is needed in the "natural look." Instead, you will choose to "spot paint" the face and not apply a full application of foundation or makeup base. Spot painting is the technique of literally painting out unwanted color from the face or body. Any spots or unwanted marks are painted out with a concealer, Dermacolor, Stacolor, or even foundation. The product you choose depends on what is to be covered. Spot painting is a part of concealing and correction, but in this case, we use it to replace foundation or base.

Example: You are instructed by the Makeup Department to "just spot paint" your actor. They do not want makeup base applied. They want you to just spot paint correction on clean skin, and only in the needed areas. This is widely used on men, children, and for all situations where you do not want to see any makeup. It has become an Industry Standard.

Stacolor and Reel Color can be used in spot painting when the makeup needs to be waterproof, sweatproof, or friction resistant. Like necks so color does not come off on shirt collars.

Working with the individual's clean skin, apply a sunblock first if working outdoors, concealing only where needed, and matching the concealer to the skin tone. The concealer or makeup is concentrated only on the spot or area that needs correction. Blend or feather out onto the skin, being careful not to overpaint or bring the edges too far onto the surrounding skin. You just want to paint the specific spot. Dermacolor (by KRYOLAN) works well with spot painting. It is noncomedogenic, and gives you full coverage (or camouflage) that you can feather or blend onto the surrounding skin with your brush. Choose a makeup brush that is small in size to prevent overpainting. Set the makeup with very little powder. Too much powder on

93

bare skin is dry looking. When spot painting a face, use Face to Face Supermatte Antishine by Make-Up International (an Industry Standard) to take down shine on the skin. Because the skin is basically clean, with the exception of the "spots," do not use powder to cut shine. Powder needs something to stick to, so on clean skin, use Supermatte Antishine, available in light, medium, and dark tones.

You can also use spot painting to correct broken capillaries, blemishes, birthmarks, and tattoos.

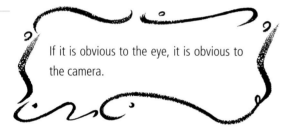

If it is obvious to the eye, it is obvious to the camera.

STEPS TO SPOT PAINTING

It is recommended that you always use a sunblock as part of your prep when working outdoors. Depending on what you are covering, you have a choice of single-layer, double-layer, or triple-layer applications.

Single-color application:

1. Prep skin (if need) for all applications.

2. With a brush, apply concealer or Dermacolor to the discolored area, matching to the skin tone. Choose a makeup brush that is appropriate in size for the area you are correcting, and check to make sure it is blended. Lightly powder.

For two-color application (for stronger color correction):

1. Prep skin.

2. With a brush, apply concealer using the opposite color on the color wheel to cancel out (neutralize) the discoloration. (See Chapter 3: Color.)

3. Layer second matching skin tone color on top, over the neutralizing color.

4. Lightly powder.

For three-color application (for birthmarks, port-wine stains, tattoos, or gray tones):

1. Prep skin.

2. Apply first neutralizing color, the opposite color on the color wheel to the discoloration.

3. Apply second neutralizing color by layering or stippling a mauve (red) or orange over the first neutralizing color. This cuts any gray that is bleeding up from the first layer. Inks, gray undertones, and intense colors will have a tendency to "go gray." This gray tone "bleeds" up through the correction colors. You will see it with your eye and in the mirror. Cut it with a mauve, red, or orange.

4. Layer the third color in a matching skin tone over colors one and two. Check your coverage in the mirror. Is the gray gone?

5. Lightly powder.

The stipple technique is an up-and-downward motion of application using a brush, sponge, or textured sponge. This up-and-down motion prevents the removal of any layers of makeup that are being applied. It is needed in spot painting, character makeup, effects, and prosthetics, but can be applied to most applications.

We want to stress how important it is to master the art of natural makeup and spot painting before moving on to beauty makeup. Practice on your models, your friends, and family. Practice until you believe it. Take photos and critique your work.

> In film, beauty makeup is character make-up. Every makeup begins with the text. Makeup is simply one of several languages used to elaborate and illustrate text. Based on the text, we make all sorts of decisions: the character's physical well-being, social and financial status, level and condition of vanity, and inclination to spend time in front of the mirror.
> —Richard Dean, New York Makeup Artist
> —(See Chapter 8 on Design)

Unfortunately some individuals will look in the mirror and want symmetry. If you are working on a film, sometimes a gentle reminder that the camera loves irregularity will help, but often you will have to accommodate individual insecurity and vanity. Every situation is different.

Beauty makeup should accentuate and not overwhelm. It is not a mask, or unnatural looking. Accentuate the positive, without re-creating the face. In the beginning of film, the custom was to blank out the face and to paint back in the desired features. This is no longer the custom or trend. Reality is the accepted beauty aesthetic.

> We no longer do makeup by the pound.
> —Randy Huston Mercer, New York Makeup Artist

BEAUTY MAKEUP

Beauty makeup in film and television has many layers to it. You are accentuating the face as well as adding character and background. We will go into more on designing characters in the next chapter. Beauty does not have to mean symmetry for film or the camera. The camera and the lens love irregularity. There will be jobs where you work for symmetry, and an equal number where you do not. This does not apply to video, HD, theatre, or to the retail world. These are media that will require symmetry. You will adjust your makeup designs and application for the medium you are working in.

Beauty does not stop at the face. You also have to do necks, hands, arms, legs, and—if needed—the full body. The skin should appear healthy—in some cases, glowing. Bring attention to the eyes, define the eyebrows, and add color to the cheeks and lips. The eyes can captivate, and are generally everyone's best feature. If you cannot see the eyes, the audience loses interest, so eyes play an important role in all media.

RICHARD DEAN'S TIPS ON BEAUTY

1. Begin with a foundation primer and any eye shadow primer. Apply with a

sponge. Areas of the face have uneven oil distribution, and will accept and hold foundations irregularly. A primer will have moisturizing effects in that it retards water evaporation from cells, and will create a more even surface for foundations and color cosmetics.

2. Liquid or oil foundation applied with a foundation brush. To keep a more natural look to the skin's surface, use foundation sparingly, do spot coverage (spot painting), and add pinker tones to the foundation with cream rouges as they naturally occur in the skin.

3. Cheeks are typically a bluish pink, never brown. Think blood vessels, the source of color. For a natural cheek, drag cream blusher down slightly toward the jawline and add a touch to the bridge (not tip) of the nose. This may be very subtle or quite heavy, depending on the situation. Example: to approximate the palest Irish skin with flushed cheek.

4. Powder with a yellow-based powder, then add powdered blush on the surface. The pink-yellow-red layer imparts a sense of depth, and therefore reality, to the foundation's finish. As the day progresses, try to blot before adding more powder. Remove as much natural oil as possible with blotting paper. Natural oil production plus powder creates another layer of a kind of foundation that gets heavier throughout the day if never blotted.

5. I use eyelashes for character effect.

In beauty makeup, the amount of attention brought to the eyes and eyebrows will depend on character and situation. There is a range to work from, but save the "smoky eye" for the glamour makeups that are more stylistic and dramatic.

Practice eye treatment and combinations of colors with as many models with varieties of eye color and shape as possible. Your eye and hand need the practical experience to develop your talent. You need to make mistakes as well as get it right to have the ability to deal with the uniqueness of each person.

Practice the art of eye shadow. Start with applying an eye shadow primer all over the lid. Try Paula Dorf. This preps the eyelid, helps the shadow last, and gives a smooth finish for eye shadow application. Using an eye shadow brush, apply a base color of shadow in cream, pink, beiges, all over the lid. Next, define the eye structure by applying browns or grays or blues in the eye crease. Placement is key, color choice is open to what looks good on the person. Start with browns until you have mastered placement. Have your model look in the mirror to check and correct placement. This is "working off the mirror." You will do this to correct and check your work in all situations. Does the eye look open and balanced, or drooped? Is there enough definition? Is the application smooth and consistent in color, or muddy? Is there too much color in the inside corner? Too much of a straight line in the crease? Take photos to critique placement and style.

FIGURE 7-3: EYE FROM STUTTERBOX

changing eyebrows is a great tool in character design and altering a look. The level of intensity and style of the brows will come from the character or situation. Brows should have a natural, unpainted look when doing a "beauty look" or "natural look." Glamour makeup has all the drama, with a precise shape to the eyebrow that is obviously drawn or painted on. There are several ways to shape brows using different products: brow pencil, brow creams or shadow, eye shadow, temporary hair color, Stacolor or Reel Color.

Choose colors that are close in shade to the eyebrow or slightly lighter. Remember, browns photograph darker. For a realistic brow, use two colors, to fill in or shape.

You can use brow pencils or brushes. If choosing brushes, pick a brow brush with stiff bristles that are cut at an angle (try Cargo's brow brush).

PRO TIP

Use a combination of brow pencils to shape, and brow powders to fill in or soften the pencil work. Follow over the completed brow with a cream or light-colored eye shadow to fade your work.

FIGURE 7-3A:

BROW SHAPING

Brow shape conveys a number of emotions and expressions, and is a focal point on the face (Chapter 1: Shapes). We use brows to draw attention to the eyes. Shaping and

Find the brow shape by taking the handle of a makeup brush and laying the handle gently on the face vertically. Starting from the inner corner of the eye at the nose, point straight up toward the brow. The general rule is to start the brow at the inner corners of the eye (or one eye length between each eye). Next, with the brush handle vertical, gently lay the handle on the outside of the iris with the handle going up to the brow. This is your highest point in the arch, or where the natural arch should be, and sometime is not. Approximately a $\frac{1}{2}$ inch from the arch is where the brow should end. For the beginning brow artist, take a pencil and lightly mark any area of the brow that you feel needs shaping.

Start with the inside corner of the brow and use light, short feather strokes in an upward or 45-degree angle (depending on how the hair grows). Move along the brow in this way, filling and shaping where needed. Use different colors. Remember not to fill in too much, just where needed. If you are using the brow pencil and brow powder technique, add brow powder in a lighter shade, and go over or fill in areas that are too harsh from the pencil. You can use brow pencil alone or brow powders alone, depending on your hand and eye.

Brow sealers can be used to tame unruly brows. Apply after you have shaped the brow. Sealers can darken the brows, so adjust your work accordingly. Sealers can also start to flake over time, so check your brows!

Brows also need trimming (just like the hair on the head). Makeup Artists trim brows on a regular basis, particularly on men. Have a small trimmer on hand (Panasonic), small round-tipped scissors, and a small-toothed comb (a mustache comb or brow comb works). Keep everything clean, sanitary, and running well. Follow the manufacturer's directions for the care and cleaning of the trimmer. Comb the brow hair upward, with your scissors at an angle, trimming any hair

that is too long. Work a little at a time until you have the desired results. It is better to make several passes during trimming than to cut too much in one pass.

PRO TIP

Facial-hair lighteners are used to take naturally dark brows and lighten them. This process is good for continuity and looks. Lightening is a simple process, but not something you would do on the same day as shooting. This should be done several days before, or at least the day before, shooting. Always follow the manufacturer's directions on how to use a product.

Blush the cheeks and the lips with colors that work with the skin tone, costume, and situations. Placement depends on the individual features, character portrayal, and current trends. Experiment with different

PRO TIP

I very much depend upon the Estée Lauder Smoothing Creme Concealer, using it under the foundation of every women's makeup that I do, and some men's. It not only works beautifully on dark circles and blemishes, but also as a successful eyebrow cover when only a small portion of the brow needs to be blocked.

—Steven Horak

colors and placement on your models to see the effects of color, placement, and shapes on the cheeks and lips. Refer to Chapter 1: Shapes.

GLAMOUR MAKEUP

Painted perfection, beautifully sculpted. Use your imagination with color, boldness in application, and dramatic placement to create a stylized look that is glamorous. Depending on the design or look you want, start with blanking out the face with a flawless foundation that has complete

FIGURE 7-4: PHOTO OF GLAM FROM SHUTTERSTOCK

FIGURE 7-4A:

coverage with correction. Re-create the desired features using beautifully sculpted contour and highlight. Add drama to the eyes and eyebrows with bold shapes and color. Consider painting in the eyebrows and using false eyelashes, with eyeliner to add to the drama. Make lips luscious with a full shape using lip pencils and lipstick; top with shine or gloss. Glamour makeup should be bold in application and color, and has to be well blended. You will be working with more makeup, both in color and texture. This look is "the full slap," also known as "beat the face" (makeup slang for painted). You will need plenty of experimentation and practice in the beginning, so go for it, work it, but blend it and powder it.

FALSE EYELASHES

Strip lashes, individual lashes, and exotic lashes are all great for bringing attention and beauty to the eyes. For subtlety in a beauty makeup, use individual lashes, which come in several lengths and styles. An alternative to individual lashes is a delicate strip lash in brown or black. For glamour, fantasy, stylistic, or theatrical productions, choose a heavier strip lash in black. Go for the flair and be as bold as the makeup design allows. Decorative or exotic lashes are wonderful in the right situations and designs.

Industry Standards: DUO eyelash adhesive (available in black and clear white), Andrea eyelashes, Ardell eyelashes. All are available in most drugstores.

Exotic/decorative/fantasy lashes: Elegant Lashes (www.eEyelash.com).

Before applying eyelashes, check for size. Always remove strip lashes from the tray from the outside in to prevent damage to the strip. Without using any glue, place the strip or individual on the base of the lashes. How is the fit? Remove and trim any excess from the strip from the outside. With the individual, you are looking for length and style with the eye. This is the time to choose. After checking the fit and style, apply a thin line of glue to the strip lash. Never apply glue to the eye directly. An alternative is to put a small amount of glue onto your clean makeup palette or wax paper palette, and then apply a thin line onto the strip using a thin brush. This brush will become your glue brush. This works well with individual lashes. Always take care in not using too much glue, as you can glue the eye shut. Center the false-eyelash strip on the eye at the base of the lashes. With the eye closed, gently press the strip onto the base of the lashes. Have a slightly wet Q-tip ready in case you have glued the eye shut. If you do not wet the Q-tip, the cotton will stick to the glue. Application can be done with tweezers or hands, or a combination of hands, tweezers, and a soft glue brush for securing the false lashes to the base of the lashes. How successful the application will depend on your hands and steadiness.

Removal of false eyelashes should always be done from the outside in. Pinch the outside of the false lash with your thumb and index finger, and gently pull in toward the nose. Clean off glue by pulling off the strip, and reshape it on a tray. You can get several days on the same actor with one pair if they are well cared for.

PRO TIP

Curl the eyelashes and apply mascara first. Apply false eyelashes. After the glue has set (one minute), "marry" the real lashes with the false-eyelash strip by combing more mascara to combine them together.

FIGURE 7-5: PHOTO OF MAN STUTTERBOX

MEN AND CHILDREN

Script, circumstances, and skin condition will dictate your choices with makeup for men and children. In most cases, you would not want to see any makeup. Healthy skin tone, definition, and believability to the eye are key. Spot painting is recommended for both. Additional definition to the eyes and eyebrows for men is noted in the section "Natural Makeup."

Bronzers and tanning products are also recommended for men. Men's grooming should be addressed first before applying any sunblock or makeup. Check for nose hair, ear hair, unruly eyebrows that need trimming (unless the character calls for unruly), shaving mistakes, sideburns, and nails. It is always best to get all the trimming done in the makeup trailer. Use lip moisturizers that are not shiny. Try Chap Stick.

Talk about sunblock with the parent or guardian of the child. Has sunblock been applied? It is extremely rare to do a full makeup on a child. There might be spot painting of a mark, or sunblock might be needed for a child. Check for dry skin, dirty face and hands, dry lips, and scrapes and bruises. Use Chap Stick so the lips are not too shiny. Make it fun for them with flavored Chap Stick.

BODY MAKEUP

Body makeup finishes and smoothes out the color of the skin. Even a sheer coat of body makeup will give the skin a beautiful finish that photographs better than skin would if clean. It polishes the skin for a beautiful look. Usually opaque body makeup covers veins, stretch marks, age spots, and discolorations. Sometimes you are doing just the neck and hands; other times, full leg, back, and chest, on men, women, and occasionally children. Widely used in all media, liquids are favored for their finish and are formulated for the body. Most come in water-resistant, sweat-resistant formulas.

Industry Standards: Visiora, Make Up For Ever, M•A•C.

Start with applying sunblock first, if needed, and allow time to absorb. Know the area of the skin that is not covered by clothing. Place tissue in all openings of clothes to protect from makeup. Avoid applying body makeup where there is clothing covering the skin. The Costume Department will appreciate your protecting the clothing.

You can apply body makeup directly to the skin with a sea sponge, large foundation brush, or your hands. If a sheer coverage is needed, mix with body lotion. Check for even application and no lines of demarcation. Let dry. Gently press with tissue to remove excess. Powder with a "no-color" powder or translucent powder and large powder puff. Buff off excess powder with the puff. Allow time for drying before removing tissue from clothing.

Body makeup using an airbrush is covered in Chapter 10.

COVERING TATTOOS

Tattoos are everywhere! You will cover millions of tattoos in your career for so many reasons: if it does not work with the character, if the Director does not like the real tattoo and wants something more appropriate for the situation . . . the reasons go on.

There are several ways to cover tattoos. We will give you two to try.

QUICK AND EASY

This is the fast and dirty method, with no prep involved, working "out of your kit" (makeup slang for using what is in your kit—and Dermacolor should be). It is for those moments of need and no time. This method uses KRYOLAN's Dermacolor palette, an Industry Standard.

1. With a synthetic precut sponge, cover the tattoo completely with Dermacolor D red B (green). Apply the Dermacolor on the tattoo itself, and not on the area around it. You do not want too much overlap, just to cover the artwork. This is the first color to start canceling out the ink, and therefore needs complete coverage. Note: some tattoos have a dimensional quality to them from the tattooing/scarring process. You will be able to camouflage the ink, but not the dimension. You need the help of lighting for dimension.

2. Stipple Dermacolor D31 (or D32, depending on ink colors) over the first layer of Dermacolor. This color prevents gray from bleeding up through the first color, and gives complete coverage. The gray is coming from the blue and black ink.

3. Stipple the third layer of the appropriate Dermacolor to match skin tone, again giving complete coverage.

4. Powder with No-Color Powder and a powder puff or clean sponge.

5. Lightly mist with Ben Nye's Sealer, holding the spray 12 inches away from coverage when spraying. Do not overspray!

TATTOO COVER-UP STEPS

by Christien Tinsley of Tinsley Transfers, Inc.

In order to set up a tattoo cover-up, I first like to prep my workstation. Materials I have with me at all times when doing a tattoo-cover application are: astringent to clean the skin, cotton pads, shavers (electric and razor), shaving cream, scissors, adhesive (Pros-Aide), latex sponges, tissue, spray bottle (water), No-Color powder, powder puffs, Q-tips, 99 percent alcohol, brushes, sealer (Ben Nye's Final Seal), hand towels, Isopropyl Myristate, Supersolv lotion (body, hand, or face), Anti Shine, Mac Crème Gloss Brilliance, tattoo palettes in flesh tones and primary colors; I use Skin Illustrator, Reel Color, W.M CREATIONS, airbrush tattoo colors from Skin Illustrator, Derma Palettes, airbrush and compressor (all items are Industry Standards).

No matter what approach you will take for tattoo cover-up application, you will commonly prep the skin by cleansing it with an astringent of your choice. Doing so removes dirt and oil, and slightly dries the skin for better adhesion of makeup and paint.

Depending on the size of the tattoo you are covering, you may choose to airbrush or paint it out using your makeup brushes. Either way, the colors you choose to use should remain the same. I like to think of this as though you were painting an opaque prosthetic (foam). The idea is to have a color that is not conducive to looking real, and it's attached to the skin. Your job is to make it imitate clean skin, and to blend by painting. When I say paint, I mean paint as though you have a blank canvas.

1. First, you need to start by blocking out all color of the tattoo. I like to go with a meaty red-orange color first. Paint the color solid over the whole tattoo, right to the edge, and then blend and feather it out only about a $\frac{1}{2}$ inch from the edge. This not only helps block out the blues and blacks used in most tattoos, but also gives you an undertone to your flesh colors.

2. Next, go in with a natural flesh tone that is about one shade lighter than the actor's own skin tone. Stipple this color over the surface—making sure it has solid coverage, but with variations of transparency.

3. Add yellows, blues, or greens to the skin to adjust the color by graying, cooling,

or warming the painted area. This should give you the overall match you are looking for.

Details:

Lightly apply a hotter red to the surface already painted to bring out the effects of capillaries and natural blush colors found in the skin tones. Freckles and the occasional browning of the skin can tie the look all together.

Adjust the shade of your tattoo cover-up as you wrap around the body. Not every angle of the body has the same degree of warmth. When working on darker skin tones, you will be using reds and sometimes yellows.

4. After you are done covering up the tattoo, a thin spray of sealer over the surface will help protect it. If your image is a little too shiny, add a little antishine over the surface. Try to avoid powders. Flesh-tone tattoo paints, lightly applied over the surface, can help. Use silicone or water-based product.

Note: Never put oils such as glycerin on top of your tattoo cover for a wet or sweaty look. This will break down the cover.

For on-set touch-ups, always have your paints and makeup colors with you in case you have to remove and reapply on set. For minor repairs, have premixed colors to match and fill in areas that have rubbed away.

For removal of tattoo cover, mix Isoproply Myristate and SuperSolv in a 50/50 solution.

Warm the mixture to a temperature comfortable to the skin. Gently rub the remover with a powder puff in a circular motion on the area to be cleaned. Follow with a dampened hot hand towel to remove all solvent.

FIVE O'CLOCK SHADOW

Painting or stippling in beard growth is done to show a "five o'clock" shadow or a few days growth without using any real hair glued onto the face. It is a basic, easy, fast technique that every Makeup Artists knows. It is sometimes requested last minute, on set, so always have your favorite stipple product and stipple sponges in your set bag. Skin Illustrator, Stacolor, and Reel Color Products make the Makeup Artist's job a lot easier to achieve a lasting, water resistant, beard stipple. These products are all activated by alcohol, are water and abrasion resistant, easy to use, clean off quickly and do not rub off on clothing. They are great for doing so many different kinds of makeups that they are Industry Standards and invaluable for realistic effects and continuity. You should have all of their palettes in your makeup kit.

You will also be working with stipple sponges. Stipple sponges are textured sponges, available in different guages and density for different stippling effects. Orange stipple sponges are softer to the touch and more elastic. Black stipple sponges are coarse and much firmer than the orange ones. Stipple is also a term used for technique as well as to describe sponges and application. It is part of the makeup industry's vocabulary. An example of this terminology is if the Makeup Artist you are assisting says, "Stipple some color into his cheeks"—they would be asking you to use the technique of stippling to add color to the cheeks with an up and down motion using a sponge or brush. It is not complete coverage; it is varied and inconsistent. The up and down motion is done with a light touch, using the wrist in a tapping motion. This gives a realistic look, that is not mask like. It is not complete coverage of color. There is an air quality to it and gives a variation of color and intensity that is organic. This technique is essential to a real-looking beard growth. You will use it often, and for many types of makeups. If you were to apply complete coverage for a beard growth it would look comical and clownish.

Stipple technique is also used to fill in real beards to make them look fuller or appear to have more growth, for long distance shots where you do not want to lay hair by hand, stunt doubles, and background artists who will not be shot in close up.

Let's look at the three products and how to stipple a beard growth with them.

coarseness and sometimes by hand with round natural bristle brushes in varying sizes.

Occasionally, I've used a dye brush and thumb technique splattering the stipple for an uneven look, then going in and removing obvious blobs. Illustrator is designed to be mixed according to the complexion you are working on. But, I'll often start with a black, white, and yellow mix from the FX Palette and make variations. It's really impossible to give a specific formula or even percentages since mixing is an individual painter's eye and art. But I would always start with black as the base tone then mix in bits of yellow, blue and white to give that blue or green cast that beard stubble can have. Adding in additional colors is for fine-tuning to suit an individual. Varying opacity and building layers rather than trying to do it in one shot (always a mistake-unless you want it to look fake) is the best approach.

FIGURE 7-6: THE SKIN ILLUSTRATOR PALETTE

Kenny Myers, creator of Skin Illustrator: I use a black stipple sponge with various

FIGURE 7-7: STACOLOR PALETTE

Matthew Mungle: Apply GBB Beard Stipple using different densities of beard stipple sponges (black beard stipple sponges) or thinned down liquid StaColors with 99% alcohol and air brush on using a splatter technique. Airbrush can be purchased through bearair.com, Combo kit with compressor and Paache H brush with #3 nozzle.

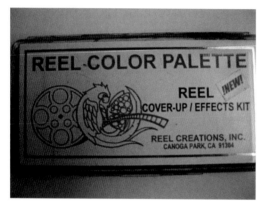

FIGURE 7-8: REEL CREATIONS REEL COLOR PALETTE

Fred Blau, founder of Reel Creations:
Using the cover-up effects palette and depending on the color, I usually use browns mixed with black. I use a coarse plastic wire type stipple sponge, and cut the hard edges off to make a semi round surface. The sponge should be about two inches. When stippling, don't try to cover large areas at once.

Dip sponge into the color then test on another surface. When density is good, you might get two to three hits on the face. Yes, it is time-consuming but it works and it lasts.

If you have any heavy deposits, use a Q-tip dipped in reel developer (99% Isopropyl alcohol), and touch the glitch once for a couple of seconds, then turn over the Q-tip and touch again; this should lift the color. Do not rub! It will smear and ruin the look.

If you have any dark areas, you may use the same type of sponge and counteract the beard stipple with a flesh-tone mix (Cover-up Effects Palette). Stipple lightly on the heavy areas and the beard will lay down to match the desired shade. This is also a good technique for a salt and pepper look.

If you chose to use Reel Body Art instead of the palette, it is a good idea to pour the colors into a wide lid (i.e., pancake lid one for each color). Let it thicken or dry. Then use the same technique as with the palette. Do not be afraid to lighten (density) color using some Reel Developer.

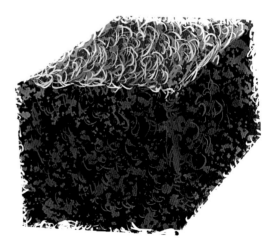

FIGURE 7-9: ILLUSTRATION OF A TEXTURED STIPPLE SPONGE

Stipple sponges are stiff sponges made in different textures used in makeup to create a variety of shapes and textures.

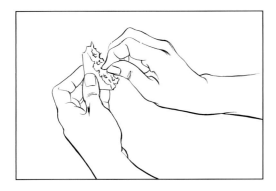

FIGURE 7-10: A COSMETIC SPONGE MADE INTO A STIPPLE SPONGE

Stipple sponges can also be made from regular cosmetic sponges by tearing a desired number of holes into the sponge. This will create texture.

Favorite adhesives to use for chopped hair applications: Extra Hold Matte Adhesive.

SUN PROTECTION

No matter who you are, you need sunblock. Everyone needs to protect their skin from the damaging effects of the sun. Makeup Artists should apply sunblock before a makeup as well as during the coarse of the day when filming outdoors. It needs to be reapplied to protect all day. There is a certain responsibility to ensure your actor does not burn while filming or shooting outdoors. It also makes your work a lot easier if you take the time to protect the skin. Covering burnt skin is a drag; it's time-consuming and painful.

The SPF (Sun Protection Factor) can be misleading and not always accurate in what the manufacturer claims. Example: waterproof sunblock has to be reapplied after getting wet or out of the water. The labels have now been changed to "water resistant," but there are still products floating around with old labels on them that say "waterproof." When in doubt, reapply. SPF products with a number larger than 30 have not been proven to have any more protection, experts say. Another misleading assumption is that a sunscreen or sunblock with an SPF 30 has twice the protection of a SPF 15: not so. SPF 15 blocks out 93% of the sun's rays and SPF 30 blocks out 97% of the sun's rays. Rays are the Ultra Violet rays of UV. The UVB rays cause damage to the surface of the skin such as: burning, tanning and other skin damage. The UVA rays penetrate the surface of the skin and damage the connective tissue. UVA long-wave protection ingredients are avobenzone, zinc oxide, titanium dioxide, mexoryl sx, tensor and helioplex (a stabilizer). Sunblocks come in creams, lotions, gels, sticks and sprays.

A MUST HAVE: board spectrum sunblock that blocks both UVB and UVA rays.

For the face try Neutrogena Ultra Sheer Dry Touch Sunblock in SPF 55. It works great under makeup base, feels good on the skin, is non-greasy, and water resistant.

For the body try Neutrogena Body Mist Sunblock SPF 45. This spray goes on beautifully and is ultra light, feels clean on the skin, is non-greasy, water resistant, and great for on-set touch-up or reapplying. You can spray it right over your makeup.

MAKEUP SAFETY TIPS

Makeup and applicators should not be shared. Use certain safety standards when working. Wash your hands in between working on each person. If a sink is not available, use hand sanitizer, or hand wipes. Always remove cream products and foundations from their container with a palette knife and place onto a makeup palette or artist's paper to use for each person. Use disposable mascara wands and applicators. Cut off lipstick from the tube and place onto your palette to be use off the palette only. Clean brushes after each use. Sharpen all pencils before and after using. Clean lipstick brushes with 99% alcohol. Use sponges and puffs only on one person.

Industry Standards: stainless steel palette, artist's paper palette, Japonesque makeup palettes, stainless steel palette knife, 99% alcohol.

REFERENCES

Thomas P. Habif, Clinical Dermatology,
Third Edition, 1996, Mosby Year
Book Inc.

www.consumersearch.com/www/family/
sunscreen/index.html

www.comsumersearch.com/www/family/
sunscreen/review.html

www.medicinenet.com/sun_protection_and_
sunscreens/pg2.html

www.medicinenet.com/sun_protection_and_
sunscreens/pg3.html

Beard stipple with Reel colors, Fred Blau
www.reelcreations.com

Beard Stipple with StaColors,
Matthew Mungle
www.matthewwmungle.com

Beard Stipple with Skin Illustrator,
Kenny Myers
www.ppi.cc

Tattoo Cover up, Christien Tinsley
www.tinsleytransfers.com

Richard Dean
Rdean1028@mac.com

8

DESIGN

TEMPORARY TATTOOS, CONTACTS, VENEERS, DESIGNING WITH ENVIRONMENT

Makeup accessorizes the character's look, mood, and style. We put the finishing touch on the actor's exterior to match the interior performance and to bring the character to life. This enables the actor to focus on the performance and not the look, and to become the character. Many times you will feel the actor start to transform before your eyes as the makeup application progresses. They are looking into the mirror and seeing the physical appearance matching the interior of their performance/character, and their body language begins to change. At this moment, both actor and artist know the makeup design (and application) is working. You know you have been successful in developing the character.

In film, every makeup begins with the text of the script. Makeup is one of several languages used to elaborate and illustrate text. Based on the text, we make all sorts of decisions: the character's physical well-being, social and financial status, level and condition of vanity, and inclination to spend time in front of the mirror. At the point the actor or actress enters our lives, his or her analysis of the same textual information meets our own. Add to this their personal needs, physical condition, areas of insecurity, and physical strengths, and we are nearly ready to put brush to skin.

—Richard Dean

We explore, examine, research, discuss, collaborate, and meet with the Director, Actor, Costume Designer, Production Designer, Cinematographer, and the Producers. From our breakdown of the script, design meetings, production meetings, and sidebar meetings, we begin to test the looks. This is the prep period of the schedule: the weeks or days (for prosthetics, the prep time is much longer) before filming begins, for both film and TV. Stage has its own prep or rehearsal period, where designs and makeup are worked out in dress rehearsals onstage with lighting. There is the same collaboration with Director, Costume Designer, and Lighting Designer—and, you hope, a chance to see your makeup "from the house" with the lighting plot or design. This is the time to see your performers from the seats in the audience ("from the house"), usually viewing from orchestra seats, midway back, to judge how your makeup is reading to the audience. It is generally a standard in theatre or opera to work from this vantage point of "middle of the house." With each theatre being a different size and capacity, you adjust your work accordingly. If you work for the back reaches of the house, the makeup will be too heavy for the seats in the front rows. If you work for the front of the house, your makeup will not be seen by anyone seated past the first few rows. So you split the difference and go for midway.

Adjustments are also made for HD filming of stage productions and live broadcasts. This has altered the products and style of makeup used for stage, and has lessened the theatricality of the makeup.

For photograhy, the design is based on conversations with the Photographer, Art Director, and client. There could be several days to create a design or look, or just one day. It is a project-per-project situation, with amount of time, research, and designing per job varying greatly—from exotic, very stylized fashion to natural, to designing the makeup for a runway collection.

There is a lot to think about in all areas of makeup, starting with what medium is being used? What is the look (style) of the project? Is there a color palette that all departments are working with? Who are the characters (and their background)? What is the movement of the story? Who is the client? Is it an editorial shoot or advertising? Where are the shooting locations? Environmental factors; continuity issues. What does the Director want? What does the actor want. Is there an arc to the story that affects the makeup movement? What research needs to be done to create realism? What creative influences do you want to use: European fashion magazines, art books, American fashion, street or local fashion, or museums? Is it fantasy or real life? What is the inspiration?

Inspiration for design can come from just about any source. It's all around you.

There is movement to makeup in film. Our work is consistently changing with the mood or emotion of the character, the situations, and the environment of filming. It can be extremely subtle or very obvious. Attention to detail brings life to the look and believability. The more believable, the less focus on the fact that it is makeup.

Read through the text several times, making notes and breaking down the script before meeting with the Director. Script breaks are done by all departments, and you must compare and defer to the Script Supervisor's version as the final word. The Script Supervisor will provide a breakdown to all department heads. Recommend reading for script breakdown "Costuming for Film: The Art and The Craft" by Holly Cole and Kristin Burke.

After meeting with the Director, meet with the other departments: Costume Designer, Production Designer, Cinematographer. This is the time of discovery and aesthetics decisions. It is also a time for research. Once you feel you have done your due diligence, talk to the AD (Assistant Director) about meeting with the actors. The AD handles all scheduling. Your first meeting could just

be a meet-and-greet (no makeup applied). If that is the case, you and the actor will discuss looks, products, and ideas. If schedule allows, then there would be a makeup day to test or work out the looks. If there are makeup designs that are still in the experimental pause, work out the design on a model first, perfect the design or products to use, and then apply this to the actor. If you are not experimenting, work out your designs with the actor. Makeup Artists also use Photoshop to design looks and to use for a show-and-tell. Prep time and money in the budget will dictate how much makeup testing there is. In some cases, you will not have access to an actor. Normally, there is at least one day of makeup testing done on-camera, called a "test day." This gives everyone a chance to put the work on film, look at it on-screen, and make decisions based on what was tested. When the tests are screened at "dailies," everyone involved is present. Discussion on the looks goes on while looking at the film, and decisions are made or more testing is requested if the looks were not what they had been hoping for. Many feel prep is the most difficult time in
the production schedule. This time of collaboration can become a time of too many cooks in the kitchen! In photography, you will develop your makeup design from directions and concepts given to you by the photographer and client. On the day of shooting, test photos will be taken (or Polaroids) and, after reviewing and consulting on the photo, any adjustments or requests that are needed will be made.

In all situations, remember to stay flexible in mind and hand. This is part of the

process of problem-solving and collaboration that go into designing looks and characters. There will be times when you will be asked to change or correct something. Do not be put off, but understand that you will not always get it right the first time. Ideally, you will have the opportunity to start out with small projects, independent films, industrial projects, and small print jobs to hone your skills, creativity, and intuition. These small projects help to develop and perfect your problem-solving ability in design. Knowing how to achieve a look with very little money or resources, or how to create a look when the environmental issues at hand will cause problems (like humidity) is an asset. You will struggle to achieve and maintain your makeup if you do not look at the whole picture. It is foolish to not consider all elements to each design situation.

You now have some idea what the Makeup Department Head or Makeup Designer goes though. In the beginning of your career, you will not be privy to all the meetings, discussions, and decisions regarding design. The bigger the budget and show, the more this is true. This is why we remind you often to follow instructions given by those members of the department that are supervising the makeup crew. This is true for all mediums; so much has gone into the design and choices for a project long before you arrive for your first day of work. If you are a daily hire, the larger the show the more likely it is that you will have very little interaction with the HOD (Head of Department). The HOD will be relying on their crew to instruct and manage a large staff. There is a temptation in a large work situation to "grand stand," or stand-out from the group. Resist the urge! When you are new and wanting to impress, all you have to do is your job! The HOD might not have the time to chat with you, but they know who is getting the work done. This is what will impress those you work for; doing the makeup asked for, paying attention, being professional on and off set, and not trying to over-step your position to get attention.

CHARACTER DESIGN

Character design can be thought of as all makeup designs; even a beauty makeup is a form of character design. For some people, when referring to character makeup, they don't realize this point. They think of an old age makeup or an obvious physical alteration to the actor to show character, and not beauty. All projects begin with text or concept; there is your character. Working subtly is just as challenging as painting with broad strokes when creating a character. Nicotine stains on the teeth and fingers of a character that smokes is an example of conveying the subtlety of a character. Many times the audience does not consciously notice these design because the look is so authentic to the physical portrayal. Richard Dean, whose artistry and brilliance in makeup design for so many films, is one of the top makeup artists in the film industry. His work gives makeup artists inspiration, and for the beginning makeup artist he will illustrate some of the thought processes for designing a makeup:

"In designing the makeup for *Fatal Attraction*, the female character Alex Forrest, played by actress Glenn Close, is clearly attractive and sensual, but with an underlying layer of terrible disturbance and ill function. Symmetry and balance could not tell this story. Instead, I made an effort to suggest that something was always hidden by emphasizing the natural lack of symmetry in the human face, by lining the eyes to stress that one was slightly smaller and by tossing a shaft of hair over one eye to create a kind of three-quarter (rather than honest full face) gaze. The lady had her secrets and her "beauty makeup" contributed to her mystery. In the retail world, balance and symmetry are more useful than they are in film.

The movie camera seems to adore the less-than-perfect if it exists within the confines of perfect reproductive health and heat. Just examine the specific features of today's biggest stars. I struggle to learn what each face wants to say about itself; unless there is a particular demand made upon one feature's emphasis over another, my habit is to let the face of the actor tell me. Or their voice if they are so inclined."

—Richard Dean

We use every trick available to tell the story and sell the look. We change eyes, teeth, eyebrows, noses, nails, skin color, hair color. We reverse age, add age, add tattoos, change facial features, and, of course, alter with prosthetics. Your designs can be sketched, done with Photoshop, tested on models/actors, or verbalized. The better your prep and research of a project, the better your work will be. There will be times that you have no prep or research time, such as last-minute jobs, on-the-spot requests because of a new inspiration by the Director or actor, or accidents that require fast problem solving. Remember attention to detail gives your makeup designs life.

Patty York prefers to illustrate her designs for film. Being a passionate perfectionist with a background as a commercial artist helps distinguish her face paintings from others. Patty also prefers illustrating her makeup continuity charts (or Face Chart). She meticulously shows a painted illustration and includes written details of her makeup designs, including a photo of the completed makeup on the actor or actress.

"One of my job requirements is makeup continuity for the film project at hand. This means reproducing the makeup designs I've created for the film on paper, a Face Chart, if you will, with painted illustrations and written details. I love doing them. I get a sort of Zen buzz from the process."—Patty York

Many times you will have to recreate looks for continuity reasons on a project. Scheduling, story line, and cost affect how often one look will be recreated throughout a shooting schedule. You need to remember what you did, how you did it, and what you use.

These Face Charts or Makeup Charts go into a makeup continuity book that is kept by the Makeup Department and turned into the studio on completion of the film. If there are re-shoots or additional photography requested by the studio to finish or change the film, the looks can be recreated by referencing the makeup continuity book—regardless of whether or not the original Makeup Department is available. These decisions are made "in post" on a project; the Powers That Be decide to change, redo, or add to a scene for many reasons, one of which is a testing audience that does not respond well to the movie. All departments on film and television keep continuity books. Everyone puts their own stamp on how the book is done. Digital photos, notes illustrated with photos, sticky notes that attach to the back of the photo, Makeup Charts (Face Charts), labeling of the cosmetics used with the scene and actor on the label, and combinations of all of the above, are some of the tools used to document continuity.

Patty's Face Chart gives you all the detail and description to recreate her makeup design for this character.

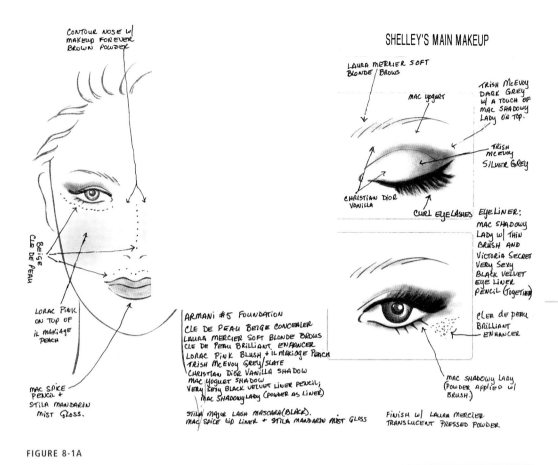

FIGURE 8-1A

Note: This is an actual working Face Chart, the photo of the completed makeup on the actress is not included to protect the integrity of the film until it is released to the theatres. The film is still in production as of this printing.

Kim Felix-Burke gives us another example of a Makeup Chart. This shows how a photo from fashion or advertising can inspire a makeup design. The photo is from a Sephora makeup ad.

EYEBROW BLOCKING

Changing eyebrow shape is a wonderful and powerful tool to developing and designing a character. The eyebrows frame the eyes, the windows to the soul, making them very influential on the focus of the facial features. Block out the eyebrows to completely alter a face or show "period" (for example, Victorian England). As with all makeup, it can be a very subtle or extreme block.

Three Techniques

Adhesive Block: To block out the brows, choose an adhesive that is easy to remove (see adhesives under product information). Spirit gum or resin-based adhesive works well. It is easy to remove, dries fairly

FIGURE 8-1B

quickly, and comes in different grades of matte formulas.

1. Apply the spirit gum, brushing into the brows to lay flat and smooth against the skin.

2. Using a soft cloth or powder puff wrapped in nylon, gently press-roll the brows until the adhesive looks matte. (Leather shammys, or Nylon or silk fabric works best with spirit gum, because they do not stick to the adhesive.)

3. When the adhesive is dry, apply a sealer over the top of it.

4. Apply foundation, choosing one that fits the character's skin tone, with full coverage and staying power.

Removal: Use alcohol or spirit gum remover.

Waxing Out: Eyebrow wax comes in several degrees of hardness, and many brands to choose from.

We use KRYOLAN's eyebrow wax.

1. Apply wax over the eyebrow with a spatula, blending the edges into the skin.

2. Cover the brow with a sealer. Dry.

3. Finish with the correct foundation color.

Combination: Combine the spirit gum and wax for more hold and block.

1. Apply spirit gum, brushing into the hair against the skin.

2. Let dry, and follow with an application of eyebrow wax.

3. Apply sealer.

4. Apply foundation.

APPLIANCE BLOCK

Eyebrow appliances will give you a total block, but you must be able to blend the edges for successful application. They are applied directly over the eyebrows. Plastic-based products are easier to work with. We will use KRYOLAN's eyebrow plastic.

Making the appliance using KRYOLAN's plastic, take a round object (such as an orange or grapefruit—they both give a nice texture) to simulate the pores of the skin.

1. Apply on the fruit a thin layer of plastic that is slightly larger than the eyebrow area and shape. Let dry.

2. Reapply a second layer. Let dry.

3. Powder with no-color powder. Lift off the fruit.

4. Apply eyebrow wax to brows to flatten.

5. Press with powder puff that is clean—no powder or talc on the puff.

6. Apply spirit gum around the edges of the brow.

7. Lay the plastic appliance on top of the brow, being careful not to fold or crease the edges.

8. Secure and glue down the plastic. Go around the edges with alcohol to blend the edges.

9. Apply foundation of choice, and powder.

PRO TIP

To prevent the eyebrow hair from "bleeding" up though the plastic, lighten the hair with Tattoo Paints or Roux 'Tween Time Color Stick, by Revlon.

LIFT OFF

The "Traynor Lift" is the beauty device used by Makeup Artists for stage, film, and TV to give a youthful look to the face. Mark Traynor Face and Neck Lifts and Isometric Beauty Bands are used for beauty, glamour, to reverse age, in character makeups (think *Tootsie,* drag queens, transvestites), and on both women and men.

The "lifts" eliminate lines around the eyes and mouth, and help give a smooth, firm look to the jawline and neck. They tighten the skin and lift the eyebrows. Many times you will use them in tandem with a wig, but lifts can also be used without a wig. The Hairstylist will work with you to incorporate the lifts into the hairstyle or wig. They are fantastic for those projects where the same person goes through several decades. You would use "reverse age," current age, and old age to show the passage of time.

Mark Traynor's lift package consist of two pieces of hypoallergenic surgical tape attached to two elastics, one of which has eyelets on it for adjusting the tension.

To apply the lifts, the pull is very important. Start with a clean face, deciding placement of lifts before doing any makeup. At some point nearing the completion of the makeup application, you will stop doing makeup and attach the lifts. This ensures that your placement of makeup is correct. Once the lifts have been attached and the skin is tight and smooth, complete your makeup. The eyebrows should be done last, when the lifts are in place, to get the proper shape.

1. With the person sitting (clean face), looking straight into the makeup mirror, stand directly behind your subject. Placing your fingers at the hairline, pull to see where the lifts should be placed. You must work off the mirror image. Check the pull by adjusting your finger placement. See where it looks too tight or just right.

2. Clean the area with alcohol to remove natural oils. Let dry.

3. Apply the tape to the prep area. In some climates, you can also add a medical adhesive to the tape for extra holding power.

4. Gently place the elastics to the side or back of the head, with a clip to get them out of the way for makeup application. You are not attaching the elastic yet.

5. When your makeup application is almost complete, attach the elastic. You

should work with the Hairstylist at this point, to coordinate elastic with hairstyle.

6. Finish the makeup, and check for any adjustments that are needed. Always follow all manufacturer's instructions.

OLD AGE

We can add age to a character by painting in lines, age spots, and broken capillaries, and by graying the eyebrows and hair. If the actor has a photo of a parent at the age you are recreating, that is very helpful in seeing the way the family genetics age. Your knowledge from the previous chapters on Shapes (Chapter 1), and the Body (Chapter 2), and Highlights and Contours (Chapter 6) are needed to guide you in hollowing out the features, adding fine lines, and giving an old-age texture to the skin. Texturing the skin is a must to complete your line work. Otherwise you have smooth lined skin. Have your model raise and lower each section of the face that you are painting to find the lines (see Chapter 2: The Body). Using a medium brown with a fine-tipped makeup brush, paint in the line where the wrinkle forms. For a very subtle aging use a taupe brown. If a heavier line is needed, blend the top edge out and leave the lower edge of your line hard (unblended), this hard edge will recede the wrinkle further. Practice and work out your aging with as many models as you can. Each face tells you how to age them, so we will not give you steps to aging. Review Chapters 1 and 2 before starting your aging exercise.

FIGURE 8-2: OLD GREEK WOMAN

The information contained within the context of this article is presented in good faith. The responsibility for the use of any material in special makeup effects rests solely with the user. The author assumes no responsibility for the use, or misuse, of any material, technique, or the informational content discussed within this article.

AGING USING STRETCH AND STIPPLE

Many times the painted technique of aging is not enough to achieve the age needed. In this situation, the professional Makeup Artist should know how to do aging using the stretch and stipple technique. This is a very simple technique using three-dimensional appliances to achieve wrinkling and aging of the skin. We are going to tell you how to do stretch and stipple with two different products. Basically, the technique of stretching is the same with both products. The key to stretch and stipple is how you stretch the skin to get realistic-looking wrinkles. There will be times that you will be asked to do this without any preparation, so having the skills and products for stretch and stipple will allow you to work directly out of your kit, at a moment's notice.

GREEN MARBLE SeLr AGING TECHNIQUE

by Richard Snell and Kenny Myers, reprinted from Premiere Products Inc. (www.ppi.cc)

Green Marble SeLr is often used as an aging product. The results are subtle and effective. A technique called stretch and stipple (or stretch and brush) is used in the aging process. These procedures were refined by Douglas Noe during a particularly brutal summer while filming in Atlanta. To mix Green Marble into an ager, you must use Green Marble SeLr concentrate and Attagel (clay powder used in facial masks).

Very important: Do not use this technique with the spray Green Marble SeLr.

Recipe: 1 oz. Attagel to 6 oz. Green Marble concentrate still works well as a fine line wrinkler when used lightly. This formula also works for lighter applications or where texture change is all that is needed. You might want to custom blend the recipe to get a desired effect for different areas of the face.

Attagel to Green Marble Concentrate Formulas:

- 1 to 3 oz.—heavy ager on most skin types
- 1 to 4 oz.—medium heavy
- 1 to 5 oz.—medium light
- 1 to 6 oz.—light ager on most skin types

Your makeup kit for stretch and stipple with Green Marble Concentrate:

- Kleenex
- Puffs
- Sponges
- Towels
- Hair dryer
- AF thinner (RCMA)
- Assorted makeup brushes
- Cups, Q-tips
- Cotton pads
- Kiehls blue astringent
- Flat white synthetic brushes ($\frac{3}{8}$, $\frac{1}{2}$, $\frac{5}{8}$, $\frac{7}{8}$, 1 inch)
- Cape
- Skin Illustrator Color Palettes
- Makeup remover
- Eyewash drops
- Moisturizer
- Hand sanitizer
- Powders
- Hand fan
- Green Marble SeLr Concentrate

- Chubs
- 99 percent alcohol
- Telesis 5 Thinner

Prep the actor:

Remove any fine hairs from the actor, and lightly wipe the face with Kiehls blue astringent (product of choice) or witch hazel. To prevent lashes from sticking while you work, apply AF Thinner to lashes with a mascara wand before you begin. Recline the actor in a chair for easier working conditions. An upright position is perfectly fine also. You might find yourself doing both throughout the process.

THE METHODS

Use a flat white synthetic bristle brush (between $\frac{3}{8}$ and 1 inch in width), depending on the area being aged. The application changes only with the tools you use to put the SeLr to the skin. Have your brushstrokes complement the directions of the wrinkles. One to four layers, and up to as many as nine layers, can be used to get the desired effect. Stretch the area being stippled. While still stretched, apply SeLr concentrate ager with a brush, complementing the directions of the natural wrinkle. While the skin is still stretched, powder the area just done. Now release your stretch. Repeat the process until you have the number of layers desired. If possible, for multiple layers and if you can hold the skin that long, try not to powder in between layers. This will enhance the finished look. But whatever you do, don't let go of the skin before your final stipple and powder are applied. Use a hand fan while working to keep the fumes away from the actor and to encourage the drying process of each layer. A hair dryer can also be used on a cool low setting. When aging an actor, don't get too close to the mouth or nasolabial area. Too much buildup of product will only cause you to have constant repairs because this is a very mobile area. Remember to keep your fingertips powdered at all times.

WHERE TO STRETCH

Furrow lines: Area between brows is pulled upward and outward.

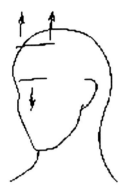

FIGURE 8-3: AREA BETWEEN THE BROWS WITH FURROW LINES

Forehead: Subject scowls to lower brow line, and hairline is pulled away from face.

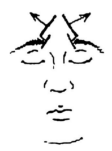

FIGURE 8-4: FOREHEAD WRINKLES

Crow's-feet: Pull away from outer corners of both eyes.

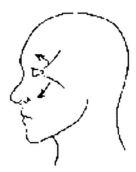

FIGURE 8-5: CROW'S-FEET

Eyelids: Pull up at eyebrows, both eyes.

FIGURE 8-6: EYELID WRINKLES

Under-eye area: Pull down and toward center of face, both eyes.

FIGURE 8-7: UNDER EYE AREA LINES

Option one: Lift area away from center of face.

Option two: Puff the area to be aged.

FIGURE 8-8A & 8-8B: NASAL LABIAL FOLD

Upper lip: Puff entire area to be aged. (Puff means having the person fill their upper lip with air and hold until application is dry.)

FIGURE 8-9: UPPER LIP PUFFED

Chin: With neck arched, pull both sides of chin away from the center of the subject's face.

FIGURE 8-10: CHIN STRETCH

Cheek: Using the subject's index finger, reach deep into the cheek and push out. This is a perfect opportunity to tie the nasolabials, under-eye area, and crow's-feet together. Do both sides.

FIGURE 8-11: CHEEK STRETCH

Neck: Begin with the head back. Do the throat first. Then, with head turned, do both sides.

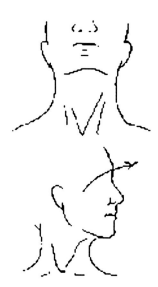

FIGURE 8-12A & 8-12B: NECK STRETCH

DESIGN

REPAIRS

Depending on how many layers you have done, areas around the mouth may crack or flake. You'll most often notice this damage around lunch and near wrap.

Repairs are easy and quick:

1. Paint 99 percent alcohol in the direction of the wrinkles.
2. Apply Telesis 4 Thinner and/or acetone (faster) with a brush. Then apply Green Marble SeLr with a brush, sponge, or spray.
3. Apply the original ager material.

Removal

Massage isopropyl myristate or IPM Gel with your fingertips into the skin that has been aged. Take your time. The material will dissolve—slowly, then faster and faster. When the product has loosened, follow with a hot towel for a thorough removal.

STRETCH AND STIPPLE WITH W.M. CREATIONS, INC.

W.M. Creations has old-age stipple available in four formulas: A, B, C, and Crusty. Neutral and dark skin formulas are available by special order.

A: Used in a perspiration-free environment. Will give slight wrinkling effect when applied to unstretched skin.

B: Perspiration resistant. Under normal use, gives heavy wrinkling effect even if the skin is not stretched. This is the most widely used stipple.

C: Heaviest wrinkling effect possible. Good for use on hands.

Crusty: Gives the illusion of deeply weathered skin. Great for use on hands. Apply a thin layer of Pros-Aide or Beta Bond before stippling hands for maximum adhesion.

Prep the skin with 70 or 99 percent alcohol.

Decant stipple into a small container, and heat in the microwave for two seconds.

Be careful not to overheat, or the stipple will coagulate.

Stretch and stipple skin area with a light coat of old-age stipple. Powder and release.

Castor oil makeup base or Stacolors may be used as translucent washes over or under stipples for a natural look.

A wash of castor oil and 70 percent alcohol may be used to remove the powdery look of latex over the stretch and stipple area.

Removal

Massage liquid hand soap into stippled area, and let soak for at least one minute.

Apply a warm, wet towel to the area for one minute and repeat the process.

Stipple may be rolled off the skin.

CONTACT LENSES

Custom contact lenses are a great way to complete a makeup design, and are sometimes necessary to sell the look of the makeup. Examples of contact lenses being necessary to complete a makeup are: a badly beaten face, illness, death, or portrait makeup (lookalike). With a badly beaten face, if there is bruising/wounds to the eye area, there would be broken blood vessels in the whites of the eye. In illness, you would show yellowness and broken vessels. In death, you would use a death lens that is cloudy. In portrait makeup, you would change the eye color of the actor to match the person they are portraying. In all of these situations, having lenses to remove the "life" in the whites of the eye, or to change the color of the iris, completes and sells your artistry. Contact lenses are a fabulous tool for the Makeup Artist.

There are many way to order contact lenses. Cristina Patterson Ceret, Contact Lens Technician and Special Effects Coordinator, takes orders from all over the world. The most common method for her is by email. Christina says:

> "Depending on the production, sometimes I am asked to actually create the designs for the contacts, or the Makeup Artist requests their designs to be painted. It's tricky when a Makeup Artist creates their own. A lot of times, they will design something that takes the lens all the way to the edge. People forget that lenses are round, so if you stretch a lens out one way, they also have to go the other way to complete the circle. It also depends on the size and curve of the actor's measurements. For instance, if the actor's measurements permit only a smaller size of the sclera lenses, it's definitely not going to the edge. Makeup Artists

should also be aware of adding any light reflection flares to the design. Although it looks nice, the reflection can be confusing to interpret during the painting process. At times, it becomes a collaboration between the Makeup Artist and myself. The Makeup Artist will give me a design that I will alter in Photoshop to better fit the contacts to be worn. This would be the easiest way to see what the Makeup Artist wants and how the design can be executed. Most designs are created in Photoshop beforehand, then emailed to me. After discussing what is doable, I'll sit down to paint. A mock-up is painted first, and, if time permits, a picture is taken to be sent off for approval."

The most commonly used contact lenses are kept in stock with different curves.

Television shows tend to need contacts at the last minute. Actors would be fitted for contacts right away to be used in same-day or next-day situations. There are times when the contact lenses are not in stock.

The Makeup Artist must have the actor fitted by a professionally licensed doctor. When contacts are being worn, you can get tunnel vision—just like looking through a straw. Everyone is different with their comfort level when wearing contacts. A properly fitting lens should be reasonably comfortable. There is no definite wearing time. It is completely dependent upon the actor's comfort level. Environmental conditions will have an impact as well. Artificial environments are all irritants to the eye, which affects contact lens comfort.

Artificial snow, smoke, wind, lots of splashing water, and the occasional sand can make all lens wearers unhappy campers.

Colors of the lenses can be adjusted or used in such a way to accommodate media such as bluescreen and greenscreen. Effects can be included with this. For example, green or blue lenses have been used to make an actor disappear on-screen.

Green or blue lenses have also been used to project an effect onto the sclera lens that is being worn. These are just a few examples.

Contact lenses should be the last thing to go on the actor, and the first to come off. Most lenses stay with the Makeup Artist after the shoot. He or she will bring them in to be sterilized and sealed for long-term storage. If the lenses are to be used again after they have been sitting for a year or so, we ask the Makeup Artist to bring them in to us or any other eye-care specialist to be checked out for imperfections, bacteria, and so on. Also, the artwork on the lenses should be checked for any fading or opacity. If the lenses are in good shape, we'll go ahead and sterilize them for use.

All Lenses Are Unique (or a word about contact lenses)

There is no such thing as a generic contact lens. Every person has a slightly different eye curvature and eyelid tension. Only a licensed eye-care professional can fit a contact lens. You are putting your eyes at risk by purchasing special-effects lenses from online auction sites, flea markets,

convenience stores, or shops, for example. Soft lenses are currently the standard of the industry. Almost anything can be painted, printed, or laminated on a soft lens. Rigid lenses are used for a variety of effects—athough the wearing time is much less than for a soft lens, and rigid lenses take longer for the actor to get used to.

Scleral Lenses

Scleral lenses cover the sclera, or white part of the eye. They are larger in diameter (18–24 mm) than traditional lenses, which generally cover only the iris (colored part of the eye) and are usually 14–15 mm. Scleral lenses work great for bloodshot eyes, hemorrhage effect, jaundice, full black, demon eyes, and other monster effects, where the entire inside surface of the eye needs to be covered to avoid seeing the edge of the lens.

Contact Lens Information

Cost: The cost of a lens is related to the difficulty and type of special-effects lens design.

Fitting and Exams: All exams include internal and external eye-health evaluation to determine if the actor can in fact wear contact lenses, plus refraction for prescription.

Getting Fitted by Another Doctor: To purchase lenses without being able to bring the actor in for fittings to your favorite special-effects lens maker, you can forward the information directly to the shop. This is what you'll need to submit:

1. Current refraction

2. Keratometric (K) readings

3. Visible iris diameter (mm)

4. Pupil size (mm)

5. Normal iris color (photo if possible)

6. An exact color rendering of effect to be created

7. If scleral contact lenses are the desired lenses, the actor must be fitted by a doctor who has the compatible fitting set. Scleral lenses must be fitted physically; they cannot be determined solely by corneal curvature measurements.

TEETH

Another great tool for the Makeup Artist is working with and changing the teeth. As with contact lens, changing a person's teeth to go with the makeup design is an essential tool to create realistic effects. It is also a wonderful choice for character design and comedy. As with contact lenses, teeth that don't go with the makeup design will take away from your makeup job. For example, you have aged an actor from 40 to 80 years old, and the actor's teeth are too white. This will detract from all of the aging work that has been done.

It is important to use a qualified professional in both areas when designing characters involving eyes and teeth. The professional's technological and medical background protects the actor that you are making the changes on.

Gary Archer of G.A. Enterprises, a specialist in dental prosthetics for the film and

television industries, explains the process and current reasons for tooth transformation:

"One of the main reasons for tooth transformation is that in today's Hollywood society, a perfect smile is essential. Unfortunately, with the latest in porcelain veneers, implants, and cosmetic bonding, we have beautiful smiles in life—but under the lights and in front of the camera, it is entirely too dazzling, and therefore unrealistic. We have had requests to darken actors' teeth to make them less perfect. We can give them gaps where no gap exists, and stains to represent neglect and poor dental care; have them missing teeth, or have them fall out on camera. We also make "grills," ranging from single teeth with faux diamonds to full arches with designs and styles on them. We make perfect teeth bad, and bad teeth good! We have also developed a range of fake braces and retainers that will fool the most critical eye. In addition, we have copied smiles of famous celebrities and influential figures of the past to transform the actor's teeth into whoever it is they are portraying. Plumpers are another specialty to help swell out or fatten a character's mouth, and are another unique product.

PRO TIP

Plumpers are a great makeup tool for changing facial shape. For example: aging or swelling from a fight or accident.

stress in the artist-actor relationship, to say the least. Not using enough material can lead to a shortened or underextended impression that doesn't capture the areas that you need.

It is recommended that you use a dental professional when transforming teeth for a character. Gary will show us the process for dental casting:

Obtain accurate dental casts of the actor. Do not use old molds that the actor may have from previous projects. They are usually older than the actor remembers them to be, have been used for a previous prosthetic appliance, and may be damaged or inaccurate.

Gary takes us through the steps of dental casting and dental molds:

1. First, an alginate impression is taken with a metal tray. Plastic trays are not rigid enough and can cause distortion.

2. Second, a cast is made in a hard yellow or blue stone.

3. Be careful loading the impression tray. Using too much material can gag or choke the patient (actor), which causes

Once the positive dental casts have been done, the design process starts. A diagnostic wax-up can be made to show the Makeup Artist and Director exactly what the teeth will look like. This helps to eliminate surprise on the set, and will enable all parties to be on the same page. It helps to bring it all (the design) together.

After the designs have been approved, a last wax pattern is cast to fabricate the acrylic veneers. Heat-cured acrylic is used to give the most accurate, color-stable, and realistic look for the veneers. Self-curing plastics tend to have a very monochromatic and dull appearance, so they should be avoided.

Once fabricated, the veneers are quite thin and delicate. Given time, the actor actually forget they have teeth in, and care must be taken to ensure that the actor does not forget they have veneers in, and go to lunch wearing them. This has happened, much to everyone's amusement.

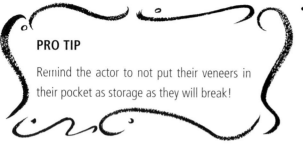

PRO TIP

Remind the actor to not put their veneers in their pocket as storage as they will break!

Normal process time from design to fabrication and completion of a set of veneers is usually one week. In some cases, GA Enterprises can turn them around faster, but there are certain rules to using dental acrylics, and attempting to rush or speed up the process usually produces bad results.

CARE OF ACRYLIC VENEERS

Gently rinse under cool tap water, and store in the case provided for each set. Add a small amount of mouthwash in the case to keep them fresh tasting.

Things to know as a Makeup Artist working with veneers:

- You will need to work with latex or nonlatex gloves on.

- Ask if the person has an allergy to latex, and what flavor preference they have for mouthwash. Mouthwash helps to keep the veneers fresh, as well as being great for a fast rinse on-set if needed.

- You will be putting in, as well as taking out, the veneers. Always wear gloves. This is also necessary on-set. Sometimes the actor will want to do this, but there are always moments when the Makeup Artist must be prepared to do this.

- To help the actor adjust to something on their teeth, they need to get the feel of them Have them wear the veneers well before going on-camera to give them time to forget they are on. This also helps with their speech. At first, they might sound a bit different, but this goes away when they forget that the veneers are on. You will need to do this only for the first few days of use. The actor will quickly get used to them, and not need to put them in early. Soon you will be popping the veneers in on-set!

ON-SET TOUCH-UPS

On-set, you will need to bring with you:

- A dental case: the veneer case for each pair of veneers working

- Latex gloves

- Nonlatex gloves

- Bottle of mouthwash

- Bottled water

- Paper towels

If you need to remove veneers on-set, put gloves on and remove the veneers, placing them in a paper towel or directly into their case. Sometimes you have to be the one to actually remove the veneers from the actor's mouth. The actor can't do it. Regardless of who takes them out, they will need to be rinsed and stored properly. Ask the actor to please not drink hot coffee or tea while wearing veneers.

BALD CAPS

Bald caps can be helpful in creating old age to show hair loss. Used in conjunction with hairpieces, they create a realistic aging. Besides old age, we also use bald caps in character design, to show illness, photo double for a bald actor, stunt double for a bald actor, and, of course, creature/alien designs. You could go years without needing to do a bald cap, but you should still know how to do one. You will need to apply a bald cap several times before being successful, and it is time consuming.

We refer to Edward French (www.edwardfrench.com) for his instructional DVD. It's an excellent source for the demonstration and application of bald caps. Ed gives great information and instruction, and it is fun to watch. We feel you will greatly benefit from a visual lesson rather than the text lesson in the area.

REFERENCES

Glavan Richard Corson James. 2001. *Blocking Out Eyebrows With Plastic Film, Stage Makeup,* Ninth Edition. Needham Heights: Allyn and Bacon, A Pearson Education Company.

Internet Resources

Archer, Gary. Dental Prosthetics Specialist for Film, dental/teeth information, G.A. Enterprises. www.gaenterprises.net.

Ceret, Cristina Patterson. Professional VisionCare Associates, contact lens information. www.fx4eyes.com.

French, Ed. "BALD CAP" The Instructional Video. www.edwardfrench.com.

Myers. Kenny. Premiere Products, Inc., Green Marble Stretch and Stipple. www.ppi.cc.

Richard Dean Rdean1028@mac.com

Huston Mercer tracterproject@aol.com Mark Traynor Lifts and BeautyBand

9

HAIR

In the film and television industries, the Makeup Artist is responsible for anything that is applied to or glued onto the face; this includes facial hair and sideburns.

> IATSE Local 706's general definition of Makeup Artists: "Makeup Artists perform the art of makeup, which includes:
>
> Application of all moustaches, chin pieces, side burns, beards, false eyebrows and lashes."

There are many professionals who do not feel that hair experience is necessary in today's market, because Hollywood has become so specialized. We disagree, and feel that in order to be a professional Makeup Artist working in film and television, you need to learn the skills for working with facial hair. If, at some point in your career, you choose to not polish these skills or to not use them, and prefer to "hire out" or not accept jobs requiring these skills, that will be your option. Not learning to work with facial hair will limit you. Until you have the working experience to know what your forte is, it will take experience and exposure to all areas of makeup artistry. So, learn all the skills that are required to be a professional Makeup Artist before deciding what suits you. Having a working knowledge of all aspects of your field not only makes you a well-rounded professional, but is extremely beneficial during conversations with Producers and Directors on how to create certain looks. It is not uncommon today to "hire out" jobs that require a high level of skill and expertise; it saves time and money to have the best. Early in your career, you

will be hired for jobs in which there is no available budget to "hire out" specialists, so the Producers will hire a Makeup Department that can handle all the makeup needs. This is an example of what can happen if you do not have all the skills required to be a professional, especially in the beginning of your career. You most likely will be working on projects that have small budgets and cannot "hire out."

Remember, those Makeup Artists that do specialize have done so after achieving a level of experience in all areas, prior to specializing in one area of makeup design that is their forte or passion. It is in your best interest to learn all of the skills required to become a well-rounded Makeup Artist before deciding if you want to specialize in one area, or that a particular area of makeup design is not for you. Doing so will give you a more complete education, and the essential background experience that you will need in the film and/or television industries.

Most Department Heads will hire a Makeup Artist that is skilled in everything, so they do not have to worry about the makeup designs that you are assigned. For example, there will be those accidental moments when an actor shows up in the morning and has shaved off his mustache or has changed the shape of his sideburns. In this instance, your film continuity will not be affected because you are able to fix the problem by laying hair or applying a lace piece. As a well-rounded Makeup Artist, you will have the skills and resources to take care of the situation—not to mention that the actor will be relieved and pleased by your ability to fix the problem. Accidents do happen.

Erwin H. Kupitz is a Makeup Artist and Wig Maker. He trained in a classic German apprenticeship, which includes a unisex hairstylist license, makeup artistry, and wig making for five years, with three examinations and one final examination. Unfortunately, there is no longer an apprenticeship program of this magnitude in the United States. This is a wonderful method of training because the learning period is long, and the practical experience is invaluable. Erwin did specialize when he migrated to the United States, after seeing the need for wig making and facial hair, and recognizing that Hollywood had evolved into an industry with specialization for each area of makeup.

Erwin will guide us through the design, laying of facial hair, and lace facial pieces. Things to think about before hand:

- What is the period of the project (current, past, future)?
- Who will wear it, and what medium are you working in?
- How many shooting days?
- Interior or exterior, rain or snow? What is the climate?

PRO TIP

The questions affect how many pieces are made, and how much hair you need.

If it is a reshoot, and you are matching something that was shot one year ago, what are you going to match to as far as shape and color? Is there a good photo for reference?

Once all the script information is collected, the design process starts. You will need:

- A template or live cast of the actor
- A hair sample from the actor
- Reference of the final look to be created
- Approval of the design
- Approval from Production on cost, and a purchase order issued with instructions for billing

PRO TIP

When ordering anything, you need a purchase order number to give to the vendor. This gives the vendor permission to start work, and is a guarantee of the agreed-upon price and payment.

TEMPLATE

When possible, have the Wig Maker do the template or face cast. This is helpful to them in making their pieces. If it is not possible to have them come to the set, or if you are on location, knowing how to make a template will save you time and money.

MAKING A FULL-BEARD TEMPLATE

by Erwin H. Kupitz

HOW TO MAKE A PROPER FULL-BEARD TEMPLATE OF AN ACTOR'S FACE

Materials and Tools Needed:

- Eyebrow pencil
- Plastic wrap
- Clear tape or matte tape

- Permanent markers
- Scissors
- Baby oil or makeup remover
- Tissue or cotton pads
- Camera (digital or instant)

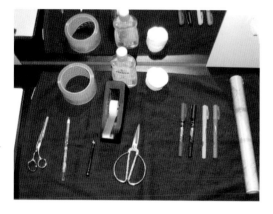

FIGURE 9-1: ERWIN H. KUPTIZ'S WORK STATION

First, cover the actor with a cape.

FIGURE 9-2: ACTOR COVERED WITH CAPE

Using the eyebrow pencil, follow the beard shadow of the actor, and mark it on his skin.

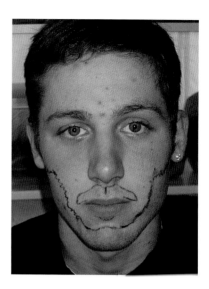

FIGURE 9-3: EYEBROW PENCIL MARKING OF BEARD SHADOW ON ACTOR'S FACE

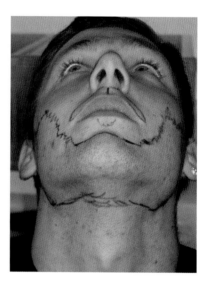

FIGURE 9-4: CHIN VIEW OF EYEBROW PENCIL MARKING

Cover the beard area (and disregard the mustache for now) with a single layer of plastic wrap, and secure with tape on the top of the actor's head. Make sure that your eyebrow pencil notes (markings) are all covered with plastic wrap.

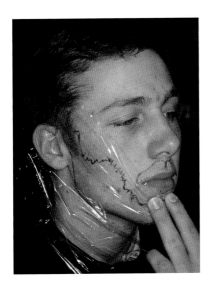

FIGURE 9-5: BEARD COVERED WITH A SINGLE LAYER
OF PLASTIC WRAP

Take special care below the chin and
around the neck, making sure that the taped
plastic wrap is tight. Two to three layers
would be appropriate.

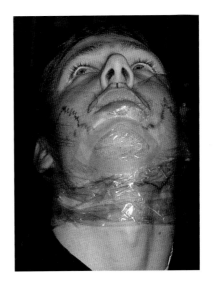

FIGURE 9-7: TAKE SPECIAL CARE AROUND THE CHIN
FOR A TIGHT FIT

Start using clear tape, and tape over the
plastic wrap. Make sure that the tape is tight
around the chin. This is very important for
a proper fitting of the lace beard around the
chin.

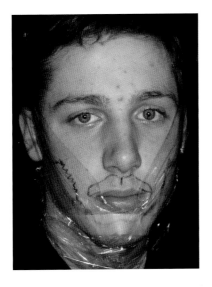

FIGURE 9-6: USING CLEAR TAPE OVER THE PLASTIC
WRAP

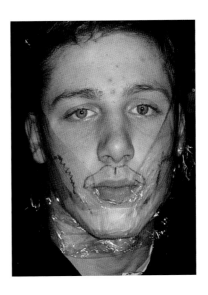

FIGURE 9-8: CHIN FULLY TAPED

Now proceed to the sides of the beard, and cover again with two layers of tape. Use a permanent marker to trace the eyebrow pencil markings onto the tape.

After the full beard is done, do the same to the mustache, lip piece, and two connector pieces between mustache and chin.

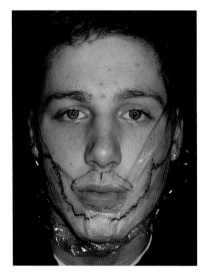

FIGURE 9-9: FULL BEARD WRAP

FIGURE 9-11: MUSTACHE LIP TAPE

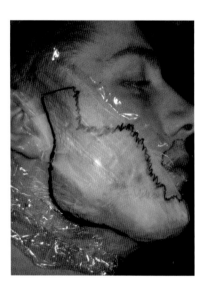

FIGURE 9-10: SIDE VIEW FULL BEARD TAPE

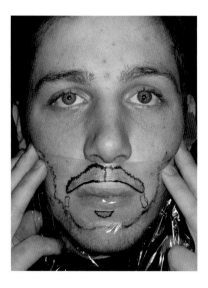

FIGURE 9-12: LIP DETAIL

Now cut out the beard template above the permanent marker lines about 2 mm to 3 mm, and try the entire template again. Take special care around the chin. The template should lay tight around the chin and below the chin, and should lay flat onto the actor's hair at the sideburns.

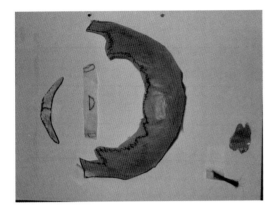

FIGURE 9-13: FINISHED TEMPLATE

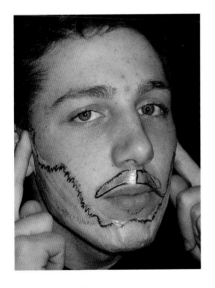

FIGURE 9-14: TEMPLATE CUT AND CHECKS

After the beard template is checked and finished, while the eyebrow pencil markings are still on the skin, take photos from all sides. Clean up the actor's face.

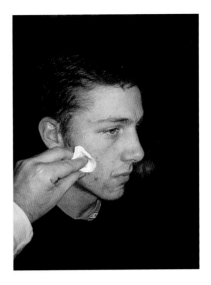

FIGURE 9-15: CLEANING MODEL

Cut out a hair sample from the actor's own hair. If the actor's hair is too short, refer to a swatch ring or hair color swatch book for reference. Sometimes sending hair from another source, such as a wig or someone else's hair, is an alternative. Try to make a base that matches the desired skin tone of the actor, or a final skin tone of a character, and spread it onto a clean white paper or in between two layers of plastic wrap. This sample is needed as a guide to color the lace.

Double-check to make sure you have all of the items needed by the Wig Maker before you release the actor. (The approximate time to make a full beard is about four working days in backup or doubles.)

MASKING TAPE TECHNIQUE

Use a lip or eyebrow pencil and masking tape to transfer markings from the face into the tape. This technique is very good for small or partial facial-hair additions. It also works well on a clean-shaven face.

Material and Tools Needed:

- Masking tape
- Eyebrow or lip pencils
- Scissors
- Loose powder and powder brush
- Towel

Procedure

Using the lip or eyebrow pencil, mark all facial-hair additions or trace the natural growth pattern and shape of the model's facial hair. If needed, different colors help to design new shapes or mark special patterns.

FIGURE 9-16: MODEL WITH MARKINGS USING A BROWN EYEBROW PENCIL

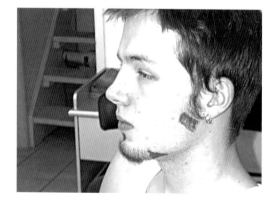

FIGURE 9-17: MARKINGS FOR SIDEBURN EXTENSIONS USING A BROWN EYEBROW PENCIL

After all markings are done, use small pieces of masking tape, and apply one or two layers over the marked areas. Try not to use more than two layers because this would be too much of a buildup. In this demonstration, sideburn and chin-beard extensions and the addition of a lip piece are created.

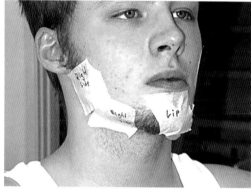

FIGURE 9-18: SIDEBURN, CHIN BEARD EXTENSION AND LIP PIECE WITH TAPED AREAS

Using a warm towel (warmed for 10 minutes in a wig dryer), the areas are wrapped and pressed down tight with your hand. The heat of the towel as well as the pressure from your hands will transfer the grease in the eyebrow or lip pencil into the adhesive. A combination of gentle rubbing and pressing for about two to three minutes is recommended.

If doing a full-beard or chin-beard pattern, special care has to be taken around the curves of the chin to make sure the tape is pressed tight against the chin curve. This will ensure the proper shaping of the pattern and a tight fit of the final lace beard.

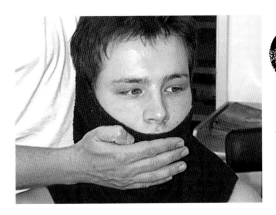

FIGURE 9-19: A WARM TOWEL AGAINST THE CHIN TAPE

After the pressing and rubbing is done, start carefully to remove the tape from the face. The markings are transferred into the tape.

Remove the tape carefully from the face.

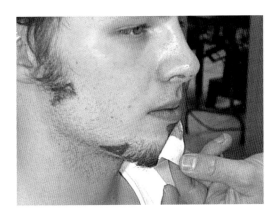

FIGURE 9-20: REMOVING TAPE CAREFULLY FROM THE FACE

The removed tape pieces are organized on a towel and are ready to powder. Using loose face powder, powder the tape pieces to prevent them from sticking together or getting messed up.

141

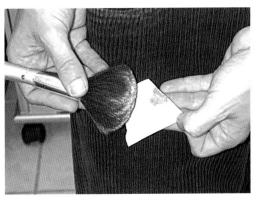

FIGURE 9-21: USING LOOSE FACE POWDER AND POWDER BRUSH ON REMOVED TAPE PIECES

The beard template can now be cut out and applied to a beard block, ready for making the lace pieces. After the lace pieces are done, it is recommended to store them together with pictures of the actor, as well as hair color and lace color swatches, in a plastic bag or box for future reference.

Tools in the photo of Erwin's workstation (Figure 9.22):

• Cutting comb for combing hair during cut

• Rattail comb for separating and sectioning

• Small hair clips to secure separations

• Lifting comb for detangling and lifting permed hair

FIGURE 9-22: ERWIN'S WORKSTATION: TOOLS AND PRODUCTS TO CUT AND STYLE FACIAL PIECES

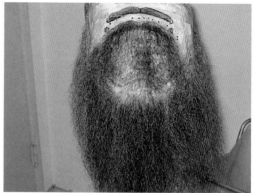

FIGURE 9-23: CHARACTER LACE BEARD PRIOR TO CUTTING AND STYLING

- Haircutting and thinning shears as well as razor for cutting hair
- Tweezers for eventual plugging and finishing of hairline
- Ceramic iron heater
- Flat curling iron for lifting and shaping
- Small marcel iron for texturizing and curling
- Natural bristle brushes for wax and tattoo color
- Pinking shears for precutting the excessive lace

Products in the photo of Erwin's workstation (Figure 9.22):

- Mustache wax or stronger hair wax
- Plastic sealer in pump bottle or a strong, fast-drying hair lacquer
- Tattoo color for detail work on finished beard
- 99 percent alcohol
- Lace pieces

CONSTRUCTION OF A VENTILATED BEARD

Ventilating is the technique used by Wig Makers to knot hair (either human or synthetic) into wig lace. It is similar to tying a rug, and has been used since King Louis XVI of France. There is single knotting and double knotting. There are many versions of lace, and quality of hair. Most lace pieces in film do not use synthetic hair—it does not look real. The quality of lace and hair and the blending of colors are extremely important.

The medium of the lace piece, as well as the design of the facial hair, will dictate what materials and hair are used. The hairline or beard line is always the finest quality of knots to create the illusion of the hair coming out of the follicle.

The Base

The base is made of one layer of custom dyed nylon lace using a blend of layers of fabric dye following the manufacturer's directions. Match the actor's skin color or the foundation makeup used on the actor as closely as possible.

Construction includes seven separate pieces: chin, two side pieces, one lip piece, two connections, and one mustache. A light coat of acrylic spray is applied before hair ventilation to the finish base. This adds durability.

The Hair

Use human hair from different origins (Asian, Indian, European), as well as yak tail and belly hair. Blends of thicker and coarser hair are used at the bottom of the beard for body. Thinner, finer hair is used closer to the edges.

All hair is custom color blended using darker colors at the bottom and lighter colors at the edges, then permed using a mild alkaline perm. The diameter of the perm rod will determine the curling result. In this case, a medium to small perm rod is chosen for a frizzy, "ungroomed" result. This will ensure that the beard keeps the shape, and restyling will be limited to a minimum.

Ventilating Hair

Knotting the preblended and permed hair into the lace base is done hair by hair (single-hair knotting), using the various color blends to design natural shading and highlighting. Lighter colors are always used around the edges of the beard (front shade), building up more volume at the bottom and in areas where denser beard growth appears, and decreasing the amount closer to the edges for a natural appearance.

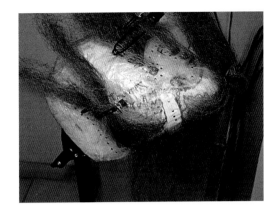

FIGURE 9-24: A BEARD SEPARATED IN SECTIONS READY TO CUT INTO SHAPE

How to Cut Facial Hairpieces

A good haircut can eliminate half of the styling and maintenance later on. Because perming is done on the hair, it needs to be treated like curly hair, which means caution is needed during cutting. Texturizing and cutting with razor and thinning shears (cutting different length into the hair) will give a more natural appearance of "beard hair." Blunt cutting a straight line, especially on the mustache, will result in an unnatural "fresh-cut look" that is very "eye-catching" for the camera. The proper cut for a beard is as important as the proper cut for a hairstyle. If the cutting and texturizing are finished and the permed hair is reactivated with water, let dry naturally.

The beard shape and style should be almost completed after proper cutting. Finishing can be achieved with curling irons.

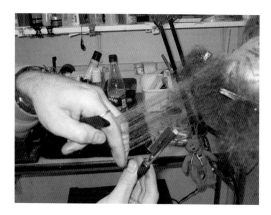

FIGURE 9-25: CUTTING A LENGTH GUIDELINE BY USING A RAZOR

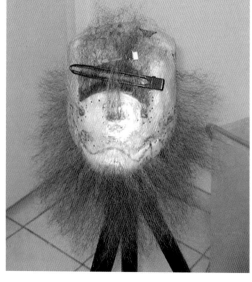

FIGURE 9-27: FINISHED CUTTING AND BASIC TEXTURIZING OF FULL BEARD

FIGURE 9-26: USING THE GUIDELINE REFERENCE, CUTTING THE HAIR ONTO THAT GUIDELINE

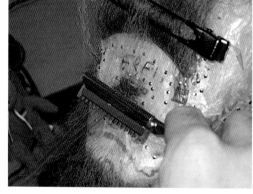

FIGURE 9-28: USING THE RAZOR FOR CUTTING THE LIP PIECE TO THE DESIRED LENGTH AND SHAPE

Elevating your hand while you razor the hair will give a layered-hair effect. All hair except for the sides of the beard is cut to this guideline. The sides of the beard are blended in length into the sideburn length of the design.

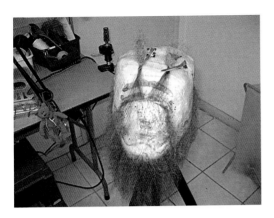

FIGURE 9-29: SEPARATIONS FOR CUTTING THE MUSTACHE GUIDELINE AND CONNECTING PIECES BELOW THE MUSTACHE

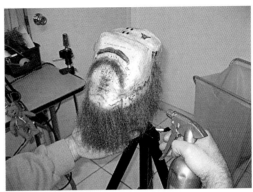

FIGURE 9-31: MISTING THE PRECUT BEARD WITH WATER AND LIFTING HAIR USING A LIFTING COMB

Mist the precut beard with water, and lift hair using a lifting comb, so the curl can go back into its permed style. The beard is then dried in a wig dryer on a low setting: 100°F, or 45°C.

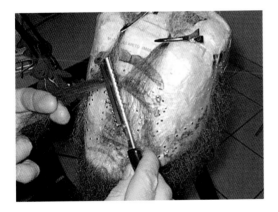

FIGURE 9-30: CUTTING A GUIDELINE TO THE DESIRED LENGTH WITH THE TIP OF THE RAZOR

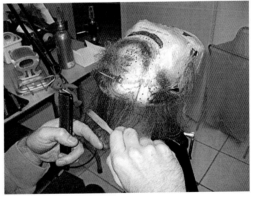

FIGURE 9-32: LIGHTLY WAXING DRIED HAIR WITH MUSTACHE WAX AND A BRISTLE BRUSH

Cutting a guideline to the desired length with the tip of the razor cuts the mustache in the same manner. Make sure that both sides are even in length and shape. All of the hair is then cut to the length of that guideline with the tip of the razor.

After the hair and the base (lace) are truly dry, the hair is then lightly waxed using mustache wax and a bristle brush. The wax will protect the hair from the heat of the curling irons and from moisture. The facial hair is now ready for final styling with the curling irons and tongs.

To bring the permed texture into shape, a small marcel curling iron and waving technique is used. Caution is to be taken that the texture does not appear like finger or marcel waves similar to the waves in hairstyles. Using artistic input as well as practice, this technique is useful for all longer beards and facial hairpieces for building texture, movement, and style.

Final touches are done on the texture of the beard prior to styling the mustache.

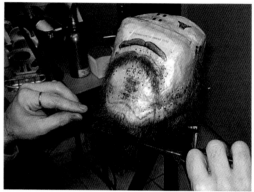

FIGURE 9-35: FINAL TOUCHES ON THE TEXTURE OF BEARD PRIOR TO STYLING THE MUSTACHE

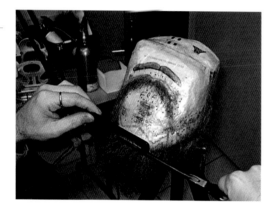

FIGURE 9-33: SHAPING THE FACIAL HAIR AND BEARD WITH A MARCEL CURLING IRON

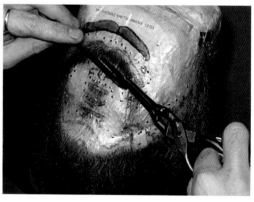

FIGURE 9-36: USING A FLATIRON OR TONGS TO SHAPE THE MUSTACHE AND LIP PIECE

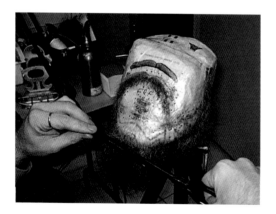

FIGURE 9-34: SHAPING THE FACIAL HAIR AND BEARD WITH A MARCEL CURLING IRON

A flatiron, or tongs, is used to shape the mustache and the lip piece. Because of the use of perm-textured hair, the mustache hardly needs curling. Only the ends at the bottom of the beard are blended under. A root lift is applied to the edges by lifting and sliding a warm flatiron to the hair.

FIGURE 9-37: USING TATTOO COLOR AND 99% ALCOHOL FOR COLOR TOUCH UPS

Final color touch-ups are done using tattoo color and 99 percent alcohol.

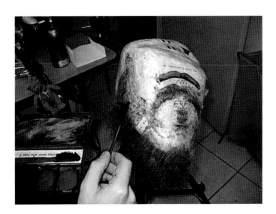

FIGURE 9-38: APPLYING TATTOO COLOR WASH TO A BEARD WITH AN EYEBROW BRUSH

Using an eyebrow brush with a lash comb attached, a tattoo color wash (more alcohol than color, like an aquarelle color drawing) similar to the beard's color is then brushed over the lighter shades around the edge (front shade). Brushing and immediate combing of the hair will make blending easy. It is important to keep the knots light, while softly blending the ends of the lighter

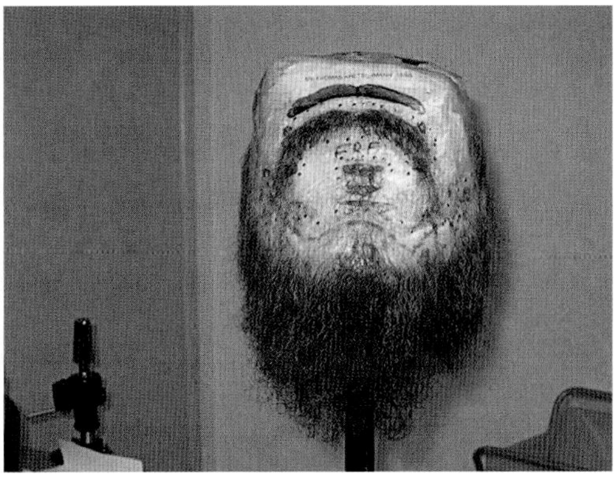

FIGURE 9-39: A FINISHED, STYLED BEARD BEFORE REMOVAL FROM THE BEARD BLOCK

hair into the beard color. Be careful not to make it too opaque or even too dark. The beard line should still be lighter than the beard for a natural effect. This technique will keep the edges soft, and knots will blend more easily around the edges with the skin color. After coloring is done, a light coat of matte clear acrylic spray is applied to the finished beard.

Figure 9.39 is a photo of the finished, styled beard before removing it from the beard block.

SAMPLE APPLICATION OF A BEARD WITH STUBBLE

Materials Needed:

- Chin lace piece
- Lower lip piece
- Sideburns
- Chopped curly hair matching beard color
- Scissors, thinning shears
- Metal tail comb
- Adhesive (W.M. Creations, Inc. Adhesive)

- Tattoo color (e.g., Reel Hair Palette)

- Hair spray

- Makeup sponges

- Brushes

- Alcohol, 99 percent

- Cotton swabs

- Makeup cape

- Concealer pencil in skin tone matching actor

Steps for Application:

1. Start with a clean face.

2. Start applying the chin beard. Check its placement, and use the concealer pencil to mark dots where the edges of the piece belongs.

3. Brush a thin layer of adhesive onto the skin, staying about 1 cm below the markings of the lace piece edge.

4. Stipple adhesive with your finger until tacky. Apply a thin second layer and repeat. Be careful not to get adhesive over the concealer marks.

5. Glue the lace piece in place using your rattail comb. It is important that you press with the tail in between the hair at the base of the lace. Make sure you do not glue down the beard hair flat against the skin. This will take a few minutes, and a bit of practice.

6. Use a cotton swab dampened with alcohol to carefully remove your concealer markings.

7. Use a new cotton swab or a finer brush to apply a very thin layer of adhesive to the skin. Tack it with your finger or a brush until flat and tacky.

8. Press lace piece gently into place using your clean rattail. Continue pressing all edges until they are smoothly glued down to the skin.

9. Apply the lip piece in the same manner. Because it is very small, you probably don't need to use the concealer pencil. Placement of a lip piece should be easier than the placement of a larger beard piece.

10. Apply the sideburns in the same manner. It is important that you position them directly at the bottom of the actor's own sideburns, without a gap in between.

11. Cut the sideburn hair to match the actor's own sideburn hair at the same length, using thinning shears.

12. Brush in a little tattoo color to blend possible color differences between the actor's hair and the false sideburns.

PRO TIP

Lace facial hairpieces for HD are much more difficult because the high definition shows every detail so crisply and sharply. The lace pieces have to be designed in sections that puzzle together onto the face, with a lower hairline edge that has to be overlaid with hair by hand to finish off the edge of the facial-hair design. The glue must be totally matte.

13. After all of your lace pieces are applied, you can start using chopped hair to create a patchy, shorter beard stubble.

Lace facial hairpieces require an investment of time and money that pays off in the long run. The work and materials used are expensive, but the result is a more natural, consistent look, with easy maintenance.

BEARD STUBBLE

As with everything else in makeup, there are several ways to create beard growth that looks like more than several days of growth. There are different products and techniques to use, depending on the situation you are working in. As with all areas of makeup, you will need to be able to answer critical questions before designing or choosing what to use. The hardest beard growth to simulate is between five and 10 days, too long to be painted in, and not long enough to use lace pieces. You will need to use one of several techniques to create the look and length needed. The length of hair for beard stubble will depend on what the length of time passage is, or how scruffy the look is designed to be, or how many "story days" in the script that the actor has not shaved. The actor's own beard growth and density will also effect your decisions.

What is the growth pattern like, what color is the hair, how old is the beard growth, and how many days will you have to recreate the look? These are all questions you will need to have answers for. Look at the growth pattern of the actor—this is your guide for placement of hair stubble. This is very important in creating realistic beard stubble. If you do not follow the natural growth pattern and beard line of the person, it will not look real.

In some cases, the actor's own beard growth and growth pattern is minimal or sparse. You will still need to follow the person's own beard as a guide. If you choose to add more to make the stubble read better on camera, be careful—your stubble will look unnatural if you add or fill too much on an actor with sparse growth.

Hair color for beard stubble needs to be a blend of colors, with highlights and lowlights—and in some cases, a bit of auburn or red added. Use caution with adding too much red to your blend—this can look too artificial, even if the actor has a lot of red in his own beard.

Careful hair color blending with proper placement will sell the look. We will look at creating beard stubble by using a hair ball, a lace net, and a makeup brush.

ERWIN KUPITZ'S HAIR BALL METHOD

The chopped hair should be no longer than 0.5 cm, otherwise it will be very hard to apply.

Prepare the chopped hair by making little hair balls of about the size of a walnut. The chopped hair is placed in the palm of your hand and then rubbed in a circular motion between your two palms until a ball is formed. This can also be done in advance to save time. If you do so, spray the prepared hair balls lightly with hair spray, and store them in a plastic box until you are ready to use them.

149

Hair Ball Application:

1. Apply only one layer of adhesive, starting close to the chin lace piece.

2. Stipple adhesive with a makeup sponge until flat and tacky.

3. Quickly pull one of the hair balls apart, and you will notice that the short hair is sticking out of the ball where it has been separated.

4. Lightly touch the adhesive with the *standing hair,* and pull the hair quickly away from the face. The short hair will adhere to the face, and it will stand out like real beard hair. *Do not press hair flat to the face. If you do, it will look very unnatural.*

5. Continue this process until you have finished your design.

6. After all of the hair has been laid, spray a light mist of hair spray over the beard. Be careful not to point the bottle straight into the actor's face. Have the actor hold his breath and close his eyes while you are spraying the beard. Make sure that you mist only the hair and not the skin, because this could create a sheen effect, and it is very uncomfortable on the skin.

For actors and beards with a curlier texture, you can use chopped permed hair, and you don't have to build a hair ball out of it. Chop the hair to about 0.5 cm length, and apply it directly to the skin. Because of the curly texture, it cannot lay flat.

Your character's beard application using lace pieces in combination with chopped hair is now complete.

FIGURE 9-40: MODEL/ACTOR BEFORE BEARD

FIGURE 9-41: MODEL/ACTOR IN CHARACTER (AFTER BEARD)

MATTHEW MUNGLE NET LACE METHOD:

1. Apply spirit gum adhesive to the surface of the beard area to be stippled.

2. Press down with a soft cloth to take out or matte the shine of the adhesive.

3. Lay down a piece of hair lace into the adhesive.

4. While the chopped hair is still wet, press it into the lace using a stiff makeup brush, sponge, or atomizer.

5. Before the adhesive dries, pull the lace up and away from the face, leaving the cut hair behind, standing straight up or at the angle the lace net is pulled off the skin.

BEARD STUBBLE WITH BRUSH

For stubble looks by hand, you can choose to use a medium-sized makeup brush or a small atomizer, with a matte spirit gum adhesive or beard stipple wax by KRYOLAN. We will show you this technique using the makeup brush and stipple wax. The wax is clear on the skin no matter what skin tone, and has no shine whatsoever. This is a huge advantage for HD and close-up work. If you use spirit gum, we recommend W.M. Creations, Extra Hold Matte Adhesive. Blend and prep your hair using at least two colors of hair.

Lay white facial tissue on your workstation or counter.

Wet your hair with a small amount in your hand. Hold over the tissue, making uniform cuts to the hair, so that the chopped hair drops onto the tissue.

Let the chopped hair dry on the tissue.

Remember, it is best to cut the hair when wet, and to take care making each cut the same size.

There is a tendency to make your cuts too long. Look at your first cut of hair to check length. Hair needs to be completely dry before being applied to the face.

Apply beard stipple wax over the beard area of the face where you want to apply hair.

With a clean, medium-sized makeup brush, pick up the desired amount of chopped hair from the tissue by dipping the brush into the hair on the tissue.

Using a quick, light motion with the end of the brush, apply at a slant to the beard area. The quick hand motion, or stipple, needs to barely touch the skin to create a raised beard area. If you hit the brush with too much pressure, the hair will stick flat. It helps to have a bit of static electricity in the makeup brush. You can get static in your brush by rubbing the brush quickly back and forth over a towel.

Go back with a small, stiff brush or tweezers, and lift any hair that is not sticking out straight. You do not want any hairs to be laying flat against the skin.

Sometimes there can be clumps or patterns that you will need to thin out.

Be gentle. This application is fragile, but easily touched up.

Remember, with all hair applications, to stand back and really look at your work, as well as getting up close to the skin and checking. Check your work in the makeup mirror from all angles, by rotating the actor around.

If you believe it up close, so will the camera.

GLUES

In film, television, and HD, use only matte adhesive. The application is very important because any shine or glow from the adhesive under the lace piece will register.

This will cause the viewer to realize it is not real facial hair.

W.M. Creations, Adhesive is lightweight but strong. It is greenish in color during application, but dries clear.

K.D. Spirit Gum is a processed spirit gum, and works very well with lace pieces.

ALTERNATE ADHESIVES

Telesis comes with its own thinner, and the application is slightly different from spirit gum. The brush usually has to be dipped into the thinner, then into the adhesive.

All of the adhesives dry very fast, and are not recommended for use by the beginner.

ADHESIVES TO AVOID

Any kind of latex-based adhesive should be avoided. It is impossible to clean it from the lace without the danger of destroying the lace piece and its edges.

Exception: If you have a new lace piece for each day, for all of the shooting days the facial hair works—in other words, the lace pieces are not reused the next day. If it is a small piece, Pros-Aide usually works better than latex adhesives.

CLEANING THE LACE

Once the lace pieces have been removed from the actor, you will need to clean the lace and re-dress the pieces. With classic spirit gum or lightweight adhesives, the actual removal of the lace from the skin also removes some adhesive from the lace. Any

adhesive left on the lace can be removed by the following steps:

1. In a saucer or plate filled with the cleaning agent about $\frac{1}{2}$ inch deep, lay the pieces in the solution with the lace facing down (hair up). Try not to have the hair covered entirely by the cleaning solution. Let it set for one to two minutes. The heavier the adhesive, the longer it needs in the cleaning bath.

2. Lay the piece on a towel, but try to avoid pressing the hair flat.

3. Dip the brush into the cleaning agent, and brush out any leftover adhesive from the lace.

4. *Important:* Always follow the direction of the knotting on the lace. Example: On a mustache, brush from the nostrils down to the upper lip.

   Very important: Never brush against the knotting. This results in opening the knotted hair, and the knots wll appear larger and eventually fall out.

5. After the entire adhesive is removed, place the pieces on a clean towel and let evaporate for 10 to 20 minutes.

The pieces are ready for blocking and any re-dressing.

The cleaning agent is different, depending on the glue and/or adhesive being used:

Classic Spirit Gum: Easy cleaning with a mix of 99 percent alcohol and acetone (1 : 1 ratio).

Matte Adhesives: 99 percent alcohol.

Silicone-Based Adhesives: Use special cleaner that often has a slight oil base in it. Lay the facial hair in alcohol after using these cleaners, and let soak for a few minutes to dissolve the oil. Remove, do not comb, and let dry without stretching the lace, on a clean towel. After the facial hair is completely dry, it can be re-dressed.

Latex-Based Adhesives: Need a heavy oil and alcohol mix. Try a mix of baby oil and alcohol (1 : 1 ratio).

A stiff bristle brush is used to brush off the residue of the latex—this is labor-intensive.

Beard Stubble Wax: Cannot be used with lace pieces as an adhesive. It is a tacky wax paste, and the lace hairpiece would not successfully stay on.

HAIR TEXTURE

All facial hair needs to be texturized before applying it to the face. The texture varies from kinky straight (Asians, Indians), to slightly wavy (European), to kinky curly (African). All hair used for knotting into wig lace is custom permed before ventilating into the lace, and therefore will not turn straight if it gets wet or during cleaning.

Quality facial hair takes all kinds of hair origins into consideration, and the texturizing creates the look of real facial hair. The color design enhances the simulation of the facial hair, again creating the illusion of a real beard.

REFERENCES

Cimuha, Inc.
Erwin H. Kupitz, Wig Maker
Design, laying of facial hair and lace facial pieces
Tel: 818-769-6465

10 | AIRBRUSH

Airbrush makeup is now a major tool in creating certain looks, especially a flawless finish to the skin. Airbrush makeup has also found a niche in the retail cosmetic world. It is used in all areas of makeup: beauty, body makeup, body art, tattoo cover, bruising, effects, and fantasy. Airbrush is used in all media—print, film, television, and theatre—and is a mainstay in HD and HDTV. Airbrushing gives a flawless finish to your makeup. The airbrush machine is a tool that is going to be a personal preference for the artist and the actor/talent that you are working with. In some situations, or in makeup design, you will have to airbrush to create the look that is needed. In other situations, the Department Head will require you to airbrush. You would be at an extreme disadvantage to not learn how to airbrush and care for the equipment.

What is an airbrush? An airbrush is a small, air-operated tool that sprays various media, including ink and dye, but most often paint, by a process of atomization. An airbrush works by passing a stream of fast-moving (compressed) air through a venturi which creates a local reduction in air pressure (suction) that allows paint to be pulled up from an interconnected reservoir at normal atmospheric pressure. The operator controls the amount of paint by using a trigger that opens a fine-tapered needle.

UNDERSTANDING YOUR AIRBRUSH

by Badger

Airbrushes have three usual characteristics:

1. Action performed by the user triggering the paint flow.

2. The mechanism for feeding the paint into the airbrush.

3. The point in which the pressure (PSI) and air mix. (PSI means measurement of air pressure, pounds per square inch.)

There are two different ways an airbrush mixes with paint, allowing you to airbrush:

Internal Mix: The paint and the air mixes together inside the head assembly to produce a thoroughly atomized fine-dot spray pattern.

External Mix: Indicates that air and paint mix outside the airbrush. Air and paint come together outside the head, or fluid assembly. External-mix airbrushes produce a larger-dot spray pattern than internal-mix airbrushes.

AIRBRUSH TRIGGERS

Single Action: Refers to airbrushes on which the trigger controls only the airflows. When the trigger is depressed, a preset amount of fluid is sprayed. The amount of fluid is regulated by turning the needle adjustment screw at the back of the handle, or, in the case of an external-mix airbrush, by turning the fluid cap on the paint tip at the front of the airbrush.

Dual Action: Refers to airbrushes on which the trigger controls both air and color (down for air, back for color). This simple maneuver allows the artist to change the width of the line, the range of value, and the opacity of paint without stopping their hand motion.

FEEDS

Gravity Feed: Refers to airbrushes with top-mounted color cups in which gravity draws paint into the airbrush. Less air pressure is required, enabling slower hand movement, which creates excellent control for fine detail.

Bottom Feed: Refers to airbrushes on which paint enters through a siphon tube or color cup attached to the bottom of the airbrush. Removable jars or various-sized color cups can be connected to and utilized with bottom-feed airbrushes. This configuration is generally more versatile and enables the user to change colors quickly. This is important when working with several colors at once. This enables the artist to move quickly when changing colors, as well as for storing colors during use.

Side Feed: Refers to airbrushes on which a small color cup fits into the side of the airbrush. The side-feed color cup rotates, enabling the user to work on either a horizontal or vertical surface. The side-feed configuration also permits the user to achieve fine detail without the possible sight obstruction of a top-mounted color cup.

Hybrid Airbrush: Airbrushes that have a combination of gravity and bottom feed.

AIRBRUSHES

Badger Model 100G: Gravity-feed airbrush with $\frac{1}{16}$-ounce color cup (Figure 10.1).

Badger Model 100MU: Airbrush with $\frac{1}{3}$-ounce color cup and makeup-specific head assembly (Figure 10.2).

FIGURE 10-1: BADGER AIRBRUSH MODEL 100G

FIGURE 10-2: BADGER AIRBRUSH MODEL 100MU

FIGURE 10-3: BADGER AIRBRUSH 360 UNIVERSAL

FIGURE 10-4: AIRBRUSH MODEL OMNI 5000

Badger 360 Universal: Airbrush is capable of performing in a gravity-feed as well as a bottom-feed mode (Figure 10.3).

Model Omni 5000: Gravity-feed airbrush with $\frac{1}{8}$-ounce color cup (Figure 10.4).

Paasche VJR #2: Gravity feed, double action, internal mix. Airbrush used to create a wider range of tinting, shading, and

FIGURE 10-5: PAASCHE AIRBRUSH VJR #2

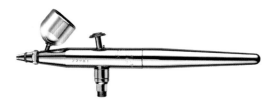

FIGURE 10-6: PAASCHE AIRBRUSH VSR90 #1

Fine-spray output and entire range of stippling effects. Airbrush has a short paint passageway.

Iwata HP-CH: Designed for artists who need control for detail work. Airbrush uses new Micro air-control-valve technology.

Iwata HP-CS: Gravity feed with 0.35 mm needle and nozzle combination for fine-detail spraying. Generous-sized cup and funnel shape.

Iwata HP-CR: Gravity feed designed for quick change of custom mixed colors. Internal-mix airbrush, ergonomic handle design, fine-detail work, and easier spraying.

details. Color cup is on top for easy color changes. Good for both right- and left-handed users (Figure 10.5).

Paasche VSR90 #1: Gravity feed. Unique two-to-one design allows for quick color changes by including two different-sized color cups. Cups attach to top of airbrush assembly and swivel left or right for unobstructed view. Suited for both left- and right-handed airbrushers (Figure 10.6).

Iwata HP-C Plus: Large gravity-feed cup with a large needle-nozzle configuration.

PRO TIP

Makeup Artists often use airbrushes that have stipple features for effects work. Temptu offers a large selection of Iwata products.

PRO TIP

Airbrush eye shadow is best applied with an airbrush with a very fine needle/nozzle ratio like the Iwata High performance HP-B, which is 0.2 mm. Although much too light to apply foundation, it gives you the ability to keep your colors focused. Fine-needle/nozzles are popular for lining eyes, and for effects artists for veining. An appropriate needle/nozzle range for most airbrush makeup, both face and body, is 8 mm + 5 mm, with the wider aper-tures leaning toward the body makeup end of things. The smaller the nozzle, the more control you have. When the nozzle is too small, the application will take longer than necessary unless you need to focus the range of space you are working on.

—David Klasfeld, CEO/Creative Director, Obsessive Compulsive Cosmetics, Inc

COMPRESSORS

Terms Used With Compressors

CFM: Measurement of airflow.

Moisture Filter: Removing water from air.

Oil Filter: Removing oil from air.

PSI: Measurement of air pressure.

Air Regulator: Adjusting air pressure.

Iwata Smart Jet Pro: Compressor shuts off automatically when not in use. It has an oil-less piston air compressor with built-in airbrush holder; moisture filters (removing water from air) with an air regulator (adjusts air pressure); and bleed-valve adjustment to release moisture.

PRO TIP

Compressors with built-in airbrush holders are extremely convenient when working in a makeup trailer, especially if you are working with an airbrush with a top color cup.

Iwata Power Jet: Compressor has oil-less dual-piston air with a 3.5-liter air-storage tank. It has zero pulsation, moisture filter, and a mounted pressure gauge with air regulator for precise air-pressure adjustment.

Iwata Power Jet Pro: A compressor with a 2-liter air-storage tank with zero pulsation and an air reserve for spraying at higher air pressures. It has dual adjustable pressure regulators plus dual moisture filters and dual mounted pressure gauges. The

compressor also has dual quick-disconnect ports and dual built-in airbrush holders.

Iwata Power Jet Lite: Adjustable pressure regulator, moisture filter, and built-in airbrush holder.

Iwata Silver Jet: Compact and quiet single-person use with working pressure adjustable from 10 to 18 PSI. The compressor has a coiled air hose, pressure-adjustable knob, handle, airbrush holder, and pressure gauge.

Iwata Sprint Jet: A mounted air-pressure gauge with a bleed-valve airflow adjustment to lower air pressure. Pressure working from 1 to 35 PSI. Zero maintenance with an oil-less piston air compressor.

PRO TIP

Makeup companies (such as Mac Pro and Obsessive Compulsive Cosmetics) which offer small portable compressors often use the Iwata Series.

Paasche DAS 00: $\frac{1}{8}$-horsepower diaphragm compressor with auto shutoff. Shuts off when airbrush is not in use.

Paasche D100: $\frac{1}{8}$-horsepower compressor delivers 15 to 25 PSI with most model airbrushes (Figure 10.7).

Paasche D3000: Oil-less diaphragm compressor with tank-mounted unit, designed for compactness and portability. Air tank stores reserve air volume and reduces pulsation. Air pressure in the tank is

FIGURE 10-7: PAASCHE AIRBRUSH D100

FIGURE 10-9: BADGER MODEL 80-3 MINI COMPRESSOR

FIGURE 10-8: PAASCHE AIRBRUSH D3000

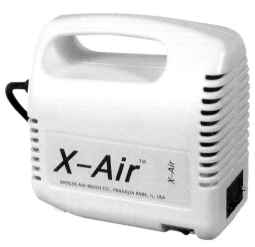

FIGURE 10-10: BADGER MODEL 80-7XAIR COMPRESSOR

regulated with an automatic On/Off switch to a maximum of 40 PSI (Figure 10.8).

Badger Model 80-3 Mini Compressor: Produces 3 to 5 PSI (Figure 10.9).

Badger Model 80-7xaIR Compressor: Produces 10 to 12 PSI (Figure 10.10).

Badger Model 80-8x Air Compressor: Produces 10 to 12 PSI with built-in regulator (Figure 10.11).

PRO TIP

In general, use compressors with a lower PSI or compressors that allow you to adjust the settings for direct airbrushing on the face. The higher the PSI, the more kickback you'll get from the product.

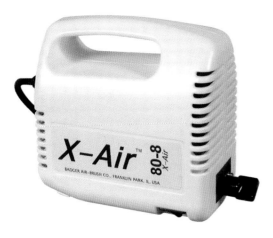

FIGURE 10-11: BADGER MODEL 80-8X AIR
COMPRESSOR

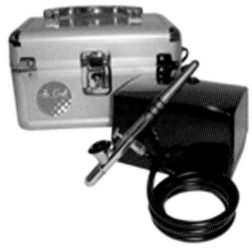

FIGURE 10-12: AIR CRAFT AIRBRUSH SYSTEM

ALL-IN-ONE AIRBRUSH SYSTEMS

Small all-in-one airbrush systems have
fantastic overall weight. Traveling with
these compressors is a snap, and using
one in small spaces is a breeze. Sometimes
you just have limited space and needs; this
size goes anywhere, a great advantage for
the professional. There are no fancy
pressure gauges or moisture meters that
make airbrushing intimidating. Air Craft,
Air Pro, and Dinair are a few of the
portable-airbrush companies on the market
today.

PRO TIP

Small compressors with an output of 6 to
8 PSI are perfect for the face and small
areas of the body, such as covering tattoos.

Air Craft AirBrush System: Consists of an
airbrush, compressor, hose, and blow-by-
blow instruction booklet. The system is
housed in a small silver case weighing a
total of 4 pounds. The airbrush is single
action with 6 to 8 PSI (Figure 10.12).

Air Pro AirBrush System: Includes two
foundations of your choice, compressor,
single-action airbrush with 6-foot silicone
air hose.

Dinair Mini-System Beauty Kit:
Compressor weighs less than a pound. The
system comes with a travel adapter (100 to
240 volts), and has a PSI of 0 to 7. The
airbrush is a Dinair 400CA. Also included
are stencils, instructions, and makeup
(Figure 10.13).

AIRBRUSHING PRODUCT LINES

by Bradley Look

People ask me all the time of the dangers
of airbrushing. There is an unfounded fear
about the airbrush. What I usually find is

FIGURE 10-13: DINAIR MINI-SYSTEM BEAUTY KIT

that airbrushing is not being properly sprayed in some of those cases, which leads to many of those problems. As a Makeup Artist, it is your responsibility to stay on top of the most current information and how products interact with each other. Airbrushes, compressors, and airbrush makeup all have instructions, plus suggestions on how to use their products so you'll get the most from airbrushing with success. Before you start using that airbrush, know what makeup is available and, more important, what kind of makeup you are buying. What is in airbrush makeup?

Here are the six formula breakdowns of airbrush makeup available:

Water Based: This type of makeup is not unlike the standard liquid variety: finely ground cosmetic-approved pigments dispersed in water. Water is the most common solvent found in cosmetics, and is usually referred to as aqueous dispersion.

Polymer-Water-Based: This cosmetic formulation is one of the more commonly used for airbrush makeups. Once the makeup is airbrushed, the polymer vehicle upon drying produces a continuous film on the skin.

Polymer-SD40-Alcohol Based: This is just like the polymer-water-based formulas (as listed above), with one major difference. SD40 alcohol is used as the solvent in place of water. The alcohol assists in the drying of the product on the skin.

Alcohol Based: This type of airbrush makeup is normally known within the makeup industry as the "temporary airbrush inks" associated with the production of faux flesh art (tattoos).

Silicone Based: This is the newest formula of all the airbrush makeups currently available. This brand of cosmetic claims that it stays looking "just applied" all day without fading or wearing away.

PRO TIP

Water-based makeup makes cleaning your airbrush equipment easy. Just clean after each use with water.

PRO TIP

Silicone-based products that you want to thin so you can alter the coverage can be thinned only with formulas that work with silicone. (Example: Mac Pro has an airbrush cleanser that also works as a thinner to their silicone-based airbrush makeup.)

DHA Based: Although technically not really considered an airbrush makeup, DHA (dihydroxyacetone) based products constitute the sunless-tanning systems. The use of the airbrush in spraying cosmetics gave the sunless-tanning manufacturers an idea: Why not produce a formula that can be atomized?

Now let's talk about makeup and what is on the market today. Products are listed by their brand name and/or by the manufacturer's name. All of the products listed are prereduced to a consistency for spraying straight from the bottle. However, if you should desire to thin the product further, check with the manufacturer first. Also, these products have been formulated to be atomized at a low PSI (pounds per square inch), usually between 3 and 6. Using the right product for the right job means a good makeup.

Airbrush Bodyart: Airbrush product available in both water and alcohol formulations. DHA tanning system offered as well.

Airmakeup Cosmetics: Polymer water based product.

AirPro Airbrush Makeup: A water-based formula. The company also has a sunless-tanning solution. Airbrush cleaner available for line.

Air Craft: A water-based formula.

Bodyair: Polymer water based line of products.

DCK Airbrush Cosmetics: Polymer water based product line.

Dinair: There are three product lines available through this company: polymer water based, polymer SD40 alcohol based, and DHA. An airbrush cleaner is also manufactured.

Duratat: A water-based tattoo ink containing no alcohol.

Fantasy Faces: Polymer SD40 alcohol based formulation. Thinner for product also available.

Fashion Aire Foundation: Polymer water based and sunless DHA formulation. An airbrush cleaner is available.

Graftobian: Polymer water based as well as polymer SD40 alcohol based. Both thinner and airbrush cleaner are available.

JanTana: DHA sunless tanner.

Jomo: SD40 alcohol based.

Kett Cosmetics: Water based and polymer SD40 alcohol based. An airbrush cleaner is also available.

KRYOLAN: Currently, kryolan has a polymer water based and an SD40 alcohol based product line.

MAC Airbrush: Polymer water based and silicone SD40 alcohol based.

Make Up For Ever: Water alcohol based.

Mancini Airbrush Makeup: Water based and offers an airbrush cleaner.

Marvaldi Makeup: Water-based formulation.

Michael Davy Airbrush Makeup: Polymer SD40 alcohol based.

Mist Mirage: Silicone SD40 based, as well as DHA sunless formula. An airbrush cleaner is also available.

O2 Cosmetics: Water-based formula. Also available in a DHA sunless tanner.

Obsessive Compulsive Cosmetics: Water based and SD40 alcohol based.

Reel Creations Body Art Inks: SD40 alcohol based line.

Safari Airbrush Makeup: Polymer-alcohol-based formula. DHA sunless tanner also in the line.

Skin Illustrator Colors: SD40 alcohol based formula line.

Stacolors: SD40 alcohol based product line.

Su-do Body Art: Polymer water based, SD40 alcohol based, and DHA in product line. Airbrush cleaner available.

Temptu: Water based, polymer water based, polymer SD40 alcohol based, and silicone SD40 based. An airbrush cleaner is also available in the line.

Totally Tattoo Party Body Paints: Polymer water based.

Trendy Tribals: Polymer water based.

uslu airlines: Polymer water based.

Remember to keep in mind that not all brands interact well with each other. So don't try mixing together two different manufacturers' product lines—their chemistry may not be compatible. A classic example is thinners. A Makeup Artist wrote to me to say she was having a hard time applying a certain makeup brand that would

not adhere or cover well when thinned with the product she was using. It turns out the makeup is silicone based, which has a chemical reaction to the product she was using as a thinner. Some silicone-based makeups do have thinners to go with their product line. The same can be said of any of the above makeup brands mentioned. Here are a few airbrush makeup tips I have found to work over the years.

1. Less is more when airbrushing. The makeup should not feel like a mask.

2. Use a PSI of 3 to 6 when airbrushing the face. If you airbrush with a stronger PSI, there will be a larger quantity of "bounce back" of the product into the air.

3. Hold the airbrush at a downward 45-degree angle when airbrushing the eye area on the talent (Figure 10.14). Of course, have the actor close their eyes!

4. If you are going to airbrush on the eyelid, use a PSI of 3 or less.

5. Using stencils when airbrushing works well for eyebrows. (Note: Freehand actually works better and looks more

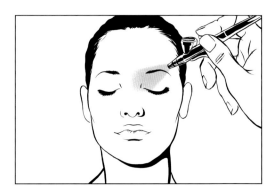

FIGURE 10-14: AIRBRUSHING AT AN ANGLE

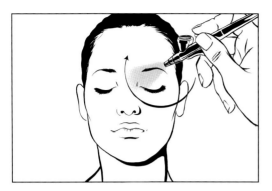

FIGURE 10-15: AIRBRUSHING IN A CIRCULAR MOTION

FIGURE 10-16: TISSUE OR SHIELD

natural if the person airbrushing is quite skilled.)

6. When airbrushing the face, spray in small, circular motions (Figure 10.15). This keeps the makeup even.

7. Have a folded tissue or shield to protect the hairline from overspray of makeup (Figure 10.16). Do not add tap water to a water-based makeup to thin. Use distilled water. Tap water contains minerals that can contaminate or compromise the chemistry of the makeup.

PRO TIP

Read the ingredients of products you buy. Many of the cosmetic and airbrush companies have products that work well with each other. Know what you are buying. You'll have the best results possible when airbrushing.

AIRBRUSH LESSON FOR BEAUTY MAKEUP

by Kris Evans and Darla Albright

Makeup Artists Kris Evans and Darla Albright developed Air Craft Cosmetics to meet the needs of the professional Makeup Artist as well as the consumer. From their vast experience in film, television, theatre, HD, and print editorial, they felt a need to develop a product that could be used with or without an airbrush. Kris Evans:

> I use the airbrush on everything and find it much faster and easier. With HD becoming so popular, there is nothing better than the airbrush. Many of my clients also do red-carpet events that are mostly shot in HD. HD can be very harsh, so it is imperative the makeup be flawless. I really believe you must use the correct color in the foundation for the look to be natural. Easy touch-ups are also essential, which is why we created Air Craft Cosmetics. On set, I usually use a makeup brush for touch-ups. Because the foundation can be used with or without an airbrush, touch-ups are a breeze.

165

What's in Kris Evans's makeup kit? "Of course I use Air Craft!" (Figure 10.17).

Primer: Air Craft Primer (shea butter based); used with a brush or sponge, not the airbrushes

Foundation: Air Craft foundations (water based)

Pressed Powders: Air Craft Perfect Layover powder

Lip Gloss: Air Craft Lip Gloss Duos

Eye Shadow: Air Craft Eye Glosses

Excellent makeup brushes

Tweezerman tweezers

Eyelash curler

Eyedrops

Cleanser

Moisturizer

FIGURE 10-17: AIR CRAFT MAKEUP LINE

PRO TIP

Keep on hand a small squeeze bottle of distilled water or spring water or suggested product by the manufacturer for thinning airbrush makeup.

PRO TIP

It's very important to clean your airbrush immediately after each use. You want to prevent the makeup from drying inside the airbrush. Not cleaned properly, your airbrush will not give the proper spray.

How to start:

1. Set up your station with everything you need to airbrush.

2. Apply the moisturizer or primer of choice to the skin first. Apply the primer with a sponge and not through the airbrush. A primer ensures a smooth surface with staying power for your airbrush. Squeeze six to seven drops of makeup into the airbrush cup. For a more translucent effect, add one to two drops of water. Remember to replace the cap on your airbrush to avoid spills.

3. Start the compressor. Position your hand on the airbrush lever as if you were holding a pencil.

4. Airbrush horizontally 3 to 4 inches from the face, pulling back the airbrush lever with your fingertip. You'll see a fine mist start to adhere onto the surface of the

skin. Keep moving around the face in a circular motion without stopping in one place. It's this constant movement that keeps the makeup even. Application should take about 15 seconds. If any areas need more coverage you can lightly airbrush a second coat of foundation to those areas.

5. Have your actor close their eyes. Then gently airbrush around the eye area.

6. Corrective spot covering is easy. For under the eyes, you can use a shade lighter than the foundation first. Then airbrush the entire face with the color you chose. For problem spots on the face, you can lightly spray a second layer of the foundation color.

7. Adding color for blusher or highlighters is easy. Blow out any leftover makeup color through the airbrush with a few drops of water. Add your next color choice to the cup. Blusher should be a soft blushcolor applied by hand or an airbrush. Lightly spray a highlighter color along the cheekbone, brow bone, under the eye, or anywhere a highlight is needed.

8. Set your makeup with a setting powder (for example, Air Craft Cosmetics' Perfect Layover Powder). You are now ready to finish the rest of your makeup application. Sweep an eye color over the lid—and, if needed, a subtle eyeliner. Top your makeup off with a flattering lip gloss.

9. When all leftover makeup has been fully blown through the airbrush, detach the gun from the hose, and place the cup under running water to rinse thoroughly. Connect your gun again to the compressor, and run through your airbrush system to remove any makeup still there.

Maintenance: After every few applications, pull the needle out and wipe clean. Be careful not to bend the top of the needle. Go to www.aircraftcosmetics.com for blow manual.

AIRBRUSHING WITH STENCILS

by Dina Ousley, Founder, Dinair

Stencils are used in beauty airbrush makeup to achieve a cleaner, softer, less made-up look. With HDTV and digital HD cameras, every detail is visible. Feature or flaw, it shows. Airbrushing an entire makeup is perfect for these technologies. Shields and stencils are used to protect areas of the face or body where you don't want colors to go, while allowing you to define perfect natural eyebrow shapes, lip shapes, and to feather and blend existing colors. At Dinair, we use shields (stencils) for beauty makeup, fantasy, glamour, and tattoos. The following sections explain how to work with and apply the use of shields in a natural beauty makeup.

FOUNDATION

Start with a clean face, and make sure that where you choose to spray the airbrush makeup is free of any moisturizers or oils. Apply a primer before the foundation. Choose a color that is in the shade range of the skin tone you are working on. The liquid must be shaken before use to correct pigment. If you want to create a custom color match, you can always mix your foundation colors using the airbrush with a technique called back bubbling.

If you were to look at airbrush makeup under a magnifying glass, you would see that the makeup consists of light, medium, dark, and blush-colored dots. Look at the actor's skin tone. If there is anything dark around the face—such as hyperpigmentation, birthmarks, or age spots—lighten with one or two shades lighter than the person's natural color before applying the natural shade. You need only five to eight drops of makeup to spray an entire face, neck, and ears. Spray the natural shade over the concealer. Spray sparingly so you don't lose your highlights.

Work in passes. A pass is every time you go over the same area, the dots fill in, and the coverage becomes more opaque. Make sure to use one pass at a time—one pass, two pass, three pass, and so on, until you have the right coverage. Dots are the ultimate in camouflaging.

Leave enough open coverage. Open coverage is the space around the dots of color (your skin) that you have sprayed. This allows you

to fill in with some blush color or use the natural redness of the skin to become the blush. We call this the window of opportunity. Spraying sparsely is the key to success. Keep the distance of your airbrush about six inches away from the skin while spraying foundation, using circular motions with back-and-forth movements. This is key to an even application.

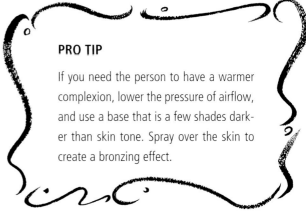

PRO TIP

If you need the person to have a warmer complexion, lower the pressure of airflow, and use a base that is a few shades darker than skin tone. Spray over the skin to create a bronzing effect.

When spraying around the eyes, note that the natural folds and squint lines must be gently opened and sprayed in the direction that they appear. If the lines and folds change direction, so should your spraying. Remember to spray especially sparingly so the airbrush makeup does not collect into the folds and squint lines. You can use the remainder of the airbrush makeup in the cup to spray the top of the hands to knock down sun spots and add tone.

EYE SHADOW

1. Put two to three drops of liquid eye shadow into the airbrush cup.

2. To create a custom color, mix them by creating back bubbles with your airbrush.

PRO TIP

When mixing custom colors in the air-brush cup, hold a tissue in front of the nozzle to block the airflow. Then pull the lever back until you see the colors start to bubble and give off a marbling effect. Remove the tissue to restore airflow, and spray the airbrush makeup into the tissue to see your new custom color.

3. Keep the eye area clean and free from moisturizers or oils. Moisturizers can cause eye shadow colors to crease.

4. Set the airflow to 3 or 4 PSI.

5. Hold up a shield (stencil) that follows the contours of the eye, and gently pull back the airbrush lever.

6. In a small, continuous motion, spray the shadow color by making several passes until you reach the level of color desired. Note: If you hold the stencil flat against the skin, your edge will be more defined. Holding the stencil slightly above the skin will give a softer feathered edge (Figure 10.18).

169

yellow   blue   green
new color

Mixing and Matching. When we mix, We mix only a couple of drops of this, with a couple of drops of that, and then suddenly, we have a endless amount of color combinations. Create your own custom colors, get creative and see what happens.

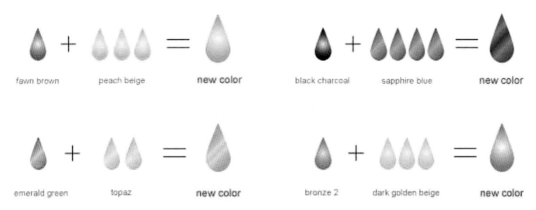

fawn brown   peach beige   **new color**   black charcoal   sapphire blue   **new color**

emerald green   topaz   **new color**   bronze 2   dark golden beige   **new color**

FIGURE 10-18: A MAKE UP CHART

EYELINER

1. Change out any color you desire for eyeliner.

2. Set the airflow on a low PSI of about 3 to 4.

3. In the same way as for the eye shadow, follow the natural lash line in a back-and-forth motion, building the color with each pass. Note: An eye shadow stencil held directly on the lid close to the eyelashes will give you defined eyeliner. A stencil held just off the lid while airbrushing eyeliner color will appear feathered.

PRO TIP

The farther away from the eye area you work, the wider your eyeliner will be.

EYEBROWS

1. You will want to put a total of two to three drops of eyebrow coloring in the cup.

2. Hold the stencil up to your eyebrow, and bring it flush against your skin for a sharp edge.

3. Distance the stencil, allowing the overspray to cover and define the brows, giving them a soft, naturally feathered look. Note: You can use the stencil to spray the entire brow, or just fill in the brow where needed. You may also want to use the front of one brow stencil and the tail of another, creating the perfect eyebrow look for you.

Dinair has hair stencils to fill in sparse areas. Each stencil has a selection of hair shapes that can be tailored for your needs. This is a particularly good way for women who have lost some of their eyebrows to again have naturally beautiful brows.

LIP COLOR

1. Change out your eyeliner color for a lip color of choice.

2. Take a lip edge and lay it flat against the lips.

3. Work on small sections at a time. Note: Laying the stencil flat against the lips will give you a defined lip line. Work closer to the lips for a narrower line.

4. Work farther away from the lips to finish the rest of the lips.

5. Apply lip gloss over the colored lips for an extra-shiny finish.

BLUSHER

1. Apply blusher color by sweeping across the cheekbone area with the airbrush. The cheeks should never look made up. A subtle hint of color is all you need.

2. Use a loose tissue to block off any unwanted color into the hairline, being careful not to hold too close to the skin—this will create a hard line.

PRO TIP

To find the natural contours of the cheeks, have the actor smile while you airbrush the cheek color. Go to www.airbrushmakeup.com for video instructions.

FIGURE 10-19: THE SET UP

HOW TO CLEAN YOUR STENCILS

by Bradley Look

Productivity and the life of your stencils can be vastly improved with regular cleaning. Just as you should always leave your airbrush clean, so should you with the rest of your equipment. This is particularly paramount when working as a Makeup Artist who's using an airbrush on talent. After all, you wouldn't use dirty sponges or brushes, would you? A stencil comes in contact with an actor's skin and should be cleaned frequently. Simple steps are all it takes to maintain clean stencils. First, you'll need the basic equipment to get started.

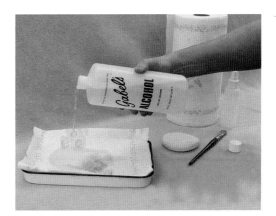

FIGURE 10-20: POURING

MATERIALS

A solvent-proof tray (such as an enamel butcher's tray, found in most art stores)

Paper toweling

Powder puffs

Isopropyl alcohol 99 percent

Spray bottle

A synthetic brush (with soft bristles)

FIGURE 10-21: WASHING THE STENCIL IN A TRAY

FIGURE 10-22: CLEANING THE STENCIL WITH PUFF

FIGURE 10-24: DRYING THE STENCIL

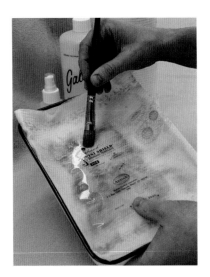

FIGURE 10-23: CLEANING WITH A BRUSH

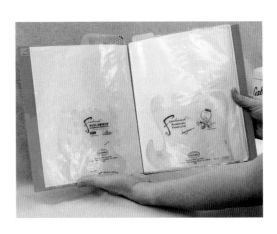

FIGURE 10-25: STORED STENCILS

TO BEGIN THE WHOLE CLEANSING PROCESS

1. Detach two sheets of paper toweling from the roll, and fold so that the toweling will fit inside the butcher's tray.

2. Carefully pour the isopropyl alcohol on top of the paper toweling so that it is entirely saturated with the solvent. Note: If you are unsure whether the solvent will affect the material your stencil is made of, check a small section before immersing it.

3. Lay the stencil facedown (dirty side) onto the toweling.

4. Let it sit there for several minutes so that the solvent can loosen all products on its surface. Note: If both sides of your stencil have dried product on them, then you'll need to flip the stencil over to soak.

5. Now flip over the stencil onto the paper toweling (dirty side up).

6. Saturate a powder puff with solvent, and lightly pat the stencil to remove product.

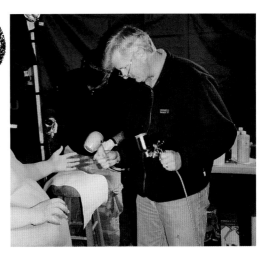

FIGURE 10-26: BRADLEY LOOK AND STEVEN ANDERSON
AIRBRUSHING

7. Once you're satisfied with the cleaning,
   rinse the stencil off with tap water in the
   sink.

8. Lay the stencil down onto some clean
   paper toweling and pat dry.

9. Store the now-clean stencil away for the
   next time you'll need it.

PREPARING FOR AN AIRBRUSH BODY MAKEUP

by Bradley Look

BEFORE THE SHOOTING DAY

Anytime a complex makeup is to be
tackled—whether it might be for a feature,
television series, and/or commercial—it is
always advisable to do a makeup test. A
makeup test is like a dry run.

Makeup testing is often done to determine
the correct order to appliance application (if
they are being used), choice of makeup
colors, and to see how the makeup reads on
camera. Makeup Artist Barry Koper and I
met at Gower Studios to test colors for a
well-known soft-drink commercial. The
concept of the ad was that two large sumo
wrestlers were to be running through a dark
forest and converge on an unsuspecting
man who was sitting on a tree stump. The
commercial spot would finish with a close-
up of the two enormous bellies of the
wrestlers squishing an unsuspecting man
between them.

Oh, and I left out the most important part.
Each of the wrestlers would need to be
airbrushed from head to foot: one yellow,
and the other lime green. We met with the
actors that were to play the wrestlers at the
studio.

SET UP YOUR SUPPLIES FOR A MAKEUP TEST

Using a vacant makeup room, airbrushes and compressors were set up along with several versions of green and yellow temporary-tattoo ink. Reel Creation product line was used because it had a suitable pigment level for the job. Other supplies for the test included a hair dryer with a cool setting, makeup cape, and additional Reel Creation tattoo colors to adjust the bases.

PREP THE ACTORS

The actors' skin was thoroughly cleaned with isopropyl alcohol 99 percent to remove skin oils so that the makeup would adhere evenly. Moisturizer was not applied—it could possibly cause the tattoo inks to streak and easily come off.

SUGGESTIONS FOR MAKEUP TESTING

After doing a number of makeup tests on the performers, it was determined that for the yellow to look concentrated enough on the skin, an underbase of white would be necessary. For the green, a mixture of white, green, and a Day-Glo green created the perfect match to the can of the soft drink that the producers wanted the colors to correspond to. After a couple of hours, the producers finally agreed to the shade of yellow and green they liked the best. Liquid samples based on those two colors were mixed in 1-ounce bottles so that a larger volume of liquid product could be produced.

The colors we found to work now had to be matched to a body makeup that would last longer and cover faster, which are tattoo inks, as mentioned earlier. We chose to work with Fred Blau, owner of Reel Creations. To airbrush both performers, we were going to need a quart of white, two quarts of yellow, and a gallon of green in temporary-tattoo ink. The yellow was easy to mix, because it was similar to canary yellow (a mix of yellow and white). The green was a much more elusive color to obtain. It took many tries for Fred to match it. Note: Because of the time involved to execute the body makeup, two extra Makeup Artists were called in who had airbrush experience.

DAY OF THE SHOOT

Before leaving, the two actors at the studio were given specific instructions to remove all body hair the day before the actual day of shooting. Further, they were told not to apply any body moisturizer and to use roll-on antiperspirant deodorant, as opposed to the spray variety. Spray deodorants will cover a wider area under the arms, and makeup will not adhere to skin coated in the product. And lastly, both actors were told not to drink anything alcoholic the night before. The alcohol would seep out of their pores the following day, and eat away at the makeup when they started to perspire.

MAKEUP AND AIRBRUSH SUPPLIES

Reel Creation Tattoo Inks were used for the complete body makeup. Ben Nye cream makeup was used around the actors' eyes in matching colors. Iwata/Medea HP-CH Hi-Line airbrushes were used on the bodies becauses that gun can operate at a low 13 PSI, which greatly reduced overspray. Iwata's Powder Jet Pro compressors were used to power the guns.

SETTING UP YOUR STATION

A tent was erected near the base camp. Portable heaters were brought in. Although the heaters were a good idea, they had to be placed a fair distance away becauses we were spraying an alcohol-based product, and safety was of utmost importance.

APPLYING THE BODY MAKEUP

1. To begin the process, everyone placed filter masks on.

2. Our first performer sat in a swivel chair as we lightly hazed the white underbase on. Note: It was extremely important that this first layer not be sprayed on too heavily—running would be visible under the yellow and ruin the effect. It was a slow process to build up this primer coat.

3. We covered the entire actor except for his hands, feet, and upper eyelids. This took about an hour and a half with two people applying the white.

4. We then lightly dusted the white tattoo product with colorless powder to remove any stickiness on the skin.

5. Then we dusted off the excess.

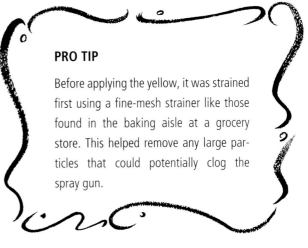

PRO TIP

Before applying the yellow, it was strained first using a fine-mesh strainer like those found in the baking aisle at a grocery store. This helped remove any large particles that could potentially clog the spray gun.

6. The yellow was applied carefully over the white. Note: Two people worked different sections of the body to save time.

7. Next, we applied a matching yellow in cream form around the eyes.

8. The edges were blended off, then set with powder.

9. We applied a base to the entire face in yellow with a Hi-Line airbrush.

10. The makeup was finished with our hands: airbrushed white primer color, yellow makeup, and colorless powder to set.

11. To seal the makeup, Reel Creations Blue Aqua Sealer was airbrushed over the entire body. A light coating of Derma Shield (a skin protector) was covered over the entire body to add a more lifelike sheen.

12. After the hair was styled, the airbrush was used to enhance the hair. This technique gave the hair a more structured look.

Lastly, a similar process was repeated on the other actor for the green body makeup.

ON-SET TOUCH-UPS

There are a few situations where you need to be properly set up to do touch-ups while shooting outdoors and for more elaborate makeups. Talk with someone ahead of time to see if it is possible to have a small tent or cover that can be put up. Set up your equipment, chairs, or small table that you'll be using for touch-ups.

REMOVING THE AIRBRUSH MAKEUP

To remove the makeup, a 50/50 mixture of isopropyl alcohol and isopropyl myristate was used on powder puffs. This mixture easily breaks down the tattoo inks.

CLEANING YOUR AIRBRUSH: PAASCHE

Follow these steps to clean your airbrush:

1. Pour any leftover color back into its container.

2. Rinse and wipe color cup or bottle assembly clean. To backflush color from the airbrush, keep bottle assembly or color cup attached.

3. If using a color cup, cover the top of it with your thumb or a cloth to keep air from blowing out.

4. Place one finger over the air cap of the airbrush, and release some air by depressing the finger button. This causes back pressure, which induces a bubble action inside the airbrush and

container. This helps clean the fluid passage.

PRO TIP

Bradley Look says: "Spray excess airbrush cleaning product into a cleaning pot, sometimes referred to as a cleaning station. The cleaning station has a filter system that helps to trap harmful solvent so as not to be introduced into the environment."

FIGURE 10-27: A CLEANING STATION

SAFETY

Certain safety issues do come up with airbrushing. Having good ventilation is at the top of the list. Although there is little or no proven risk of airbrushing with makeup and low-PSI compressors, you as a professional are responsible to know all the facts and safeguard yourself and the actor's health. One of the first defenses for protecting yourself in the trailer is having your station near one or two open doors at either end. Windows should be open, and any built-in ventilation systems running. There should be a limit on how many people in the trailer are airbrushing at a time. Airbrushing has little or no risk, but spray-on tanning is more of a concern. Good websites to research the latest findings on cosmetic ingredients or workplace-safety issues are the FDA at www.fda.gov and OSHA at www.osha.gov.

REFERENCES

Internet Resources

www.airpromakeup.com

www.arttalk.com

Badger: www.badgerairbrush.com

Evans, Kris, and Albright, Darla. www.aircraftcosmetics.com

www.fda.gov

www.iwataairbrush.com

Klasfeld, David. Obsessive Compulsive Cosmetics. www.occmakeup.com

Look, Bradley: Original articles written for Airbrushtalk web magazine

Mandor, Samantha. www.temptu.com

www.osha.gov

Ousley, Dina. www.dinair.com

Paasche: www.paascheairbrush.com

II

EFFECTS

Prosthetics is the process of creating an effect in makeup by sculpting, molding, application, and painting. Prosthetic makeup is widely used today for wounds, to simulate illnesses, to change the shape of a face, or to create a whole different face. Countless monsters and creatures are created using prosthetic makeup. Your imagination is all you need, plus skills in the art of mold making, applying, and painting the final outcome. Finding the right tools and products will help you to create anything the Director has asked for. You might find yourself behind and in trouble on occasion if you can't produce or help a department head in making, laying, or painting a prosthetic piece. Directors and Makeup Artists are much savvier and expect high-end, quality work. The process in prosthetics starts with molds, making molds and casting chosen materials to go into the mold to cure. There are many different ways to do this, and we'll go over the steps later on in this chapter. In today's market, there are many ways to shorten the path of mold making because of the advances in products being used. There will be many times when you need to rush something out, a request has been made for a last-minute makeup effect, or you need to reuse a prosthetic piece over and over again. Whatever the case, there are easy ways to do this right on location.

As a Makeup Artist, you should also learn where to turn for help in achieving realistic prosthetic applications. Not everyone needs to pour a body cast or to sculpt masks. If you know the process and who to call, then applying the final piece is what counts.

MOLD MAKING FOR TODAY'S MARKET

by Smooth-On

Many products on the market are used for mold making. Most use a variety of flexible rubber products. These products can mimic fine details, are easy to remove from the original piece being cast, and can be used over and over again, which makes these products cost effective. The following rubber products are often\ used by Makeup Artists.

Latex: A natural rubber found in rubber trees, mainly in Southeast Asia. Raw rubber is processed with ammonia and water to make the rubber usable as a molding material. Latex is often brushed or slushed into a mold, but not poured. The advantage of using latex is that you don't have to weigh the product. You can use latex right out of the container. It's not too expensive, and has a high elasticity. Latex molds are also good for casting wax and gypsum. The disadvantage of latex is the drying time. Most latex products need to dry for four or more hours between each layer when being brushed on. Some projects can take up to 20 brushed layers. Also, there can be a strong ammonia odor, but there are products out there today that have addressed this problem.

Silicone Rubbers (Smooth-Sil Series): Silicone rubbers are two-component systems, and are available in ranges of hardness from very soft to medium. Silicone can be cured with a platinum catalyst or a tin catalyst. You can make molds that are poured, brushed, or sprayed onto a model. Silicone can have negative results when coming into contact with other products such as sulfur clays. Silicone also must be accurately mixed by using a scale.

Gelatin: Can be poured into a silicone mold. The appliance picks up more detail from the mold if the silicone is slightly heated before pouring the hot gelatin.

SAFETY TIP
by Smooth-On

Materials are safe to use when following directions by the manufacturer. Federal law requires that manufacturers provide important information in the form of a material safety data sheet (MSDS). The MSDS provides all pertinent information on a product—ranging from directions for proper use, to safety precautions, to a list of active ingredients, to associated hazards, to combustion levels, to storage requirements.

FIGURE 11-1: PRODUCT SUPPLIES

181

FIGURE 11-2: A MODEL BEING POURED WITH A CONTAINER WALL

PROBLEMS THAT MIGHT ARISE WHEN MOLD MAKING

If the mold has soft spots (partial cure):

1. It was not mixed correctly (premixed).

2. It was not mixed thoroughly.

3. The product was contaminated.

4. It was not correctly measured.

If your mold stuck to the model:

1. The wrong release agent was used; not enough was applied; or it was not used at all.

2. The model was not properly sealed.

QUICK OVERVIEW

1. An original model can be made with almost any material. This includes clay, wax, wood, plaster, stone, metal, bone, or cement.

2. If you are pouring, use a container wall around your model (Figure 11.2). If brushing, no wall is needed.

3. Seal all areas of the mold and model if using porous materials: plaster, wood, sulfur, or water-based clays.

4. Use a release agent for all sealed areas. If you are using silicone, a release agent is not necessary.

5. Follow manufacturer directions suited for your project.

Have good ventilation. Do not inhale fumes, rubber products, release agents, sealers, fillers, resins, and plasters, and so on. Wear good rubber gloves, and minimize skin contact while working. Wash your hands with soap and water, or anywhere there has been contact with products.

Protect your surfaces from spills with wax paper, brown paper, or your own favorite setup towels. Keep your station clean by keeping utensils clean, and surfaces washed with acetone or alcohol to remove any materials that have spilled. Gelatin can be simply washed off.

What should you have in your kit for mold making? Smooth-On suggests the following:

Wood or acrylic pieces for container walls (this is for containing any product from spilling over). Mold boxes can be homemade.

Scale

Modeling clay

Mixing containers

Stirring sticks

Sealing agent

Release agent

Mold rubber or molding material of choice

If you find that your mold did not set properly, it could be for one of the following reasons:

1. Wrong mixing measurements

2. Wrong type of scale (should be a gram scale or triple beam balance)

3. Temperature too cold

Steps to Silicone Mold Making with Smooth-On:

1. Sculpt (Figure 11.3).

2. Release (Figure 11.4).

3. Mix product (Figure 11.5).

4. Apply thin layer (Figure 11.6).

5. Apply second coat (Figure 11.7).

FIGURE 11-3: SCULPT

FIGURE 11-4: RELEASE

FIGURE 11-5: MIX PRODUCT

6. Apply third coat (Figure 11.8).

7. Remove mold (Figure 11.9).

8. Scrape clay (Figure 11.10).

9. Measure out (Figure 11.11).

10. Mix flesh tone (Figure 11.12).

11. Mix (Figures 11.13 A and B).

12. Mix quickly (Figure 11.14).

13. Spread in mold (Figure 11.15).

14. Release with powder (Figure 11.16).

15. Done (Figure 11.17).

FIGURE 11-6: THIN LAYER

FIGURE 11-8: THIRD COAT

FIGURE 11-7: SECOND COAT

FIGURE 11-9: REMOVE MOLD

FIGURE 11-10: SCRAPE CLAY

FIGURE 11-13: A,B MIX

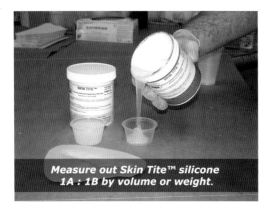

FIGURE 11-11: MEASURE OUT

FIGURE 11-14: MIX QUICKLY

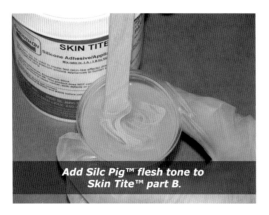

FIGURE 11-12: MIX FLESH TONE

FIGURE 11-15: SPREAD IN MOLD

Demold Skin Tite™ scar using powder.

FIGURE 11-16: RELEASE WITH POWDER

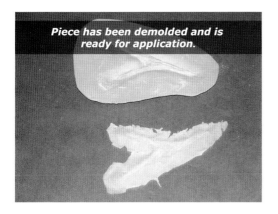

Piece has been demolded and is ready for application.

FIGURE 11-17: FINISHED DONE PIECE

TERMS

You should know the following terms as they pertain to mold making and appliances:

Adding Color: Mixing pigments or flocking materials to a product before being cast into a mold.

Alginates: Seaweed-based products used to take an impression of an object or person to be used in mold making.

Chavant NSP Clay: Sculpting clay that holds fine details, sculpture free and available in soft, medium, or hard grades.

Casting: A product being used in a mold to create molded reusable appliances.

Cure: A chemical reaction that occurs when you mix two ingredients together that finish.

Cure Inhibition: Certain casting products can be inhibited by contaminants used in or around a work area, causing the molded product to remain tacky or not to cure.

Demolding: When your product has cured enough to be taken out of the mold.

Green Marble SeLr: Makeup sealer, used in aging techniques and for multiple layers.

KRYOLAN Crystal Clear: Protective coating with clear finish that doesn't yellow.

Myristate: An additive for high-grade cosmetics. Also used as an emulsifier or moistening agent.

Mix Ratio: The proper mix of products.

Plastics: Products such as W.M.Creations, Inc. A.M.E.K. based liquid plastic. Not to be used directly on the skin. Use in stone or silicone molds.

Pot Life: How long the product mixed will last for usage.

Pros-Aide: A prosthetic adhesive that can be mixed with acrylic paints. Has a strong bond.

Pros-Aide Bondo: Pros-Aide mixed with Cabosil.

Platinum Cure Silicone Rubber: Abrasion and heat resistance in a versatile product for

185

mold-making productions. Materials such as plastics, concrete, wax, low-melt metal alloys, or resins can be cast into silicone-rubber molds.

Release Agent: An agent used to help release the product that was cast from the mold.

Rigid Gypsum Molds: Known as stone molds.

Slush Casting: Products that are to be used in a mold, poured and worked around the inside of the mold until all areas are covered. You can slush several layers on top of each other, Each layer must be cured before applying a new layer.

W.M. Creations, Inc. Soft Sealer: Product used to seal wax, gelatin appliances, and as a sealer on the back of gelatin appliances to prevent moisture from attacking gelatin.

SILICONE MOLD MAKING

Matthew Mungle will explain how to make a simple silicone mold, casting, and applying your finished piece. This is a technique that can be done on location with professional results. Matthew Mungle: "Silicone is a flexible material, and easy to demold appliances. Once a silicone mold is made, it should last indefinitely. Silicone molds can be made quickly and on location."

What should you have in your makeup kit to be able to create silicone molds and their appliances? Mold-making kit:

Silicone mold-making materials

Small spatulas

Throwaway brushes

Liquid soap such as Ivory clear soap

Pros-Aide Bondo

W.M. Creations, Inc. Soft Sealer

Medical mixing cups

Chavant NSP Clay

Sculpting tools

Steps to Silicone Mold Making:

1. Set up your station, Make sure there are no latex gloves or sponges near the work area. Wash your hands and lay down setup towels (preferably paper towels).

2. Sculpt the desired form out of Chavant NSP clay (nonsulfur clay). Spray the clay with one light coat of Krylon Crystal Clear, and dry thoroughly (about three minutes). Mix the silicone material (Third Degree molding material or Skin Tite by Smooth-On). These two products are platinum-silicone based, and are affected by latex or sulfur products. Paint the silicone material onto the sculpture with a finger or throwaway brush, making sure not to trap any bubbles in the cast. Build the material up at least 1 inch to avoid warpage. Let dry at least 30 minutes, then demold.

What to Pour into the Mold

Suggested materials that can be poured into the mold would be plastic, Pros-Aide Bondo, and silicone products.

Applying the Finished Prosthetic:

1. Set the appliance in place on the skin area, holding tweezers if necessary (Figure 11.18).

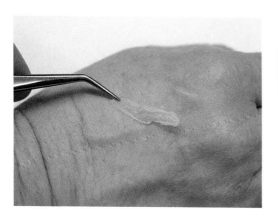

FIGURE 11-18: STEP ONE

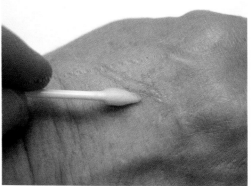

FIGURE 11-20: STEP THREE

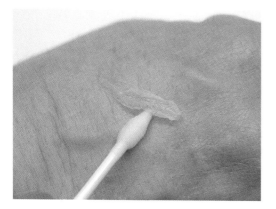

FIGURE 11-19: STEP TWO

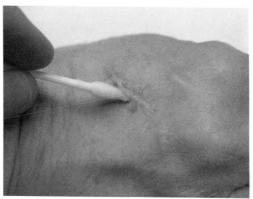

FIGURE 11-21: STEP FOUR

2. Applying a small amount of 99 percent alcohol under the appliance with a brush or cotton-tipped applicator, let the appliance blend (melt) into the skin (Figure 11.19).

3. Blend off any soft sealer edges with 99 percent alcohol (Figure 11.20).

4. Color with Stacolors, activated with 99 percent alcohol (Figure 11.21).

5. Paint with cut example (Figure 11.22).

6. Finished painted cut (Figure 11.23).

7. Adding blood (Figure 11.24).

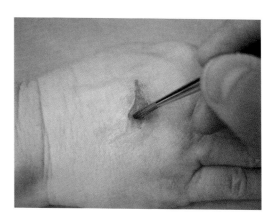

FIGURE 11-22: STEP FIVE

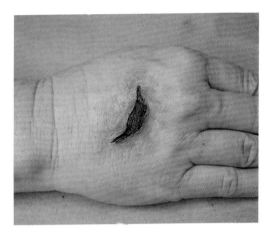

FIGURE 11-23: STEP SIX

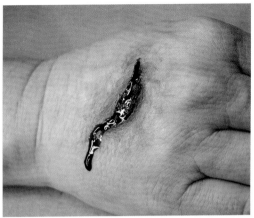

FIGURE 11-25: STEP EIGHT

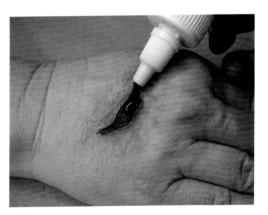

FIGURE 11-24: STEP SEVEN

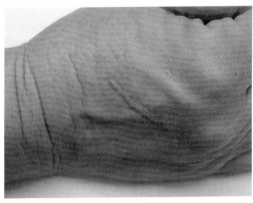

FIGURE 11-26: STEP NINE

8. Cut and blood (Figure 11.25).

9. Finished scar (Figure 11.26).

10. Seal with a soft sealer if necessary.

PAINTING PROSTHETICS

When an appliance is translucent, there is a realistic quality that shouldn't be painted over. Stacolors, which are activated with 99 percent alcohol, give you the flexibility to paint in thin layers like a wash (translucent) or opaque (dense so it cannot be seen through). Apply Stacolor with brushes, sponges, or cotton-tipped applicators. Stacolors also come in liquid form, which you can use in an airbrush without having to thin the product first.

Remove products with Isopropyl Myristate, Super Solv, or baby oil. Clean skin first with 70 or 90 percent alcohol. Do not use near the eyes.

PROSTHETIC TRANSFERS

by Christien Tinsley

Some of the wonderful attributes these prosthetics offer are undetectable blended edges, translucency (so they look like flesh when a proper tone is mixed), and incredible tenacity to hold during the long day of a shoot.

In order to set up for a prosthetic transfer application, I first like to prep my station. Materials that I like to have with me at all times when doing a Transfer application are:

Transfer prosthetic to be applied

Transfer paper

Astringent to clean the skin

Cotton pads

Shavers (electric and razor)

Shaving cream

Scissors

Adhesive (Pros-Aide)

Latex sponges

Tissue

Spray bottle (water)

No-color powder

Powder puffs

Q-tips

99 percent alcohol

Brushes

Sealer (BenNye Final Seal)

Hand towels

Isopropyl Myristate

Super Solv

Body, hand, or face lotion

Smashbox Anti-Shine

Tattoo palettes (flesh tones and primary colors)

PREPPING THE SKIN

Depending on what approach you will take for prosthetic transfer application, you will commonly prep the skin by making sure it is free of hair, oils, and dirt. Hair can be tricky if applying a prosthetic transfer because it won't allow full contact of the piece to the skin. Try to remove all hair if possible. Prep the skin by cleaning it with an astringent of your choice. This removes dirt and oil, and slightly dries the skin for better adhesion of paint or adhesive. Sometimes a layer of adhesive can be applied to the skin before the prosthetic transfer, helping in the adhesion.

PREPARATION:

1. If prosthetic is powdered, gently wash prosthetic transfer with antigrease soap and water. Note: This step is not necessary if prosthetic transfer is already clean.

2. Stipple a light coat of Pros-Aide over surface of prosthetic transfer all the way to the edges.

3. Let Pros-Aide dry until clear.

Steps 4–8 should be done only when ready for application to actor:

4. Place prosthetic facedown onto shiny side of transfer paper.

5. Press firmly onto paper, paying close attention to the edges. This is the most important part of the preparation.

6. Trim as close to the edge of the prosthetic as possible.

7. Peel off plastic top sheet slowly. If parts of prosthetic pull away from paper, lay the whole piece back on paper and repeat step 4 until prosthetic comes off clean.

8. Now you're ready for application.

APPLICATION:

1. Place prosthetic transfer face down on skin, and press firmly.

2. Wet back of prosthetic transfer generously with a Tinsley Transfer moistener (filled with water).

3. Continue wetting the paper for approximately 30 seconds, and slice or peel the backing off. Smooth transfer gently with water, and let dry well. Any visible edges can be blended away using 99 percent alcohol.

4. Powder generously with no-color powder of your choice. Gently wipe any excess powder, and seal prosthetic transfer with a spray of makeup sealer (we recommend Ben Nye Final Seal).

PROSTHETIC TRANSFER APPLICATION STEPS WITH CHRISTIEN TINSLEY:

1. Lay down with water (Figure 11.27).

2. Peel (Figure 11.28).

3. Blend visible edges (Figure 11.29).

4. Powder (Figure 11.30).

FIGURE 11-27: STEP 1: LAY DOWN WITH WATER

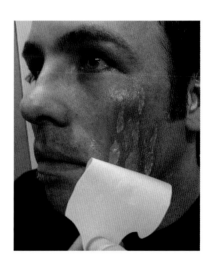

FIGURE 11-28: STEP 2: PEEL

5. Seal (Figure 11.31).

6. Paint (Figure 11.32).

ON-SET

In order to maintain prosthetic transfers on-set, be aware. As with any makeup, things can happen with prosthetics. An actor sleeps hard over lunch, or he rubs his arms on a table while eating, or the scene requires actors to wrestle or sweat or run,

FIGURE 11-29: STEP 3: BLEND VISIBLE EDGES

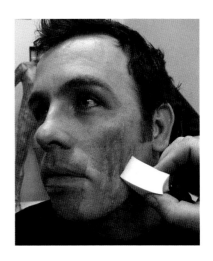

FIGURE 11-31: STEP 5: SEAL

FIGURE 11-30: STEP 4: POWDER

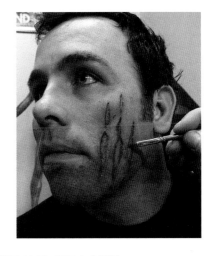

FIGURE 11-32: STEP 6: PAINT

etc. Always have backup transfers with you, and alcohol, in case you have to remove and apply a new one on-set. Do not remove with oils in the middle of the day because your next one won't stick. For minor repair, have a premixed color or colors to match the tones and to fill in areas that have rubbed away. If an edge has pulled up or rolled over, you can fill it in

using any kind of filler of your choice (bondo, wax, etc.). Remember, it is always best if you have time to remove and apply a new piece. Things happen—just be resourceful and prepared.

To Remove

Saturate prosthetic transfer with adhesive remover of your choice (Super Solv,

Isopropyl Myristate, Detachol, etc.), and rub gently with remover and dampened powder puff.

APPLICATION OF GELATIN PROSTHETICS

by Kenny Myers

The information contained within the context of this article is presented in good faith. The responsibility for the use of any material in special makeup effects rests solely with the user. The author assumes no responsibility for the use, or misuse, of any material, technique, or informational content discussed within this article.

WHAT IS GELATIN?

Gelatin is a colorless protein formed by boiling the skin, bones, and connective tissue of animals. It is used in food, pharmaceutical, photographic, ballistics, and cosmetic manufacturing. The end result is a protein derived by rendering the remnants of the animal down to a powder that is composed of about 84 to 90 percent protein, 8 to 15 percent water, and 1 to 2 percent mineral salts, free of additives and preservatives. It also contains about 18 different amino acids joined together in a chain.

In the film and television makeup industries, gelatin appliances are an alternative to foam latex in that gelatin is a moldable, flexible, and translucent material that simulates human flesh in a more natural way than latex. Gelatin for prosthetic appliances has a much higher

Bloom, or stiffness, (around 275–300) than the gelatin used for food consumption (around 200–250).

When you purchase gelatin from a supplier for appliance construction, you shouldn't have to concern yourself with the Bloom. Though it is useful to know that gelatin's "Bloom," is the relative strength or rigidity of that brand or grade of gelatin, as well as its water-binding capacity. The higher the Bloom number, the denser it will be. Gelatin is hydroscopic, which is a fancy way of saying it likes and absorbs water, swelling to many times its weight of dry gelatin as you mix in liquids, turning the dry gelatin into a slurry. The higher the Bloom, the higher the price as well. The Bloom scale was created by Oscar T. Bloom. He must have played with an awful lot of gelatin in his time!

HOW TO MAKE GELATIN

Many companies sell pre-made gelatin blocks that come in a variety of colors which you can use "as is." As well, many provide a clear block that you can add your own colorants to. This would be the best place for any Makeup Artist to start until you understand the processes and the medium.

Gelatin formulas are as unique as the artists that use the material; however, if you're determined, understand that whatever formula you find that works for you may not work for your friend across town. Why? Many reasons. For example, you may not buy raw materials at the same place, so the gelatin may be a little different, Or the sorbitol or glycerin may be formulated differently and your method of processing the gelatin into your mold may differ. Any or all of these things may throw a wrench into your "formula," but you'll learn this as you go.

A general place to begin would be to have on hand some gelatin, sorbitol (which increases the tear resistance while being less affected by humidity; usually sold as a 70 percent solution), and glycerin (which replaces much of the water that would be used in food formulas), along with a good scale to measure out your ingredients. These three ingredients are used in most basic formulas, and can be obtained from internet special-effects supply houses or any of the brick-and-mortar special-effects supply houses across the nation. As a side note, sorbitol is sold in two forms: a powder and a liquid. The liquid is the sorbitol already in solution, and it's the form I like better for its ease of use. The liquid is usually sold as a 70 percent solution.

Reiterating and many words of caution: ingredients are not necessarily the same from vendor to vendor. The supply of gelatin, the mix of sorbitol, the glycerin—can all vary. I can't urge you enough to make a chart of your ingredients and procedures, and to write down everything—including proportions of ingredients, time of day, time of year, weather conditions, type and wattage of microwave. All these things can have an effect on the end result. The object of all this work is to create a batch size that works for the appliance you're making— let's say, a prosthetic nose.

Gelatin, like a lot of makeup processes, came from many artists and many years of contribution and sharing their knowledge with each other. Much of what is outlined here is from the contributions of Dick Smith and Kevin Haney, who did a great deal of experimentation early on, with many successes and failures that many people today take for granted. It's not an exact science, and as an artist you can be surprised by all kinds of problems, usually at the wrong time. There is no shortcut to experimentation and experience. Keep a record of each formula, and network as much as possible.

Here is a starter formula: to 20 grams of gelatin, add 40 grams of sorbitol (70 percent solution) and 40 grams of glycerin. Other ingredients to consider by testing their effect on the finished appliance: water, zinc oxide, face powders, flocking, pigments,

CAUTION: Pigments should be FDA approved for use in cosmetics. Pigments from an art-supply house may not be suitable for cosmetic use—so don't use them! Safety is your responsibility.

Heating the Gelatin
Melting the gelatin into a liquid is necessary to both homogenize the mixture and break down the powdered gelatin so that it can be poured and molded. Usually this is done in a microwave for both convenience and speed. CAUTION: hot melted gelatin is dangerous, and can blister and severely burn your skin. So be extremely cautious, and protect yourself with both gloves and goggles.

Microwaves come in different wattages, so a setting of #4 for 15 seconds on one machine is not the same as #4 on another machine. Read the ratings, usually written on the back of the appliance somewhere, and write this information down.

A double boiler can also be used, but will take a bit more time. Remember to put your gelatin into a metal bowl or container, and place it into the water of the lower boiler. Do not use bare hands—it will burn you. Instead, use gloves for hot work, or a long gripping tool (pliers) to place and remove your container of melted gelatin. If you allow gelatin to boil with either method, the gelatin will break down, making it useless. So don't burn it. Allow your gelatin appliance to cool in the mold. Most artists will put the mold in a refrigerator (not the freezer) to speed up the process.

Molding Gelatin

UltraCal 30 Molds are the best place to begin because they are economical, and many people are still using them today. For the advanced user, Epoxical gives a better release and won't break down as easily. But it is more expensive, and needs more time and skill to make. Silicone molds are also used, so there are a variety of techniques to choose from. All have advantages and disadvantages, as with any material—you just have to find what fits your situation, pocketbook, and skill level.

Keep in mind that your molds should be kept warm. A cold mold will solidify your gelatin before it can flow into all the areas you require. It's also best to fill your molds with the negative side down, placing your positive

side into it. You will probably have to vent your mold to eliminate voids, air traps, or to prevent hydraulic back pressure from squashing your mold's halves together. Many Makeup Artists use a sealing coat on their UltraCal molds, but some do not. Some use a thin film of Vaseline for a mold release. Others may use PAM cooking spray or Epoxy Parfilm.

Assuming that you've flashed your mold as you would for a foam latex appliance, powder the gelatin as you remove it from the mold. Use no-color powder, talc, or cornstarch. Leave any flashing on the piece after removing it from the mold. This will be a great help in maneuvering the gelatin and handling the piece for application. Gelatin appliances should be kept on a form to keep them from losing their shape, so have either a vacuform copy of the positive or just a plaster copy. Remember to clean the finished pieces thoroughly with alcohol or acetone before application.

What your makeup kit should contain for gelatin applications:

Acetone

Brushes

Sponges

Green Marble Sealer

Pros-Aide

Witch hazel

No-color powder

Skin Illustrator

Prepping the Appliance:
1. Flip over the wound so the bottom side is up.

2. Clean the gelatin piece with acetone using a brush or sponge.

3. Let dry thoroughly.

4. Lay flat on underside, then apply two to three layers of Green Marble, drying each layer.

Applying the Gelatin Piece:

1. Cleanse (using toner) the area of the face or body that the gelatin piece is being applied to.

2. Fit the gelatin appliance to its intended position; in this case around the jawline (Figure 11.33).

3. Lift areas of the appliance, and apply Pros-Aide with a sponge (Figure 11.34). Allow to dry most of the way clear. Press into place. It's best to start from the inside pressing outward. If you fold an edge, use a little alcohol on a brush, and lift the edge to replace it correctly.

4. Have chin slightly down, and attach one side at a time (Figure 11.35).

5. Take flash off with witch hazel (Figure 11.36).

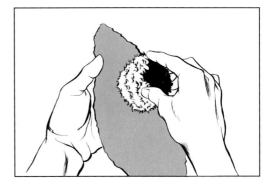

FIGURE 11-34: STEP 2: LIFT APPLIANCE AND APPLY PROS-AIDE (ROBERT ILLUSTRATIONS)

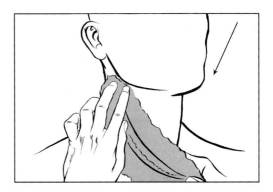

FIGURE 11-35: STEP 3: CHIN SLIGHTLY DOWN AND ATTACHING SIDE (ROBERT ILLUSTRATIONS)

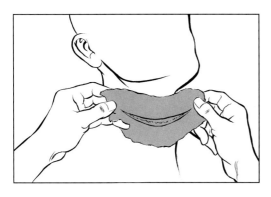

FIGURE 11-33: STEP 1: GELATIN APPLIANCE UNDER JAW LINE (ROBERT ILLUSTRATIONS)

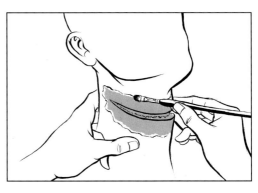

FIGURE 11-36: STEP 4: TAKING FLASH OFF WITH WITCH HAZEL (ROBERT ILLUSTRATIONS)

6. Gently blend edges with witch hazel—it's easy to overdo this step and dig a hole in your appliance edge.

7. Blend the edges with stipple sponge and Pros-Aide (Figure 11.37).

8. Apply Pros-Aide all over the whole piece.

9. Let dry completely.

10. Use no-color powder around edges.

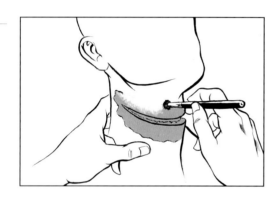

FIGURE 11-37: STEP 5: BLEND THE EDGES WITH PROS-AIDE (ROBERT ILLUSTRATIONS)

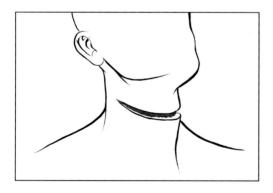

FIGURE 11-38: STEP 6: PICTURE OF FINISHED APPLIANCE (ROBERT ILLUSTRATIONS)

PAINTING GELATIN

by Kenny Myers

Now that your appliance is prepped and applied, you're ready to paint. If you've done your homework and have properly made your appliance (including the intrinsic coloring) and paid attention to translucency (the balance on intrinsic coloring to the mass of gelatin), the piece should require only a series of color stipples and wash passes using Skin Illustrator (my favorite). Taking a standard wedge of white makeup sponge and tearing holes in a random pattern on the application side of the sponge gives an excellent pattern on the appliance. Overstippling with this sponge will result in a natural soft skin pattern. Be careful not to use too opaque a mix of color, but instead, soft washes of color on the sponge.

Another favorite technique of mine is a hand-painted scumble, instead of using orange or red stipple sponges. This technique uses a round natural-bristle brush, usually around a #8, and the color is placed on the appliance in what may seem like a random pattern. However, if you closely study most skin, you'll see variations of color density and color placement everywhere. This will help "sell" your paint job! Most Makeup Artists are people watchers—not only for behaviors, but also character traits and, most of all, variations in individual colorations. This is a great pastime when sitting around a mall or at any event gathering.

This brings up an issue for those of you wishing to move into the professional end of the industry. I say this only because, if you are planning a career in the makeup industry, have a "for sure" before you have a "maybe." I've seen many Makeup Artists ignore a tried-and-true method to keep themselves in the technological limelight—only to fail miserably in the 11th hour, when it was too late to correct the situation, and get themselves a reputation for irresponsibility. This warning cuts across all material usage or processes, no matter what they are. This is an issue of responsibility for your contract with your employer.

By permission: Kevin Haney, published in Dick Smith's Advanced Professional Make-Up Course, Update #3, page 4.

Kevin also notes that sorbitol makes gelatin firmer and less elastic. At the time of *The Believers*, Kevin used a formula that included 7 grams of gelatin (275 to 300 Bloom), 38 grams glycerin, $2\frac{1}{2}$ grams water, flocking, face powder, and zinc oxide.

Internet Resources:

www.gelatin-gmia.com/index.htm

www.gelatin.co.za/

FOAM

Gil Mosko created GM Foam in 1987 to meet the needs of the Makeup Artist for a more user-friendly foam latex. Mr. Mosko has numerous awards, and has developed foam latex that has become the standard in

the industry. Gil explains how to approach working with foam latex, and how to make a gypsum mold.

MAKING A GYPSUM MOLD AND FOAM LATEX

by Gil Mosko

To make a gypsum mold, the mold maker needs to take a life cast of the actor and reproduce his or her face in gypsum (the positive mold). The most popular type of gypsum is Ultracal 30 from United States Gypsum, which is bought in 100-pound bags, or in smaller amounts from makeup-supply houses (such as Motion Picture Effects Company, in Burbank, California). The mold maker would now need to complete a sculpture on the positive. There are many types of clay to sculpt with. Plastilina is the generic name for oil-based clay that never dries out. Common types are Roma Plastilina, and Chavant Clay.

Once the sculpture is completed, it is important to use more plastilina around the outside of the sculpture to provide "relief" from the negative. In other words, by using this "flashing clay," a thin strip of contact between positive and negative is created. Having a thin strip of contact creates less surface area of contact, and therefore needs less pressure to squeeze foam out of this contact area. The finished foam piece will now have a very thin edge, which is most desirable for the Makeup Artist who is applying the appliance to hide in the final makeup application. The finished sculpture, complete with its flashing and setter points of contact (to prevent rocking), is now sprayed with Krylon Crystal Clear Acrylic Spray. This creates a barrier that prevents the positive and negative from sticking to each other during the molding process. Many mold makers also use a very light spray of MR 1500 (spray Vaseline) or Parfilm spray.

The simplest form of foam mold is the two-piece squash mold. It has a simple positive, free from undercuts. To match it, there is a one-piece negative, containing all the information from the original sculpture, but in the reverse, or negative. These two mold pieces fit together intimately. The mold-making steps are simply put: make a wet clay floor and walls around the sculpture, which sits on the mold positive; splash a coat of wet gypsum; add a second splash coat, hemp or burlap coats, and a finishing coat; including three feet.

Our lab has a steadfast rule: "Feet on every mold." Having little feet on the negative means that the mold will sit in a stable manner on the table, without rolling or rocking. This will enable the user to adjust the mold strap without having the resistance of the mold sitting on the strap. This is especially helpful in light of having a full foam injector and many molds to fill. The user can save precious seconds by not having to fiddle with mold straps that are rubbing against the bottom of the negative mold.

The most popular form of gypsum for these molds is Ultracal 30, from United States Gypsum. Although many people use burlap as a mold-strengthening fiber, we prefer using hemp fiber. The simple reason is that hemp has many more fibers per inch than

burlap, and the number of fibers adds to the strength of the mold. Once the mold is finished, it is always best if you have the time to allow the mold to sit overnight before opening it. GM Foam likes to heat the mold to about 120 degrees Fahrenheit, so the plastilina inside will be softened. In this way, the positive and negative can be separated with far less resistance from the rock-hard, cold plastilina.

In extreme cases, preheating before opening a mold will actually save the interior of the negative, which would otherwise be chipped and broken by the hard, cold plastilina. After opening the two mold halves (positive and negative), all of the plastilina must be carefully removed. Use wooden tools to scrape away the plastilina. Never use metal tools, which will scratch the interior of a mold. When the mold is fairly clean, it is time to scrub the interior with 99 percent isopropyl alcohol with a chip brush. This will wash out any remaining plastilina residue and oil. Your mold is now ready to be prepped for foam use.

New damp molds should be sealed before attempting to run foam in them. Use a thin solution of Johnson's Paste Wax, thinned with 99 percent isopropyl alcohol. The ratio is about 4 to 5 parts alcohol to 1 part wax. Mix well, then strain out the lumps through cheesecloth or window screen. Paint this "Alco wax" into both sides of the mold, all over the interior. Mop up any pools, and place the mold in front of a fan to dry. After the alcohol has evaporated, repeat this sealing process. It is always wise to bake out wet molds at this point. A convection oven works much better than a plain oven that does not have circulating air. We bake out molds at 140° Fahrenheit, but many of our friends use temperatures as high as 180°F. The moisture will stay in the mold for much longer than you think. It often takes a minimum of six hours to truly bake a mold.

After baking the empty mold, a third painting of Alco wax is done. When that is dry, the interior mold surface can be brushed out with a chip brush, or polished with a towel. This will make the surface shine. Use GM Foam Mold Release around all of the edges, where the mold pieces contact each other. Just paint a very thin layer of the white GM Release all around the perimeter of the piece, and let dry to white film. Your mold is now ready to be used with foam.

STEPS TO MOLD MAKING:

1. Little feet (Figure 11.39).

2. Little feet (Figure 11.40).

3. Sculpture (Figure 11.41).

4. Clay walls (Figure 11.42).

5. First splash coat (Figure 11.43).

6. Second splash coat (Figure 11.44).

7. Hemp coat (Figure 11.45).

8. Finished coat (Figure 11.46).

9. Two pieces (Figure 11.47)

FOAM MOLDS

All of GM Foam's latex kits come with excellent instruction sheets. For this

FIGURE 11-40: 2ND LITTLE FEET

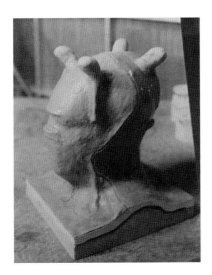

FIGURE 11-39: 1ST LITTLE FEET

FIGURE 11-41: SCULPTURE

FIGURE 11-42: CLAY WALLS

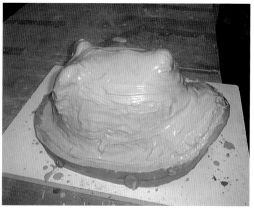

FIGURE 11-45: HEMP COAT

FIGURE 11-43: SPLASH COAT

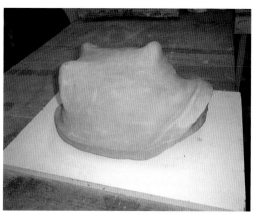

FIGURE 11-46: FINISHED COAT

FIGURE 11-44: SECOND SPLASH COAT

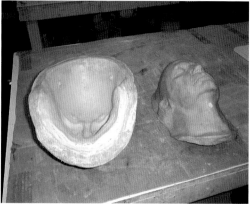

FIGURE 11-47: TWO PIECES

illustration, let it suffice to say that liquid latex and other ingredients are weighed into the mixer bowl. The mixer is turned on low for a minute to mix all the ingredients, and then turned to a high speed to whip the foam to a desired volume, usually four to five times the original volume. When the foam reaches this height, the mixer is turned down to a lower speed to pop large bubbles and "refine" the foam. All the while, ammonia is escaping from the mixer bowl. As a function of this ammonia loss, the foam will have a steady drop in pH. When a certain point is reached (usually pH 10.4), the user carefully pours in a preweighed amount of gelling agent. This begins an acid-producing reaction in the foam, which will eventually coagulate into a solid mass, or "gel." Before the foam actually gels, the user will have ample time to fill the foam molds and close them. It is important to gel the foam before putting it into an oven to cure, because ungelled foam will collapse if it feels the heat of the oven. Cells will start popping, and the resulting foam will look like Swiss cheese.

Curing the foam will cause the rubber molecules to cross-link, or "vulcanize." This transforms the raw foam into a springy sponge. Most small appliance molds will need three to three-and-a-half hours in the oven at 185° Fahrenheit. Then the molds are cooled slowly to a comfortable temperature for handling. When removed from the oven, the two mold halves are pried apart, and the resulting foam piece is removed, taking great care not to tear it during removal from the mold.

PRO TIP
DO NOT USE YOUR HOUSEHOLD COOKING OVEN FOR FOAM USE!

Please keep in mind that during the curing process, toxic vapors are given off, which will poison your oven for food use.

It is recommended that you wash the completed foam pieces in warm water and a few drops of baby shampoo, or a few spoonfuls of Simple Green. Then the pieces are gently rinsed, pressed between two towels, and placed on a form that keeps the natural curve of the piece intact. Never wring a piece of foam. If the foam is not allowed to dry in its own natural shape, it will "take a set" from any wrinkles or folds. These set-in flaws will almost always be permanent, ruining the piece, so please be careful to always store foam pieces in their natural curvature.

For long-term storage, foam pieces should be powdered, then sealed into plastic bags or airtight food containers. If kept in airtight containers, away from light, foam pieces can be successfully stored for years.

A WORD ABOUT THE STATE OF LATEX IN THE WORLD

All foam latex systems are a combination of natural latex (concentrated sap of rubber trees), a soap to make the foam whip up to desired volume (foaming agent), a vulcanizer (curing agent), and a coagulant (gelling agent). Some of the ingredients are extremely safe, such as the foaming agent, and others are toxic. Both the curing agent and the gelling agent are poisonous. Therefore, the entire system should be treated with respect, and basic safety precautions should be used. It is important to note the following: Up until last year, there was one major plantation in Indonesia that manufactured natural creamed latex. Their largest customer was an elastic-thread manufacturer. When the thread manufacturer went out of business, the rubber plantation chose to discontinue the production of natural creamed latex. Several companies have begun making a replacement product. This new product is concentrated centrifuged latex. Normally, centrifuged latex has a solids content of 60 percent, which is too low for our type of foam making. But now the new product being produced makes this centrifuged latex about 67 to 68 percent, which is perfect for making foam. To my knowledge, all the major foam companies are using this evaporated centrifuged latex.

At GM Foam, we still believe in natural creamed latex. Through difficult dealings, we have contracted a plantation in another part of the world to start manufacturing the original type of creamed latex for us. We believe the physical properties of this type of latex to be superior to the evaporated centrifuged latex. Remember that the centrifuged rubber has been exposed to heat for hours. The latex in the huge drums turns to a thick glop. All of the ammonia preservative has long gone, and we believe that oxidation is occurring during this process. Of course, ammonia is added back into the latex before it is sold, but in the time the latex was a thick paste, it lost some

of its physical characteristics, due to oxidation of the evaporating process. Our new creamed latex is as good as anything we have seen in the past 20 years. When we see cell structure that is strong and resistant to breakdown, and a smooth, shiny surface on gelled foam, we know that our rubber is performing the way it did back in the 1980s, when we started. Creamed latex is back, and we have it!

SAFETY:

1. Read the instructions before starting. Refer to the material safety data sheet (MSDS) for more information.

2. Have adequate ventilation to remove ammonia fumes.

3. Wear safety goggles and gloves when working with foam.

4. Do not let foam components come into contact with skin. If this happens, wash with soap and water as soon as possible. Clean up spills.

5. Wash your hands after working with foam. Never eat, drink, or smoke without washing first.

6. Anyone working with foam latex should keep a set of material safety data sheets nearby in case of emergency.

GM FOAM WARNING: Never use a household oven for curing foam. Fumes given off by curing foam are toxic for food use. Keep these and all chemicals out of reach of children and pets.

PREPPING ULTRACAL 30 AND OTHER STONE MOLDS

New, damp molds should be sealed with wax before applying GM Foam Mold release. An effective wax sealer can be made using Johnson's Paste Wax (or any carnauba wax) that has been thinned with 99 percent isopropyl alcohol. We use a ration of 4 parts alcohol to 1 part wax.

Liquid latex and other ingredients are weighed and placed in a mixer bowl. The foam is now whipped at high speed, until it rises like whipped cream. When the desired height is reached, the mixer speed is turned down, and the foam is refined to make the bubbles or cells smaller. This also allows the ammonia content of the foam to decrease. At just the right time, gelling agent is added to the slow-turning mixer. After about two minutes of slow blending, the mixer is turned off, and the foam is poured into the negative mold. The positive is carefully placed on top of the negative. Now pressure is applied to squeeze the two mold pieces together. With small molds, simply pressing with the hands will suffice. Larger molds require mold straps to create a good pressing action. Often the negative requires a wooden board to be placed on it and then be strapped. This increases the leverage of the strap, and gives a greater squeezing action.

FILLING MOLDS

Curing

Once the foam has gelled, in a few minutes the mold can be placed into the oven for curing. During this process, vulcanization occurs. The latex molecules chemically cross-link, and give the foam piece a memory. Once demolded, the foam will spring back into shape after being pressed.

Demolding

Specific instruction and product knowledge can be acquired by contacting GM Foam, Inc., directly: (818) 908-1087.

HOW TO PAINT FOAM APPLIANCES

by Gil Mosko

The gluing of a foam appliance is more or less a mechanical process. There are many different adhesives, but an appliance is built to sit on the face or body in one specific way, and is never stretched. Let us assume that your appliance is glued to the face, and it is time to paint. The goal of course, is to make the paint job not only look like the surrounding skin, but to also make an opaque medium appear translucent. This is achieved by building up layers of thin wash of color, so you can see through the layers and see depth.

We all learn by watching other artists. In my case, the truth is that the very gifted artist Greg Cannom had me visit his lab, along with my model, and literally showed me how he painted a bald cap. This was during the period in the '80s when I was studying for my union exam. I applied a bald cap to my model, and Greg painted it. That simple act of generosity has, since that day, changed the way I look at painting.

Everyone has their own style. Todd McIntosh begins with a base coat of reddish color, and paints everything over the red. This lets the painting have the feel that there is blood under the skin, and you can barely see it, once again creating depth. I like to use a base coat of paint that closely resembles the actor's or actress' skin. I use full-strength Pax Paint (a term coined by our dean of makeup, Dick Smith). I might add that GM Foam, Inc., has a complete line of Pax Paints in two palettes: Dark flesh tones, and Light flesh tones. Each palette also has a red appropriate to the other colors. Once the piece is painted, I gently feather a very thin layer of the base coat onto the skin, using a white makeup sponge. From this point on, I use what artists call "scumble sponges." Take a white makeup sponge, hold it in both hands, and pull until it breaks into two pieces. This edge is then picked at with your fingernails, until little holes have been picked away. The sponge is now a stamp of sorts, and can be used to create a mottled surface.

PAINTING STEPS:

1. After the full-strength base coat, I never again use full-strength Pax Paints. I thin them with water until they are mere washes of color.

2. After the base color, I paint a thin coat of red by dabbing the scumble sponge, constantly turning it as I dab, so the pattern of the sponge cannot be seen repeating itself. I dry each coat after it is applied.

3. After the red, use a shade one or two shades lighter than the base.

4. Next, use a color that is two shades darker than the base.

5. Then I use greens and blues.

6. Finally, a last coat of the original base as a wash over everything.

7. Once all the Pax colors are dry, I like to use a thin layer of RCMA Appliance Foundation that matches my base color. Incidentally, my Pax colors are keyed into the RCMA color scheme, with such colors as Olive 1, Shinto 2, and so on, so when you are ready to harmonize all of your Pax layers, you just smudge a little RCMA over the Pax Paints, in the same shade as your base coat. If you use a thin enough layer, it will not hide all of your hard work, and also it will actually bite into the Pax Paint, making the use of powder unnecessary.

8. If there is more shine than you desire, you can use Origins, Zero Oil. Use this product in a sweeping motion. Do not use a stipple technique, or it will dry in little white spots.

9. Finally, if you have the time, you can paint freckles and blemishes, either with greasepaints, or aqua colors.

I can tell you in all candor that there is a point, if you are lucky, when the paint job ceases to be layers of paint, and suddenly becomes skin. For a Makeup Artist, I can think of no greater thrill than to have an appliance painted so accurately and artistically that one cannot distinguish it from the surrounding skin. And believe me, the Director and the Cinematographer will notice.

PRO TIP

As with anything else, this technique requires practice. What I wish for the readers is that you have a good time learning these techniques, and someday do a makeup that is so flawless that you earn the respect of your peers.

—Gil Mosko

BLOOD

There will be many times in your career when you will need to create blood effects. What you use and when to use it will have a big impact on how successful the outcome will be. When a scene requires the use of artificial blood, there are many departments that are involved in creating a realistic effect. In some cases, you will need to camera test the color of your artificial blood. Some blood products will register too dark or too bright under certain lighting and film-processing conditions. These situations are classic examples of working with other departments on a film or television set. You will need to coordinate with the Costume Department, the Prop Department, the Special Effects Department, and, in some situations, the Stunt Coordinator. Discussions about the blood effects start during the prep with the Director. Then, at the production meeting, the First Assistant Director will address any issues, with all departments present and having input.

After the production meeting, there are sidebar meetings with the various departments, at an agreed-upon time, to further discuss the issues.

PRO TIP

Sidebar meetings provide excellent opportunities for fine-tuning conversations and designs with other departments involved, and not subjecting departments that are not involved to a long discussion.

The blood products that the Makeup Artist chooses should be color checked with the Prop Department and Special Effects so that the color of blood will be consistent. A sample of the blood product you have chosen should be given to the Costume Department, to ensure that it is washable and to check for stain factor. The Prop Department and the Art Department will also need to know the products, particularly how to clean the blood products off props and how to remove the blood from the set. If the props or the sets are expensive and cannot be damaged or stained, this will be discussed in the production meeting, and will affect your product choice. In some situations, the Makeup Department will provide the blood products for other departments (such as the Costume Department), or will give the other departments involved the name of the blood product and where to purchase it. If the Makeup Department does purchase products for other departments, just note on the invoice or receipt showing which department it is going to, so that the Accounting Department is able to allocate the cost to that department. Doing so will keep the makeup budget intact.

If you do not coordinate with others, there will be no continuity in the color or texture of the blood, as well as leading to confusion among departments on the set. These are moments in production and on-set when everyone works together to help each other out to achieve the desired effect. Before we talk about choosing the right blood products to use, it is a good idea to understand how blood functions in the human body.

What Is Blood?

The human body has about five liters of blood. Blood transports oxygen from the lungs to body tissue, and then transports carbon dioxide from body tissue to the lungs. Blood contains cells and is about 55 percent plasma. Plasma is a liquid and contains 90 percent water. Plasma is a vehicle for blood cells and platelets. Plasma also functions as a carrier of minerals, potassium, and antibodies. Red blood cells also keep blood clean and deliver oxygen throughout the body. Hemoglobin is a protein that is red in color. Blood is constantly recirculated throughout the body. White blood cells are there to fight off infections or germs. Blood platelets are also found in blood. Platelets help to block blood flow around wounds. Clots can form in blood. For example scabs are clots found on the outside of the body, whereas bruises are clots formed inside the body. Clots that are dangerous form inside blood vessels.

How to Choose

You will need to know the answers to a few questions before making any choices on what products to use and how the blood should look. Start with how the script reads. The scene description will get you started with a description of what the action is. Car accident, fight, murder, crime scene, gunshot, bloody nose, illness or death, and cause of death.

- Is there a written description of what it looks like?

- Where is the blood coming from, and why?

- What is the medical implication?

- What does the trauma look like in real life?

- What happens to the texture of the skin?

After reading the script, research and think about how to achieve wounds to match the action. This is one example of using your knowledge of the body, and medical resource books. If the wounds are extensive, consult with a medical doctor. An emergency-room doctor is always very helpful in researching wounds and trauma to the body. Be organized in your questions when consulting with a doctor. Their time is limited, but they are normally happy to help. Most of the time, you will have to schedule an appointment, either over the phone or at the office. If you need medical slides, you will have to go to the office.

Medical slides and photos are protected for privacy reasons, therefore you will need to obtain special permission to access them, as well as a designated area within the doctor's office where you can view them in privacy. Not only are doctors great resources for wounds, but also for all illnesses, diseases, and death, including how long it takes to die from certain diseases or wounds.

If you can answer these questions before meeting with the Director, you will be able to bring ideas to the discussion of how to achieve the desired effect. After reading the script and doing preliminary research, meet with the Director to discuss what he or she wants. Your Director will have a visual idea of what the scene or action should look like. The Director might also want you to show research on the type of wounds that are required to match the action. In most cases, the Producers will want to be involved in discussions. Producers will also have a say in how much blood is used. This is for reasons related to film and television rating issues, as well as creative choice. There will be jobs where you will have a meeting with the Director before reading the script. This could be during the job interview. They will be looking for how you would achieve certain effects. Ask questions about the action and story line, and what they want— or do not want—it to look like. In some cases, the Director will not know what he or she wants, but they will know exactly what they do *not* want.

MEDICAL DESCRIPTIONS

Busted Eye: Bruising, swelling, an open cut often seen if the person has been in a fight. A freshly bruised eye has just happened and is black and blue in color. A days-old eye injury will be green and yellow in color. This wound effect could be used for many different situations.

Abrasion Wound: Abrasions are surface skin lesions, such as scratches or small cuts, where the skin has been scraped. There is usually no need for stitches to close the wound.

Animal Bites: Animal or people bites are laceration wounds where the skin is torn.

Stab Wounds: Stab wounds or penetrating stab wounds are deep, and often fatal because of the harm done to vital organs.

Broken or Fractured Nose: When the nose has been broken, there will be swelling and bruising. There is also a good chance of the nose becoming deformed. You can also experience eye hemorrhaging and bruising around both eyes, as well as nosebleeds.

Broken Jaw: This is a serious wound for several reasons. The swelling of the tongue can affect the breathing. With facial swelling and bruising, there is a strong possibility of lacerations in the mouth. Blood from these lacerations can cause dangerous choking.

Compound Fractures: There is a big concern with compound fractures that a blood or nerve vessel could be injured. Fractures of this nature leave the bone exposed due to skin lacerations.

Hemorrhaging in the Eye: Same as the bruise, but located in the eye. Blood vessels that have broken in the eye area become trapped under the corona and give the eye a bright red stain effect. As the bruise starts to heal, the area will develop a yellow greenish tone.

Burns:

First Degree: Burns that affect the outer layer of the skin. First-degree burns are red with swelling and pain.

Second Degree: Burns that affect both the outer and under layer of skin. These burns cause pain, redness, and blistering.

Third Degree: Burns that affect deeper tissues, resulting in white, blackened, or charred skin that causes numbness.

Airway Burns: These burns can occur when inhaling smoke, steam, or toxic fumes. Symptoms to watch out for are burned lips, burns on head, face, or neck. Eyebrows and hair can be singed. Dark mucus can occur.

Thermal Burns: These burns can occur when scalding liquids, radiation, or flames or hot items come into contact with skin. Symptoms are blisters, peeling skin, red skin, shock, swelling, white or charred skin.

Gunshot Wounds: Your wound size will depend on the caliber of the gun and the shooting distance. The entrance wound is cleaner than the exit wound. The entrance wound is smaller in diameter, with burned edges of skin at the bullet entrance. The exit wound is larger and messier, with the greatest amount of blood and body matter dispersed outward.

WHAT TO USE

Ken Diaz knows the importance of realistic blood. Finding nothing on the market that worked under the many different shooting conditions, he created his own. Ken:

"There always are several factors to take into consideration when creating a makeup. First, you need to determine what type of wound you are creating. Does the wound have arterial or vascular bleeding? With arterial bleeding, the blood is oxygen enriched and bright in color. With vascular bleeding, the blood is oxygen depleted and dark in color. How old is the wound? Is the blood dry or starting to dry? Many times you will have a combination of all three types of blood in one makeup. For example, the center of the wound may have bright, oxygen-enriched blood. As you move away from the center of the wound, the blood would become oxygen depleted and darker. As you move to the outside edges or on smudges, the blood would be dry or starting to dry. Weather elements and on-set conditions can also affect the wound. Is the actor sweating? Is it so cold that the blood is freezing? Is it raining out so the blood could wash away? To get really good at dressing blood to wounds, you need to start thinking organically. Do your research and study medical books. Watch and record true-life medical-emergency shows, boxing, and full-contact matches. Take photos of real-life injuries."

The following are blood conditions and what to use.

Lighting Conditions

When filming in low light, dark-colored bloods will not show up. You need to use a brighter-colored blood for it to be visible. Also use bright-colored blood when applying the blood to any dark surface. The opposite is true when working with light-colored surfaces. Dark-colored blood looks much more realistic on white porcelain than does bright-colored blood.

Blood Viscosity

There are now many blood products available that come in a variety of viscosities or thicknesses.

Heavy: A very heavy or paste consistency blood (such as K.D. 151 Blood Jam) is used when a nonflowing blood is needed. This type of blood can be applied with a dental spatula, and works very well when used at the base of cuts. You can create very realistic scratches with this type of paste-consistency blood when applied with a coarse stipple sponge.

Less Heavy: A slightly lighter-viscosity blood (such as K.D. 151 Blood Jelly) should be used when a slow-moving blood is desired to help maintain the continuity of a bleeding wound from take to take.

Medium: Medium-viscosity bloods are the consistency of syrup. These are probably the most commonly used type of blood. Some of these bloods have been formulated for specific uses.

Light: Light-viscosity bloods (such as K.D. 151 Pumping Blood) can be used when matching the viscosity of real blood. Also are good to use when pumping blood through small-diameter tubing.

To create a thinner, realistic dry or drying blood, you need to use a medium-viscosity drying blood (such as K.D. 151 Drying Blood Syrup). When a thick, realistically dry or drying blood is required, you need to use a heavy-viscosity drying blood (such as K.D. 151 Drying Blood Jelly).

When applying blood over prosthetic appliances, you will need a blood that contains a wetting agent (such as K.D. 151 Flowing Blood). Blood that contains a wetting agent will help keep the blood from beading up over slick surfaces.

Working outside with conditions that could be hot, cold, or windy, theatrical bloods tend to have an unrealistic skin that forms on the surface. Applying a little bit of glycerin over the top of the blood keeps it looking fresh and wet. To help avoid this problem, you can use a blood that already contains a glycerin base (such as K.D. 151 Stay Wet Blood).

Mouth Blood

Blood that runs into the mouth should be specially formulated (such as K.D. 151 Mouth Blood).

PRO TIP

Always keep a small can of shaving cream in your kit on-set. Shaving cream removes stains on the skin ranging from blood to permanent markers. It is fast and easy.

There are products out there now that make all the difference in continuity and how a blood effect can be used, without the mess involved with cleanup. Skin Illustrator, developed by award-winning Makeup Artist Kenny Myers, is a water- and abrasion-resistant, alcohol-activated makeup that is available in palettes and liquids. Makeup products such as Skin Illustrator are a must-have in your makeup kit. Throughout the book, we mention different Skin Illustrator palettes, and for now, we'll talk about the Skin Illustrator FX Palette and a few ways it is used in blood effects (Figure 11.48).

The FX Palette was designed for just about any injury or illness imaginable. The Skin

FIGURE 11-48: SKIN ILLUSTRATOR FX PALETTE

FIGURE 11-49: SKIN ILLUSTRATOR FLESH TONE PALETTE

Illustrator FX Palette can simulate first-, second-, and third-degree burns; cuts; scrapes; scabs; and bruises. The FX Palette seamlessly integrates with the flesh-tone palette to create varying degrees of injuries and illnesses (Figure 11.49).

Blood tone is a realistic natural blood color that can be easily altered to a deeper, more theatrical color blood with the addition of ultra blue.

Skin Illustrators are made to mix. If you mix yellow and blue, you will produce a different green than what is already in the palette. Remember color mixing? Refer to the color wheel if you need to refresh your memory. Use the burnt orange to provide a rust tone. The aged blood is a mid-ground aged blood that is not too blue or purple.

By taking the aged blood and adding it to any of the other colors in the palette, you will get a whole new range of color.

For Continuity: If you have an actor with dripping blood, and you'll need to do the shot over and over again, you'll want to keep track of exactly where you applied the blood the first time or at the beginning of the take. Between each shot, there will be a few moments to clean up the actor so you can start fresh again.

PRO TIP

Know what part of the scene each take starts from in order to match the blood, and any changes of the blood, during filming. Sometimes there is a progression to the blood. You will need to take a continuity photo at the beginning of the take and at the end of the take.

If you have laid down blood with Skin Illustrator FX color before the wet blood, you have safeguarded exactly where the wet blood needs to go. If, during shooting, the blood lifts, Skin Illustrator colors will keep the wound looking bloody, even without the wet blood or little of it. Skin Illustrator is also a good way to paint blood on a wound when you don't want to get blood on the wardrobe. For example: a female stunt driver had to match the principal actress. The stuntwoman's arm would be in the shot for a long stretch of time. The principal actress did have wet blood applied to the wound, and the Costume Designer did cut the wardrobe to expose the wound.

Shooting the stuntwoman to match became an issue when wet blood was to be applied. The Costume Designer did not like the idea of the mess that wet blood would make, and the amount of wardrobe that would be used. The solution was to use blood trails made of Skin Illustrator colors, which, on camera, looked just like real blood. Add a little shine on top of the Illustrator color with KY Jelly. This is a product that will maintain its shine without lifting.

Everyone was happy with the results of not having to use wet blood on the stunt driver. Saves you from having to run in over and over again to clean and reapply blood. With this in mind, you can see why distance shots, working in the rain or elements outside, painting your wound for a more three-dimensional look, and keeping continuity are all good reasons to use Skin Illustrator FX Palettes in your work.

PRO TIP

Other products you can use to get the same effect as FX Skin Illustrator: Stacolor and Reel Color.

TEMPORARY TATTOOS

by Christien Tinsley, creator of
Tinsley Transfers, Inc.

When approaching a tattoo job, research is always important. You have to consider the character and the character history and time line to where and when they got the tattoo.

Also, with so many themes and mixture of themes, having a good direction or vision

from the Director can be helpful in scaling down the possibilities. Let's not forget that tattoos are symbols and representations sometimes of more than just expressive art. Sometimes there are meanings with deep ties to them, and the last thing you want to do is have your actor with something that is offensive or says something about himself that isn't in the character's description. Tattoo books, magazines, tattoo parlors, photography books, and the internet are all good sources to find thousands of ideas.

Today, in feature films and TV, the techniques of HD, bluescreen, and greenscreen are being more commonly used. The trick to a good makeup, tattoo, or prosthetic is to make it look real. If you can fool the eye standing two feet away, you will most likely fool the camera. Don't rely on video monitors—they can be misleading and not a true image for corrections.

Make sure you have a good relationship with the Director of Photography. In HD cases, there are digital DPs (not Video Assistants) monitoring the recording. Go to dailies. Ask to see them even if they give you a DVD copy. Know what you are looking at. Find out from the Director or DP how they are processing the film in post, so you can be aware if you need to punch up certain colors. There are no disclaimers in film and television for a Makeup Artist.

PREPPING THE SKIN

Depending on what approach you will take for tattoo applications, you will commonly prep the skin by making sure it is free of hair, oils, and dirt. Hair can be tricky if applying a tattoo decal because the hair won't allow full contact of image to the skin. If you are drawing the tattoo on, hair can just be in the way. Try to remove hair if at all possible. After hair is no longer an issue, prep the skin by cleaning it with an astringent of your choice. This removes dirt and oil, and slightly dries the skin for better adhesion of paint or adhesive. Sometimes a layer of adhesive can be applied to the skin before the tattoo, helping the adhesion of any image or ink being applied.

APPLYING THE TATTOO:

1. Lay the tattoo decal on the skin and apply water (Figure 11.50).

2. Slowly remove the paper (Figure 11.51).

3. Let dry (Figure 11.52).

4. Powder (Figure 11.53).

5. Seal the finished piece (Figure 11.54).

If you are applying tattoo decals, then you first want to cut close to your tattoo image,

and then remove the protective plastic coating. This coating protects the adhesive that has been preapplied to the tattoo images. Next, place the tattoo facedown onto the skin and press firmly over the entire surface. Apply water to the back of

FIGURE 11-51: SLOWLY REMOVING THE PAPER

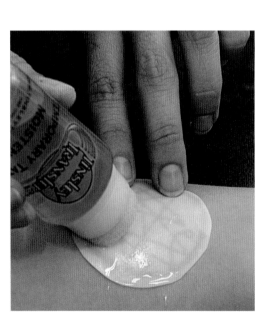

FIGURE 11-50: LAY ON SKIN AND APPLY WATER

FIGURE 11-52: LET DRY

FIGURE 11-53: POWDER

entire image. Make sure the water is completely dried, and then powder generously.

I always let the powder stay until last looks. After you are finished with the makeup, you can be sitting for hours before your first shot, and I prefer to let the powder protect the image. What I have found is that after a while, the powder falls away and absorbs with natural oils in the skin. You may find, by the time you get to shooting, that you require very little sealer. Never put oils such as glycerin on top of a wet or sweaty look. Always use a silicone- or water-based product.

APPLYING SEALER

When applying sealer, spray into a sponge and first wipe against your own hand. Then take the dampened sponge and lightly rub over the surface of the tattoo until all the powder is removed. You should in most cases not require antishine. If your image is too shiny, then a little antishine rubbed over the surface can help. Try to avoid powders.

FIGURE 11-54: SEALING FINISHED PIECE

APPLYING TATTOO PALETTE COLORS OR TATTOO INK COLORS

Flesh-colored tattoo paints painted over the surface lightly can help dull the surface and give your tattoo a more aged quality. If you need to add color or image to a transfer, then any sort of tattoo palette paint or tattoo makeup inks will work. I try to do this additional work after the tattoo has been applied and before powdering or sealing. Ideally, you have done your research and

the decal, and soak the paper. Allow this to sit for 30 seconds or so, and slowly remove the paper. After the paper is removed, wet your fingers or a sponge, and gently—without stroking the surface—press over the were lucky enough to get approval from all parties (Director, Producer, and actor) in time, and the transfer you have made should include all the aging and color you require.

MAINTAINING TATTOOS ON-SET

In order to maintain tattoos on-set, be aware. Like any makeup you do—but even more like a prosthetic makeup—things can happen. An actor sleeps hard over lunch, an actor rubs his arms on a table while eating, the scene requires actors to wrestle or sweat or run, etc. Always have backup tattoos with you, and alcohol in case you have to remove and apply a new one on-set. Do not remove with oils in the middle of the day because your next one won't stick. If it is a minor repair, have a premixed color or colors to match the image and to fill in the areas that have rubbed away. Sometimes just throw your hands up in the air, assess the shot, and say: "Hope we don't see that!" Things happen—just be resourceful and prepared.

REMOVING TATTOOS

To remove tattoos, I mix Isopropl Myristate and Super Solv 50/50, warm it up in the microwave so it is comfortable on the skin, and use a powder puff. Continue to apply remover with the powder puff, gently rubbing the area, and periodically use a dampened hot hand towel to break up the rubbing cycle. Continue this until the area is clean. Finish off with a hot towel, and then apply lotion to the area to help moisturize before the next day of shooting.

TERMS

Adhesives

Cabosil Mixed with Pros-Aide: These two mixed together form a thick paste that is often used to blend appliance edges into the skin and to repair damaged appliances. There are other usages, too numerous to mention.

Duo Adhesives: A latex-based product often used for eyelash application. Also used for fixing small areas on appliances, building small wounds directly onto the skin, blending edges, and applying jewelry or decorations to the face and body. This is one of those items you have in your kit that becomes an all-purpose product.

Liquid Latex: Also in clear. Used for many different reasons. Liquid Latex can be used to build appliances directly onto the skin, blend the edges of appliances, pour or paint or slush into molds. Is also used as a skin for some foams.

Prosthetic Adhesives: Pros-Aide, for example, is a Prosthetic Adhesive that has many other uses. You can find Pros-Aide or No Tack Pros-Aide formulas. No Tack Pros-Aide dries without a tacky surface, so the product can be used to blend edges and prepare appliances for painting. It is also used as a Pax, and seals work already done. Pros-Aide Adhesive has a milky white texture, a strong hold, dries clear, is waterproof, and can be thinned with water or thickened, but needs a correct remover.

Resin-Based Adhesives: Spirit gum is one of the least expensive resin-based adhesives. It is easy to remove and has a medium hold.

Spirit gum does take longer to dry than other adhesives. Spirit gum is good to use for short time frames or in fashion, applying objects to the skin (beads or crystals, for example). You can find spirit gum in different formulas—regular, matte, extra matte, or extra hold. Spirit gum in matte formulas is often used for lace pieces because the adhesive dries with no shine.

Silicone Adhesive: In its raw form, silicone adhesive is composed of minerals. Silicone adhesive is also found under medical adhesives. It has a strong hold and is fast drying. Silicone adhesives in general work well on sensitive skin and are resistant to water. They are used often by Makeup Artists.

Tapes: Can be thin, wide, double sided, textured, and transparent. There are many usages for tapes found in different materials. There are medical-grade adhesive tapes; tapes to apply hairpieces; to secure bald caps; and to hide or protect small cuts, wounds, and body art on the face and body—just to name a few.

Water-Soluble Adhesive: Adhesive that is easily removed with soap and water.

Thinners
Thinners are made to dilute or thin adhesive products. Most adhesives have a matching thinner to go with their product. For example, Telesis 5 Thinner works with thinning Telesis Silicon Adhesives.

Skin Primers
Primers protect the skin from adhesives or products. They set and preserve the makeup.

Removers
Most often, to be safe, you should buy the remover that goes with the adhesive you are using. Many products are made to be used together in this way. Removers can be solvent based, alcohol based, hydrocarbon based, soap based, oil based, non-oily, made with flammable solvents or nonflammable solvents, and can be thinned with water.

There are removers that have emollients to protect the skin for drying. They can be odor free, hypoallergenic, in cream or gel form for easier use.

REFERENCES

Diaz, Ken www.kd151.com.

Haney, Kevin, published in Dick Smith's Advanced Professional Make-Up Course, Update #3, page 4.

Mosko, Gil. www.gmfoam.com.

Mungle, Matthew, WM Creations, Inc.. www.matthewwmungle.com.

Myers, Kenny. www.ppi.cc.

Tinsley, Christien, Tinsley Transfers. www.tinsleytransfers.com.

Internet Resources
www.burmanfoam.com.

www.dow.com.

www.fxwarehouse.com.

www.gelatin.co.za.

www.getspfx.com.

www.naimies.com.

www.sculpt.com.

www.smooth-on.com.

12

HOW TO BE A PRO

DAY CHECKING: FILM AND TELEVISION INDUSTRY

Sometimes Makeup Artists work on a day-to-day basis; this is known as day checking. Working as a daily hire takes a certain amount of responsibility and know-how. If you are someone who is talented plus have the ability to think on your feet and are a good observer, you'll go far. Department heads look for someone they can trust on-set, to do the job asked and not use the time at work to advance your own career. There is a real need for good daily hires, or Day Checkers. Once you have worked with someone a number of times, you'll get an idea of how the department heads run their Makeup Department. No matter how chummy and laid back it might seem, try to remember that you are at work and this is a real job. Don't allow yourself to be careless with what you say and too chatty with the Makeup Artists in the main trailer. One of the biggest mistakes a Makeup Artist can do in any situation is not follow directions! Please leave your ego out of the equation when given directions on how and what products to use for the job you are on. There have already been many decisions made by the department heads in charge about the look of the shoot. Do as you're told! On top of being called to work without much information, walking into a job that might already be in progress with a group who have already established a relationship with each other can be tough. There are ways to make sure you are on the right track. The following will help you to understand the dos and don'ts of a Day Checker for daily hire, and how to watch the set.

DAY CHECKING DOS: DAILY HIRE FOR FILM

When called in to work, ask the Production Department to fax or email you a call sheet for the day you are working (Figures 12.1 and 12.2). If you have been contacted by a department head or another Makeup Artist, be sure to get the information you need, such as a production number. Sometimes the Makeup team already working has a full plate. You can help by contacting Production yourself to let them know who you are. Inform Production that you are on-board and in what department. Production can then add you to the list of Crew members to be contacted for call times. Wait about an hour after Production wraps the night before you are to work. If you have not heard from someone by then, call to remind Production that you need a call time. Note that it is the AD's department with the help of the production department to give call times, but in some cases a member of the makeup department will make the calls.

Many times department heads will contact you to ask if you have your call times. It is a plus to say yes because that makes one less thing for the Makeup Artist to worry about. They know you will be reliable to find your way to the Makeup trailer and on time. Sometimes you can sense a crazy, hectic situation, so be proactive and get the information you need yourself to get to work the next day. Expect a call from an AD. When you do get your call sheet, read it carefully. Take mental notes on what is being shot, how many background players there are, what is the

DIRECTOR: PRODUCERS: EXEC. PRODUCER: **PROD OFFICE:** 110 LEROY STREET, 5TH FLR NEW YORK, NEW YORK 10014 **P.O. PH# 212 555 1212 FAX # 212 555 1212** Weather:	"THE DUMMY" CALL SHEET	DATE: DAY: OF CREW CALL: SHOOT CALL: SUNRISE: SUNSET:

NO FORCED CALLS OR EARLY CALLS, WITHOUT PRIOR APPROVAL OF U.P.M.

SET	SCENES	CAST	D/N	PGS	LOCATION
			TOTAL		

CAST	PART OF	MAKE-UP	SET CALL	TRANSPORTATION
#1				
#2				
#3				
#4				

ATMOSPHERE		SPECIAL INSTRUCTIONS	
SI #	RPT TO LOC @	PROPS:	
SI #			
BACKGROUND TO INCLUDE:			
		SET DRES:	
		ADD. LBR:	
		SP EQUIP:	

ADVANCE SHOOTING NOTES

DATE	SET	SCENES	CAST	D/N	PGS	LOCATION

UPM	1ST A.D.	2ND A.D.	2ND 2ND A.D.

FIGURE 12-1: CALL SHEET FRONT

"THE DUMMY"

CREW CALL: DATE:

#	STAFF & CREW	NAME	Call Time	#	STAFF & CREW	NAME	Call Time	#	STAFF & CREW	NAME	Call Time
	PRODUCTION				**MAKEUP / HAIR**				**CATERING**		
1	Director			1	Makeup Dept Head			x	Company		
1	EP/UPM			1	Key Makeup			x	Chef		
1	Prod. Supervisor			1	Makeup				Caterer		
1	1st A.D.							x	Breakfast Ready @		
1	2nd A.D.								Crew:		
1	2nd 2nd A.D.			1	Hair Dept Head				B.G.:		
1	Set P.A.			1	Key Hair			x	Lunch Ready @		
1	Set P.A.			1	Hair Stylist				Crew:		
1	Set P.A.								B.G.:		
1	Set P.A.								**SET OPERATIONS**		
1	Set P.A.							x	Craft Service		
	Addl. P.A.				**WARDROBE**						
	Addl. P.A.			1	Costume Designer						
	Addl. P.A.			1	Asst. Designer				Ready @		
	Addl. P.A.			1	Cost. Supervisor				Crew		
				1	Key Costumer				B.G.		
				1	Costumer				**ASSISTANTS**		
				1	Costumer			1	Assist to Director		O/C
1	Script Supervisor	Mariana Hellmund						1	Assist to Producer		O/C
	CAMERA							1	Assist to Producer		O/C
1	D.P.							1	Assist to Director		O/C
1	"A" Cam. Operator							1	Assist to		O/C
1	"A" Cam. 1st A.C.							1	Assist to		O/C
1	"A" Cam. 2nd A.C.										
1	Loader								**TRANSPORTATION**		
					PROPERTY			1	Transpo. Captain		O/C
1	"B" Camera Operator							1	Transpo Co- Captain		O/C
1	"B" Cam 1st AC			1	Prop Master						
1	"B" Cam 2nd AC			1	Asst. Prop Master				**VEHICLES & EQUIPMENT**		
1	Stills Photographer			1	Prop Assist				Single Trailer (s)		
	GRIPS								Prop Truck		
1	Key Grip								Grip Truck		P
1	B.B. Grip				**SET DRESSING**				Electric Truck		E
1	Dolly Grip			1	Set Decorator				Camera Truck		R
1	"B" Cam Dolly Grip			1	Leadman				Wardrobe/MU Trailer		
1	Company Grip			1	On Set Dresser				Honeywagon		T
				1	Addl On Set Dresser				2 Banger (s)		R
				1	Addl On Set Dresser				15 Pass Vans		A
									3 Banger		N
									Director's Car		S
1	Key Rigging Grip								Hair Make Up Trlr		P
1	B.B. Rigging Grip				**ART DEPARTMENT**						O
	SET LIGHTING			1	Prod. Designer						
1	Gaffer			1	Art Director				**PRODUCTION OFFICE**		
1	B.B. Electric			1	Asst. Art Director			1	Prod. Coordinator		O/C
1	Electrician			1	Art Dept. Coord.			1	A.P.O.C.		O/C
1	Electrician			1	Art Dept. P.A.			1	Prod. Secretary		O/C
1	Electrician							1	Office P.A.		O/C
1	Electrician							1	Office P.A.		O/C
1	Genny Operator							1	Offfice Intern		O/C
1	Base Camp Genny Op.										
								1	Publicist		O/C
1	Rigging Gaffer								**ACCOUNTING**		
								1	Production Acct.		O/C
					CONSTRUCTION			1	1st Assistant Acct.		O/C
				1	Construction Coord			1	2nd Asst Acct.		O/C
				1	Constuction Foreman			1	Payroll Accountant		O/C
				1	Key Carpenter						
				1	Key Const. Grip						
	SOUND & VIDEO			1	Const. Grip				**EDITORIAL**		
1	Mixer			1	Shop Electric			1	Editor		O/C
1	Boom				Shop P. A.			1	Editor		O/C
1	Cable							1	1st Assistant Editor		O/C
									LOCATIONS		
1	Video Playback							1	Location Manager		O/C
					SCENICS			1	Asst. Location Mgr		O/C
	SPECIAL EFFECTS			1	Scenic Charge			1	Locations Coord.		O/C
1	SFX Coordinator			1	Stand By Scenic			1	Location Asst.		O/C
1	SPFX							1	Location Asst.		O/C
								1	Location Asst.		O/C
								1	Location Asst.		O/C
								1	Location Asst.		O/C
	VISUAL EFFECTS							1	Locations Scout		O/C
1	VFX Supervisor				**CASTING**			1	Locations Intern		O/C
1	VFX Producer			1	Casting Director				**ADDL EQUIPMENT**		
1	VFX Coordinator			1	Casting Associate						
				1	Casting Assistant						
	MISCELLANEOUS										
1	Product Placement			1	Extras Casting						
1	Dialect Coach			1	Extras Casting Dir.						

TRANSPORTATION		DIRECTOR & CAST PICKUPS
		P/U
		P/U
		P/U

FIGURE 12-2: CALL SHEET BACK

time period, whether it day or night, interior or exterior.

Why is it important to know these things? If the weather is bad, bring the right things to wear. Are you outside all day? Be prepared to work under any weather situations and for long lengths of time. Layered clothing is a must when working outdoors; bring items such as scarves, rain boots, coats, and sweaters. Maybe your set bag needs to be plastic or covered to protect it from the rain. Should you bring an umbrella? What if you are outside all day and it is hot? Sunscreen will be a must to apply on yourself and on the actors you are working on. Hats also protect you from the sun. Sunglasses help with the glare. Working indoors can mean cramped spaces, humid air, and possible excess sweat. Indoors, you might want to stay compact and bring a small portable fan for a little airflow. How many background players are coming in? Reading this information will tell you how busy it is going to get. The call sheet will also tell you what time period the movie is in for that day. Adjust your makeup kit to what you'll need. Don't bring in natural makeup colors if you are creating 1980s characters. Use common sense. These are just a few examples of why it is important to read the call sheet and to figure out how to prepare for the day.

ON THE JOB

How to Read a Call Sheet

Reading the call sheet gives you valuable information. If you are day checking, reading what scenes are being shot, how many background artists will be working, and what parts they will be playing is important information for preparing what you will need to bring to work. The call sheet will also tell you where to go and what time to be there, who to call in cases of an emergency, and who else will be working with you. The following numbers correspond to the numbers on the call sheet and explain what they mean. A film call sheet is two sided; a commercial call sheet typically is one sided. This is a film call sheet.

- Name of the production company, their location, and phone numbers. In case there is an emergency, you can contact the Production office to find out what your call times are or where you are supposed to be.

- Names of all the Producers, Assistant Directors (ADs), Writers, and the Director. It is good to know who the ADs will be. Besides the makeup department, you will be dealing with AD department. They control the set, the schedule, and the environment on the set.

- The first time listed is the crew call. This is also called the general crew call, and is the time that most of the crew reports for work. Not the makeup department, we have a separate call time, usually much earlier. Do not confuse the crew call with the Makeup call, they are usually not the same. The second time listed is the shoot call. This is the time that production has scheduled to starting filming. Makeup call times are on the back of the sheet for film and on the front of the sheet for commercials.

- Date of the day of work. Amount of days the production has already been shooting.

This is good to know because you can judge how fresh or tired the Makeup Department might be when you first start working. The more days they have been filming the more tired!

Crew Call: the time the Crew is called into work.

Weather forecast for the day of shooting. Helps you decide what to wear to be comfortable and protected. This would also include any protection you might need for your makeup kits, or for your actors.

Closed Set: A closed set means no visitors. Please remember this rule. You are there to work. It is not a time to show your friends the set. There will be names listed for you to contact to get permission to bring someone on-set.

SC(scene): Scene numbers in the script being shot that day.

Set Description: What is being shot and what the shot looks like. If the shot is indoors or outdoors.

D/N: Day or Night. Indicates if the scene being shot is a day scene or night scene.

Pages: The number of script pages for the scene being shot.

Cast: The cast members appearing in the scene being shot.

Locations: Where the scene(s) is/are being shot.

Holding and Catering: Where the extras are being held, and where the food is located.

Total Pages: Total number of pages being shot that day.

Cast: Actors working that day.

Character(s): Name(s) of the character(s) the actor(s) will be playing. Each character is assigned a number, this number is used to show the character on the call sheet and shooting schedule.

Stat: Work status of the actor. Shows if they work that day or are on hold, or traveling or off.

Reh: Time of rehearsals for the actor(s).

H/MU: The time the actor(s) will go to Hair and Makeup.

Set Call: Time the actors are expected on set.

Remarks: What time the actors will be picked up from their hotel, or home, or if they self drive.

Atmosphere Stand-ins: How many stand-ins and background actors are working that day. Also, what characters they play.

Report: What time stand-ins and background actors report to Hair, Makeup, and Wardrobe.

Set Call: The time stand-ins and background actors report to set.

Remarks: Directions on where to report and at what time for stand-ins and background actors.

Department Requirements: Notes on what each department needs to have for scenes being worked that day. Example: Makeup Dept. blood for scene xx.

Advance Schedule: What scenes will shoot and where for the next few days.

Producers, Production Supervisor, and first AD sign off on (approve) the call sheet. Set phone number and contact in case of an emergency.

Flip side of the call sheet: All Departments and the names of the Crew members listed and their call times.

DAY CHECKING: DAILY HIRE FOR COMMERCIALS

Being called in as a daily hire for commercials is similar to film. There are a few changes that you would need to be aware of. Call sheets are not as extensive, and tend to have all information on the front, sometimes with a storyboard attached so you know how the commercial is being shot. You do not have to worry about bringing in copies of your IDs. Copies might be made for you by production, but even that might not happen. A day rate is also decided on between yourself and the Producers. What you charge is up to you, but never go below the asking rate. Remember that the less you charge, the more people perceive you as someone who is not in demand. When assisting another Makeup Artist, he or she will tell you what they have in the budget for you. Working with another pro is a good experience. Working by yourself means more responsibility, so remember to keep your rates where they should be. You'll be asking for a flat day rate, with overtime after 10 hours and a kit fee. If you are with a makeup agency, your representative will work out everything for you. After a rate is agreed upon, the agency or Producers might ask for a résumé, reel, or CD of your work. This happens mostly if you have never worked with the agency or Producers before, and they want to get an idea of what your makeup looks like in print, and who you have worked for in the past.

Makeup Kits for Day Checking

Day checking, or daily hire, means you are called in one day at a time. Even though you might get a heads-up on more days, don't count on it. Anything can happen. Although there are people who consider day checking to be the least important part of the Crew, that way of thinking is a big mistake. Department heads recognize the importance of their daily-hire Crew. In general a department head that values their crew, runs a more efficient crew and gets better results in the final outcome of the makeup look desired for the film. As a matter of fact, on a large feature film or project that Makeup Artists want to be involved with, they often work as Day Checkers. Skill is so important on this level, for often you are left alone to make your own judgment calls.

The right makeup kit for the right job is also important. If a department head has phoned ahead to recommend bringing very little or just what is needed, take heed to that request. The department head knows what is going on with their shoot. There is always time to bring in a larger makeup kit if you are hired for more days, or if you are assigned a specialized makeup procedure such as laying down sideburns for a period piece. You most likely have had conversations with the department head on any special makeup to bring with you. Every now and then, a production comes to town and the Makeup Department has not expressed to you what it is you will be doing or what to bring. Doing a little research on the production gives you a feel for the time period of the movie, and you can bring what you feel is needed.

The following Makeup Kit will cover you in all your needs as a Day Checker or union Makeup Artist (Figure 12.3). If you are working a non-union production, this same Makeup Kit would apply, but with the addition of hair products. Every Makeup Artist has their favorite products, and no one or another is wrong. The products listed below are listed because they are popular with other working Makeup Artists—we are constantly trying out or using products that have been suggested by other professionals. I would also suggest that you buy small sizes that can be refilled, or products in tubes, or use small labeled

FIGURE 12-3: A TREATMENT BAG AND FILM DAY-CHECKER BAG AND CHAIR

containers to fill with your favorite products. Remember to stay portable!

NOTE: most artists have a makeup kit or case, a makeup bag with additional supplies (including a treatment bag), a set bag or case, and a set chair. The average pieces are three. Some artists are great packers and have it down to two!

Gretchen's Treatment Products for the Treatment Bag

- Kiehl's Ultra Facial Moisturizer for all skin types
- Kiehl's Sodium PCA Oil-Free Moisturizer (for those who do not want any oil added to the surface of their skin)
- Kiehl's Cucumber Herbal Alcohol Free Toner (transfer to a smaller bottle, or use the travel size and refill from the large 16.9-ounce container when needed)
- Kiehl's Blue Astringent Herbal Lotion (transfer to a smaller bottle, or use the travel size and refill from the large 16.9-ounce container when needed)
- Kiehl's Close Shavers Shaving Formula #31-0
- Kiehl's Ultimate Brushless Shaving Cream
- Terax Body Moisturizing Shaving Cream
- Kiehl's Men's Alcohol-Free Herbal Toner
- Clinique Skin Supplies for Men, M Shave Aloe Gel
- Remington Face Shaver Pre Shave Poudre
- Kiehl's Washable Cleansing Milk for Dry, or Normal to Dry, or Sensitive skin types
- L'annine Hand and Body Crème
- Kiehl's Lip Balm #1 with Sunscreen

- Fresh Soy Face Cleanser Makeup Remover
- Lancôme Bi-Facial Double Action Eye Makeup Remover
- Evian Eau Minerale Naturelle Spray
- DHC Coenzyme Q10 Water Mist
- Travel-size container of witch hazel
- Sephora Makeup Brush Cleansing Wipes
- DHC Makeup Off Sheets
- Wet Ones Moisture Wipes Travel Pack
- Murad Day Reform Treatment (works well to apply on the skin before airbrushing)
- Sunscreen SPF 45 or higher
- Rubbing alcohol in a small bottle
- Natura Bisse Sponges
- Small, clean towels
- Eye Tees Precision Makeup Applicators
- Small scissors for cutting cuticles
- Larger scissors for all-around use
- Diamancel Nail File
- Disposable shavers
- No shred cotton pads
- Sugar-free gum or mints in a variety of flavors and brands
- Norelco trimmer
- Tissues

Set Bag

The contents of a set bag or case is an individual's preference. You can be on-set for long lengths of time, and might not be able to get back to base camp if you have forgotten an item. Also, it depends on if you are watching large background scenes or one or two individuals. Try to keep your set bag lightweight and portable for easy maneuverability while on-set. If you are shooting outdoors, be sure to check the weather conditions. You might need to use a case that is waterproof or covered if rain is expected. A hard, portable gym locker bag works well because it is compact and has a long strap for shoulder use, as well as handles for carrying. It is also waterproof, so it works well outdoors in rustic conditions that may include rain, snow, or high temperatures. Indoors or on smaller shoots, use a clear, larger set bag with long straps, and that rests close to the body. With a clear bag, the contents are readily visible, which makes it easy to find a specific product. (You'd be surprised at how hard it can be finding items when you need them fast!)

Along with the products mentioned below, a small, clear cosmetic bag containing the products you will need to use on the actor for touch-ups on-set is useful. Large freezer bags would also work. If you have several actors to watch, use individual bags marked with each actor's name so there is no sharing

PRO TIP

Makeup Artist Jenny King Turko suggests covering up your powder puff with a Kleenex tissue. After touch-ups, toss the tissue away and put a new one around the powder puff. This way, you can touch up large crowds without contaminating other people.

products between the actors. Most of all, this will keep brushes and powder puffs separate.

I usually load up three or four puffs ready to go. Bottom line is whatever works for you on deciding what products you like to use.

Gretchen's Set Bag: Contents for Film Set Day Checker

(See Fig. 12-03 for Picture of Film Day Checker Bag)

- Kleenex tissues
- Peter Thomas Roth Clinical Skin Care Max Anti Shine Mattifying Gel
- Sponges
- Powder puffs
- Wet Ones Travel Pack
- DHC Body Cleansing Cloths
- Evian Eau Mineral Spray
- Pointy Q-tips
- 1 package of disposable mascara wands
- Remington Face Saver Pre Shave
- 1 small bottle of glycerin
- 1 small pair of scissors
- Band-Aids
- Small eye pencil sharpener
- Tweezers, Laura Mercier by Tweezerman
- 1 eyedropper
- 3 Cutex Nail Polish Remover Pads
- Refresh disposable eyedrops
- Visine
- Gum and mints of choice (regular and sugar-free)
- Small Jao Antibacterial Hand Refresher

- Small Bliss Body Butter
- Small Lise Water Solution Double Instant Eye Makeup Remover
- Kiehl's Lip Balm SPF 15
- Small Kiehl's Intensive Treatment Moisturizer
- Carmex
- Small Kiel's Creamy Eye Treatment
- Andrea Eyelash Adhesive
- 2 containers of individual eyelashes in dark brown and black
- 2 eye shadow palettes with the following colors (black, dark brown, light brown, off-white, rust, gray blue, taupe); eye shadow palettes by Make Up For Ever and Viseart
- Yves Saint Laurent Touche Esclat Radiant Touch
- Lancôme Dual Finish Powder Makeup
- Natural Rice Oil Absorbing Rice Paper Tissues with Rice Powder and Bobbi Brown Blotting Papers
- No color powder pressed compact
- Peter Thomas Roth Anti-Shine
- SmashBox Compact Anti-Shine
- 1 red eye pencil
- 1 black eye pencil
- 1 menthol vapor for the eyes
- 1 color each of Tween Time colors for hair
- Small squeeze bottle of Ken Diaz KD151 Flowing Blood Syrup, Drying Blood in Dark and Light
- Skin Illustrator Flesh Tone Palette
- Skin Illustrator FX Palette
- Reel Color Palette Cover-Up/Effects Kit
- Braun electric shaver

The last five items of the above list I store in my set chair (if not needed) and then they are readily available on set.

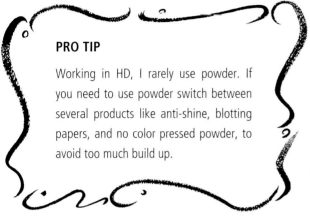

PRO TIP

Working in HD, I rarely use powder. If you need to use powder switch between several products like anti-shine, blotting papers, and no color pressed powder, to avoid too much build up.

Gretchen's Makeup Bag for Film Day Checker

The makeup you bring as a Day Checker on a film set can be contained in a bag or case of some sort. If you are directed to bring makeup for a certain character or time period, you should adjust the contents of your makeup bag to fit the need. If the job is going to entail helping out the department head most of the time, and is not so much about applying a lot of makeup, you won't need to bring a bulky case. A clear bag with a large strap and handle that can accommodate only what is necessary should work. What you do and how you transport your makeup becomes a personal challenge. Changing out your makeup to fit the job at hand happens no matter how well you think you're organized. Having at home a few different makeup bags or cases already set up and ready to go helps cut down the "What to bring?" question.

(See Fig. 12-03 for Picture of Film Day Checker Bag)

- Air Craft Airbrush Makeup in all colors
- Shiseido Stick Foundations
- RCMA KO/MB Palette by Vincent Kehoe
- Sehora makeup brush cleaning wipes
- Visiora MV in all colors
- DermaColor Camouflage System
- Mellow Yellow by Ben Nye
- A few setup towels
- 1 metal palette to blend makeup
- 1 book of artist paper to blend makeup
- 1 palette knife
- RCMA No Color Powder
- Laura Mercier Secret Brightening Powder
- Lancôme Dual Finish Powder Makeup
- Iman Pressed Powders
- Guerlain Bronzing Powders
- Tarte Stick Color Stains in all colors
- Eye shadow palettes in various colors (I like to have a shadow palette that is compact that I can use on anybody for large crowds. Colors in black, dark brown, taupe, creams, white, blue, violet, green, and gray. Personally, I have every NARS compact that has come out! My favorite for on-set is Skin Deep.)
- Eye shadow palettes in frosty gold tones
- Eye shadow palettes in frosty silver tones
- Blushers (Blushers should be simple. Light pink, coral, burgundy, red if needed, and a warm neutral color. Again, I can usually find this combination of colors in a palette, therefore I don't need to bring a

lot of loose colors. Make Up For Ever has a good combination of colors you can put together. I have one or two creams that I can use if someone has a dry skin tone.)

- Kiehl's Lip Balm SPF 15 in hues 30G and 58B

- Kiehl's Lip Balm SPF 15

- Laura Mercier Brow Powder Duos in all colors

- Bobbi Brown Long Wear Gel Eyeliners in all colors

- Brow pencils in all the brow colors

- Eye pencils in black, dark brown, dark blue, dark green, and white

- Lip Pencils: M•A•C Rosewood, Trish McEvoy Deep Nude, T. LeClerc Tendre, M•A•C Mahogany, Guerlain Rouge #2, By Terry #11, #12, Lancôme Lip Coloring Stick Inspire, Mauvelle, Lancôme LipColor Cherub. Plus a few colors that will work in any situation: pink tones, coral tones, reds, burgundy, and a rust color. Yves Saint Laurent Touche Éclat, all of the colors

- A variety of lip glosses in tubes

- Bobbi Brown eye brightener

- Laura Mercier Secret Brightener

- Laura Mercier Eye Basics Liner

- Lancôme Definicils Waterproof Mascara

- Lancôme Definicils High Definition Mascara

- Trish McEvoy High Volume Mascara

- Brush roll with a variety of brushes

- W.M Creations, Inc. Stacolor palette (full palette)

- Hand held fan (for those hot days or sets)

Set Chair

There is not always a reason you have to use the set chair, but it is good to have if you are sitting long lengths of time. In film, it is important because of the amount of time you do spend shooting. Everyone has their favorites. Every day, new bags and chairs surface that we all like to check out. I still like my larger chair that has a pocket below that I can stock up with extra items. You will find yourself storing those extra pieces of clothing for different weather conditions. The chair is compact and easy to move in a hurry. Feel out your department heads and observe what they are doing. In some cases, the Production or Makeup team does not believe in sitting down on the job. Although this is rare, don't assume that everyone brings their chairs to the set.

COMMERCIAL VERSES FILM

Makeup kits for the commercial world are similar to film. There are a few differences between the two. For one thing, you probably will need to bring a hair kit as well as the makeup kit. In many cases one person does makeup and hair for a commercial. Do not do hair if you are not qualified or comfortable with it. If you are working on a non-union shoot, you most definitely will be doing both. On a union shoot with a budget for two or more artists, they will hire a Makeup Artist and a Hairstylist. The union requires that all hairstylists are licensed in cosmetology and keep their license current.

Just as with film shoots, someone should be contacting you with your call times the day before you are to work. Call sheets are usually faxed or emailed. Follow the directions and get to work on time!

When you reach Crew parking, you'll be escorted by a van to the Makeup setups. In commercials, RVs are usually used instead of Makeup star trailers. There can be several locations in one day, so traveling is easier for Production in RVs. Plus, the number of actors you'll be working on at one time can be smaller. Of course, this isn't always the case.

Once you have set up, an AD should start bringing in your actors. Once done, you're off to set! On commercials, clients who are representing the company that is being filmed are on-set. Clients are there to make sure the company is getting what they need out of the shoot. Be professional at all times. You never know who is listening or who it is that you might be talking to.

At the end of the shooting day, make sure you've filled out your time card. Turn in your time card to Production. Be sure to stay for the actors to help remove any makeup if needed. If there is room, I like to have hot towels available.

Now you can find your way back to Crew parking. Drive carefully and slowly going back home. You've worked long hours.

TIME CARDS AND KIT FEES: INSTRUCTIONS

Get your start paper documentation in order to bring with you. On union shoots, you will need a copy of your makeup kit rental inventory, which includes a total value and product list, an invoice for your makeup kit rental fee (or Box Rental), and a copy of your IDs. Whatever you do, don't forget to bring these in. Everyone is so busy; for Production to hear your reasons for forgetting is beside the point. They need the information to process your start papers so you can get paid. Try to make life easier for everyone. I usually have several copies ready to go ahead of time. Fill out the correct information for that job. I put the papers in my makeup kit so not to forget. The Makeup Department should have your start paperwork on the first day to fill out and turn in. The combination of the papers you brought in and the start papers you'll fill out are turned in together. If the Makeup Department does not have start papers for you, find the Production trailer and get the papers yourself. Again, it looks good for you to know where to go and what to fill out correctly. If you have any questions about your rate or pay, if no one has told you, or if they don't know, ask your local union. If the Makeup Department is from a different Local they might not know your rate. Rate of pay fluctuates with regions and union locals. If you think about it, not knowing what your salary will be isn't very professional.

A Kit Fee is also called a Box Rental and is based on a daily fee paid to you to cover the cost of working out of you kit. It covers your makeup brushes and makeup products—your kit. Almost always, expendables are provided by the makeup department (in film), but always pack plenty of supplies in case they are not there when you start work. Always be ready to work!

Expendables are tissue, cotton balls, sponges, puffs, alcohol, brush cleaner, Q-tips, etc. In commercials you provide everything. If something is needed for the commercial that you have to purchase, you can turn in the receipt for reimbursement. Kit Fees are negotiated for each job; most artists have a standard fee they charge along with their rate. In day checking on a film, the Kit Fee is set by production and the makeup budget; it is not negotiable with day checking.

FIGURE 12-4: AN EAST COAST MAKEUP TRAILER—OUTSIDE

FIGURE 12-6: A WEST COAST MAKEUP TRAILER—OUTSIDE

FIGURE 12-5: AN EAST COAST MAKEUP TRAILER—INSIDE

FIGURE 12-7: A WEST COAST MAKEUP TRAILER—INSIDE

When arriving on-set for the first time, if you do not know where to report, check in with the department head so they know you are here. Knock softly and peek in. There isn't really any need to go into the trailer unless invited. Remember, the Makeup team could have already been working for hours before you got there. Keep your energy calm and soothing. Makeup trailers bounce, so watch how much you need to go in and out. Do not slam a door. Lift the handle gently to open and close. If invited in, keep most of your things outside the trailer until you get an idea of where you will set up and what you'll need. I usually leave my set chair outside. If you have already been told where to report, do not go to the Makeup trailer. You do not need to check in with the department head. They have assigned a member of the makeup department to "run" the additional hires or day checkers, and this is the person you will be checking in with.

This way it is great to get notes or directions on where you are supposed to report and what makeup you will be doing that day. Many times you will be asked to go and set up, and the Key Makeup Artist will find you to explain what they want. This could also be the Third or Fourth Makeup Artist. Whoever is in charge of supervising the additional makeup artists and the look of the background artists will be the one to go to with questions.

A typical makeup department has:

1) Makeup Department Head (Chief Makeup Artist in Europe) in charge of designing and running the department

2) Assistant Makeup Department Head

3) Key Makeup Artist

4) Makeup Artist

5) Additional Makeup Artists.

There can also be a Makeup Designer. If there is a Makeup Designer, the department head will work with them in running the department and implementing their designs.

CROWD SCENES

Background refers to background artists (actors) or extras working in a scene.

You will hear many terms for background: BG, extra's, background players, background artists, and background actors. There can be from 1 to 500 or more background in any given scene. Imagine a park scene with two principal actors sitting on a bench. Everyone around them has been placed by the ADs, with directions from the ADs for their actions and motivations. These background actors have already gone through the Costume, Hair, and Makeup Departments before being brought to set.

Instructions you will hear are:

Working With Background: That means you are hired to do makeup for the actors in the background.

Report to Background Holding or Extras Holding: Where to show up for work, or where to go. Usually a large room or tent away from set, designated for the background.

Check the Background: You are being asked to look at the background that the AD has assembled for you, and to decide who needs makeup and who is ready to go to set. The department head will decide who has this responsibility.

Working in background, you will often work on many actors in one day. The department head will give you directions on what he or she wants as far as the look for the actors. Descriptions of special background can be found on the front of the call sheet. In some cases, the Supervising Makeup Artist will give you a list of the different looks for the background that day. Swiftness is important when working in large crowd situations. Having an idea of what makeup colors and products work or do not work speeds up the process. Always follow specific directions from the department head or Supervising Makeup Artist.

On set note: never touch up a principle actor on set unless you have been asked to cover that person! You do not know the actor's continuity, so never assume that they need to be powdered or touched up. You are there to take care of the background artists that are around them. So know who the actors are and who you are responsible for, and don't try to impress your department head by being an over achiever and powdering everyone in sight. If you are unsure, ask!

There are certain makeup looks that are used regularly in film and television. A few of those would be police officers, homeless people, drug addicts, pedestrians, diners in a restaurant, waitresses, bartenders, news reporters, news anchors, and children. The other common makeup situations are for period makeup.

WORKING OUT OF YOUR KIT

You will need a variety of products and palettes in your makeup kit so that you can create any of these looks. "Working out of your kit" is a term used by makeup artists to tell you that you will be creating looks with what is in your kit, and not specially purchased products that are given to you by the Makeup Department. You rely on Industry Standards that are in your kit. As we've mentioned before, the palettes from Skin illustrator, stacolors, and Reel Creations are Industry Standards that encourage mixing to create a more realistic makeup that is long lasting and abrasion resistant. They are essential in working out of your kit, and for those unplanned makeup situations where you have to work quickly, on set. There will also be many times that instructions are given to you in "makeup slang" for products. Example: you are asked to "use MV005" or "use

Visiora005," or just "use 005." These three terms are referring to the same one product, that if you do not know what it is, you will not know that you are being asked to apply foundation using this specific color (Industry Standard). Makeup and film slang abbreviate just about everything, including products, and sometimes instructions. It is confusing at first, but you will get the hang of it. Remember, if you don't know, ask!

Having trouble remembering what colors to use or which looks to do for a certain period makeup? Tape a color chart and notes on each period inside your makeup kit for a quick reference guide.

Remember color mixing from Chapter 3?

Red: You can mix yellow and magenta to get red.

Blue: Mix magenta and cyan.

Green: Mix cyan and yellow.

Purple: Mix violet and magenta.

Black, White, and Gray: Mix white into black until you get the desired shade.

Knowing combinations gives you so many choices to work with!

Now separate the three background actor looks of homeless (Figure 12.8), drug addict (Figure 12.9), and illness (Figure 12.10) to see their differences.

Homeless
- Red or sun-damaged skin with various sizes and colors of sun spots.
- Skin tone has rough, leatherlike surface due to exposure to the elements.

FIGURE 12-8: A HOMELESS PERSON

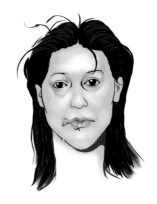

FIGURE 12-9: A DRUG ADDICT

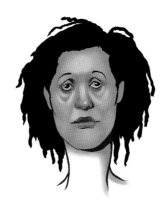

FIGURE 12-10: A PERSON WITH A COLD

- Broken capillaries around the nose and cheeks to reflect substance abuse and weather damage.

- Lesions of various sizes due to illness and injury.

- Ground-in dirt on the body, under fingernails, and even built-up grime from lack of grooming.

- Facial hair would be untrimmed, unshaven, oily, and dirty.

- Darkness, puffiness, and redness under and above the eye.

- Small cuts or scabs on the face, with weathered lips.

- In some situations, the feet must be done as well. The soles of the feet should be blackened with heavy grime, cuts, and bruises.

Drug Addict

- The skin tone tends to be pale and clammy from drug abuse.

- Darkness forms under the eye area from lack of sleep.

- Skin lesions form from drug abuse and illness.

- Track marks on the body from shooting up.

- Bruising on various parts of the body, old and new.

Illness

There are many possibilities for illness: cold, flu, high fever, and disease. You will be directed as to what the illness is, and what the desired effect should be, from the department head or Supervising Makeup

Artist. For this example, your instructions are for a cold/flu.

Cold/Flu: Red tones around the nose with dry, flaky skin. Eyes can appear red and droopy, even watery. Paler skin tone that could be clammy. A dryness to the mouth.

Would you apply foundation or do any corrective makeup on these characters? No. The worse they look, the better, in all three scenarios; and you do not want an even skin tone

Red pencil can be used for rimming the eye area or applying right on the lower lash line for irritated eyes. Several shades of red makeup colors are used for broken capillaries, red noses, and lesions. Have on hand different colors of brown or colors to mix browns for dirt and grime. One black is used to deepen or darken an existing color, plus one white to lighten any existing color or to make grays. Yellow is used for nails, skin tones, and festering lesions or old bruises. Care needs to be taken when working around the eyes. Use a cream-based makeup or a freshly sharpened pencil.

Police Officers

One of the first things you'll do is clean shave all law-enforcement characters. There should be no facial hair, with exceptions given only by your department head. Mustache's are allowed for most Police Departments. Sometimes sideburns need to be trimmed. The back of the neck needs to clean shaven. The officers should have a clean-cut appearance. On all shoots, be prepared with a good electric razor, shave powder stick, astringent of choice, and a small groomer for eyebrows, ears, and nose.

News Reporter and News Anchors

News anchors and reporters usually have a clean-cut appearance as well. If there is a time period issue, you will be told to address that issue. If it is present time, the anchor look is what to aim toward. Work quickly, and spot cover up only the problem areas. Apply a slightly heavy beauty makeup; to achieve a matte, perfect look. Most of the time, lipstick, blusher, eye shadow, and brows are all you will have to do to achieve a news anchor look. The Hair Department will pull the look together. Reporters and anchor types sometimes are pulled ahead of everyone else to go through the Makeup Department because they are usually featured in the scene.

Period Makeup

Refers to a specific time period for the look or trend of that time. Say you are asked to do a period makeup, taking five minutes for each actress because the actresses are in a large crowd scene. If you could do only three things on the actress, what would you do to execute the makeup properly for the following time periods? And what sets each time period apart from the others? We will give you some very general looks for each decade. You must do your own research for each decade to recognize and know a more detailed history of the trends.

1950s (Figure 12.11): Red lips, pale eye shadows applied to the upper eyelids, nice liquid eyeliner across the upper eyelid next to the lash line, no eyeliner on the lower

FIGURE 12-11: A 1950S MAKEUP LOOK

FIGURE 12-12: A 1960S MAKEUP LOOK

eye lash line, beautifully shaped and filled in eyebrows. Apply lipstick, eyeliner, and brows. A very clean, sometimes innocent, classic look. Note the shape of the lips.

1960s (Figure 12.12): Pale flat or frosty (but never glossy) lipsticks, strong upper and lower eyeliners, contrasting eye shadows on the eyelids. For example: light shadow on the lid; a deep, dark eye shadow in the crease; followed by a light eye shadow applied on the brow bone. The look is about eyes, so note the style in eye shadow, eyeliner, and brows, as well as the lips. Apply lipstick, eyeliners, and eye shadows.

FIGURE 12-13: A 1970S MAKEUP LOOK

FIGURE 12-14: A 1980S MAKEUP LOOK

1970s (Figure 12.13): Women and men in the early 1970s were riding the wave ushered in by the counterculture from the 1960s. Freedom of expression through fashion and makeup was seeping into mainstream society. Men had cast off the "above-the-collar" hair restrictions of previous decades, and began wearing their hair much longer. In addition, facial hair had become popular, which included long sideburns that often widened as they extended down the face, and full mustaches. Hence, facial hair is a large part of re-creating the '70s look for men. By the mid 1970s, women kept their hair natural whether long or short. Natural, meaning that it was devoid of hairspray, hairpieces, and setting gels of any kind. Eye shadow was colorful and warm (greens, blues, brown) with or without eyeliner; blush and lips in corals, pinks and frosts. Sun-tanned skin.

Example of a Decade in Makeup:

Makeup varies from the early '70s to the late '70s, so questions should be addressed to the Makeup Department head on what look they are trying to create. In general

blues, greens, and brown colors were worn as eye shadows. Makeup was applied, but not heavy or over-the-top. Dark brown tones or black would be used around the eye area as liner, but much softer than in earlier years. Lipstick colors were found in corals, pinks, oranges, and soft reds. If you had only three things to do to create a '70s makeup, what would they be?

1980s (Figure 12.14): In the 1980s, no matter what colors you were using, makeup was applied heavy. Makeup and hair were used as an art form. Depending on who it was that you hung out with, everyone today has a different take on what colors were used in the '80s. The colors ranged from the punk look (with black liners and dark eye shadows) to the preppy look (girls with rust or fuchsia-colored lipsticks with purple eye shadow). Of course, Madonna always comes to mind when one thinks of an '80s look. Three things to use for an '80s makeup: colorful lipstick, full eye shadow, and blusher. Use lipsticks in pinks, purples, fuchsia, rusts, and reds. Apply eye shadows all over the lid and crease, with a dramatic but lighter shade to the brow bone. Complete the look with a dramatic contouring blusher across and just under the cheekbone in a matching color to the lipstick.

LESSONS FROM THE FIELD
EXAMPLE OF A BEAUTY MAKEUP (STORIES) SHOOT IN PARIS

by Daniela Eschbacher

When I started out in the fashion industry, I contacted as many Photographers and Stylists as possible to do "test shooting" first to build up my portfolio and contacts. In the beginning, it's hard contacting everybody and running after magazines. But all that hard work pays off. After working for magazines and commercials, people will get to know you and pass your name and number along. That's what happened to me. Still, in a city like Paris, it is hard to break in. In fashion, sending out your newest editorials to Photographers and magazines will keep them updated on your work.

Preparing for the Shoot

For commercial shoots, it's important to have all the information necessary from the client or Photographer. The client normally knows exactly what they want, and they expect the Makeup Artist to realize it. When I get a call for a commercial shoot, I will ask the theme of the shoot, the makeup look wanted, if it's an inside or outside shoot, and how many models. For beauty, it is important to ask the Photographer the reference of the model. The Photographer can either send her portfolio to you by email, or you can look on the agency's website for the model's portfolio book. Once you have all the information, it is time to start thinking about the makeup, products, and to double-check to make sure you have everything you'll need for the shoot. A lot of times, the Photographer, or even the client, does not know how to express themselves in the form of makeup and colors, so it's up to me to find the right look. Working in fashion is different from cinema. It can be spontaneous.

Even if you agree on a certain look before shooting, it might all change on the actual workday. On larger, more-complicated shoots, there are meetings before the job. The Stylist knows the clothes, so he or she gives a direction and theme of the shoot. It can be really helpful to work with an Art Director or Stylist because they see the overall image. Sometimes a simple makeup works much better than one too sophisticated or creative. Meetings are important for meeting the team—it makes the whole process interesting, fun, and human to take the time to sit down and discuss the project. Of course, for commercial jobs, meetings do not always happen.

Designing the Makeup

Designing the makeup—especially if I'm working on personal shoots or beauty stories where everybody counts on the creativity of the Makeup Artist—can be stressful. Even so, I love the work and preparation behind it. Before you start to design, get as much inspiration as possible. The internet is one, but mostly books and paintings. For myself, I love to work with color, so before I think about my makeup, I think about all the colors that will be used and what atmosphere or feelings those colors will cause to come across.

Once the colors are fixed, I start with effects: shiny or matte, graphic or shady, simple or complicated. Try to prepare as much as possible, but a lot of inspiration is when you first see the model sitting in the makeup chair.

Makeup Kit

Many Makeup Artists have a separate kit for commercials and photography. That includes me. Commercials are not only very tiring, but you work with actors, which is different from working with models. Actors need much more products and attention throughout the day. Therefore, I always have a security kit with me that includes eyedrops, different bases, a nail kit, body cream and a first-aid kit, to name just a few items. For photography, the makeup kit has a lot of products to create effects, such as glitter, different textures of glosses, all sorts of eyelashes, powders, stones, jewelry, and stencils. Stencils I make myself if possible; the rest I pick up here and there.

Prepping the Model

For fashion or beauty shoots, start with cleaning the model's face with a mild liquid cleanser (Ciealine), and apply, depending on the skin, an appropriate moisturizer. I'm not a fan of heavy creams or moisturizers. Natural oils and vitamins work well without affecting the foundation afterward. Nuxe Multiusage Dry Oil hydrates very well and won't make the model sweat. It's very important to check the hands. Nails have to be in good shape. No old nail polish or dry skin. Apply the hand cream. Lips are very important because most models have dry lips. There can be a disaster once the model is in front of the camera, unless you take the time to prep the lips properly. Sometimes I do a soft peeling to take off the dead skin, and afterward apply Elizabeth Arden Eight Hour Cream—a must for every Makeup Artist.

Beauty or Stylized Makeup

Natural colors work best in most beauty makeup. From creamy white to chocolate brown. Warm colors also work well: pink, rose, peach, and oranges. In beauty makeup, you want to look for textures that could be interesting. Glosses on the eyes create a very fresh look. On the cheeks, eyelashes, and eyebrows, gloss will attract light. Because I work with an airbrush, Temptu products mixed with an SB solution work well.

There are no limits in beauty and fashion. Here are a few examples of different makeups for editorials or a beauty story.

Location Shoot: a Luxury Hotel in Paris

The photographer used artificial light with an emphasis on strong contrasts. So makeup needs to reflect well in the light.

Glosses, Oils, and Shimmers: After cleaning the model's face, apply natural oils onto the skin and the rest of the body that will be seen. Your goal is to have smooth, shiny, and elegant skin. Let the oils absorb before applying foundation. Use eye products that are moist and creamy in texture, with soft eye pencils to work your shape for the eyes, blending and adding as you go. Purples and chocolate colors work well for this. To increase the contrasts, use a powder shadow in gray or black in only the areas that are needed.

Mascara and individual false eyelashes applied to the outside corners of the eyes add drama and depth. Foundation is applied next. Follow with loose powder to set. Chanel has a good loose powder. A bronzer was used to sculpt and shape the face. Creating depth and contours is important in a shoot with contrast. The brows were shaped by using three pencils in a mix of brown, black, and gray. Colors you use will depend on your model, but a mix of three colors mimics the different colors of hair found in the brows.

FIGURE 12-15: DANIELE'S LUXURY HOTEL SHOOT

Theme Shoot: Madonna theme

The difficulty was to create color combinations that would express and strengthen the atmosphere and theme of the shoot. I found my inspiration from religious paintings and books. The colors dark red, golden, gray, white, and silver were used. Because wardrobe and hair had such a strong look, I didn't want to complicate the makeup. When this happens, use a matte, lightly applied foundation, no blush, and no contouring. White eyeliner applied on the inside of the eye will accentuate any color just under the eye. In this case, a red and yellow matte eye shadow from Make Up For Ever was applied on the eyelid and below the lower lashes. No shaping or contouring was used. Shadow was just posed on the lid. When such strong colors are used, a tissue laid under the eye you are working on protects the rest of the face from falling shadow. Loose powder can also be used. Natural lip colors help keep the makeup from being overwhelming. Shape the lips with a nude lip liner. Mix beige, purples, and pink lip glosses to achieve a natural look. Don't forget to finish off with a strong brow.

Remember, with both makeups, you want to work in layers. Work the shapes and slowly go darker. It's like working on a painting. To create something luminous and strong, it's always the combination of colors that accentuate the intensity of another color.

TIPS

To glue anything on the skin or eyes, I use transparent eyelash glue. The only thing you have to be careful of when you glue objects on the skin is to clean around the object afterward. Any sort of glue remaining on the skin tends to shine in photo lighting, and can be obvious in close-ups and beauty stories.

Do not powder the face, especially for close-ups. It's really difficult for the retoucher afterward to correct it. Powder only certain areas—around the nose, forehead, and chin—at the last minute.

FIGURE 12-16: DANIELE'S MADONNA SHOOT

ON-SET

When working in photography always check your makeup in the light of the studio. The makeup preparation room is always bright, and the light is quite yellow. The studio could be completely opposite. Ask the Photographer to do a test photo to see how the makeup comes across. Most Photographers now work with digital cameras that download right to the computer and show the results straight away. This is very helpful. The Photographer appreciates your taking charge and knowing when it is a good time to redo lips, add some gloss, brush the eyebrows, and powder the skin. It's so much more interesting to participate in the whole process of making a good photo.

Take Down the Makeup

For makeup removal I normally use Crealine, which is easy to use and good for all skin types. But prepared, de-makeup pads are fast and efficient, too. Some models prefer to take off their own makeup, especially around the eyes and lips. Others have their own products with them, which is understandable because of the amount of makeup they wear for work. Many models prefer not to mix all kinds of skin-care products.

Black-and-White Photograph Tip

In fashion shoots, it is not always said if the job is going to be color or black and white. Sometimes it's during or after shooting when the Photographer works with Photoshop to see what it could be in black and white. Then the decision is made. If you are told ahead of time, here are some hints to think about. Work much more with the contrasts, and even exaggerate the intensity of colors and shades. There is a lot more "graphism" in black and white than in color photography because we concentrate on the contrasts, shadows, and lighting instead of the color. Graphic lines and structure work very well for the makeup, such as strong eyebrows, eyeliner, nice colored matte lips, nicely posed blushes. Still, it's important to ask the Photographer exactly how he or she is going to work their light. Maybe the Photographer wants the image to be contrast and sober, or something luminous and mild. Try to avoid too much gloss or shiny skin, except if it's desired to create a strong and wanted effect. For black-and-white photography, it's important to have a nice balance between warm and cold tones to make the skin look alive and beautiful.

THINGS TO KNOW

Makeup Brushes
Types of Bristles
Badger: One of the most popular and easiest to find. Badger hair quality depends on an array of factors. The highest quality is the neck hair, which is the softest and most expensive of all badger hair.

Boar: Stronger and thicker than badger hair.

Goat: Strong and soft. It's used alone or mixed with other hairs in makeup brushes. Goat hair can be found in white, brown, or red.

Pony: Also known as camel hair. This is a term for brushes made from a variety of hair such as squirrel, goat, ox, or pony. Usually

brushes made with these bristles are inexpensive and are made in large quantity.

Raccoon: North American animal with a multicolored tail in grays and browns. Raccoon brushes have a really soft texture.

Sable: An animal from Siberia and Japan. Sable is strong, flexible, and takes to products well. Sable can be found in brown, white, or yellow. Kolinsky sable is a mink found in Siberia and China, and is considered the best. Red sable is from the weasel family, and is often used in place of Kolinsky sable.

Squirrel: Hair that is soft and holds water effectively. It works best with liquids.

Synthetic or Taklon: Brushes that are made of nylon or polyester. Synthetic brushes are considered reliable and strong.

Types of Brushes
Angled Brush: These are cut to use at defined angles. Blush brushes, shadow brushes, brow brushes, powder brushes, bronzers, and contour brushes are examples of brushes that can be found cut at an angle. In some cases, the bristles are stiffer.

Blush Brush: Soft, wider, rounded brush used to apply blusher color. Blush brushes are made from a variety of bristles.

Brow Brush: Angled or slant brushes with a stiff bristle for application of brow powders. It's also possible to find lash combs and brow brushes as duos.

Concealer Brush or Flat Brushes: Concealer brushes are usually flat brushes in a variety of sizes used for cream-based products. These brushes are good for spot touch-ups, heavy coverage with multiple products, under-eye concealer, and blending products. Many flat brushes can be used wet or dry.

Contour Brush: Is used to get under edges and contours of the face to create definition. The bristles are usually cut blunt or at angles.

Crease Brush: Smaller, with a blunter cut in the bristles. Crease brushes are used to apply eye shadows in the crease area and to blend existing work.

Eyelash Combs: Wire or plastic combs that are used to separate the lashes after mascara has been applied.

Eyeliner Brushes: Come in a variety of sizes and bristles. Bristles usually taper to a point, which works well for lining, detail work, powder, liquid, or water-activated makeup such as KRYOLAN or MAC. There are liner brushes that have several different bristles that can be used effectively wet or dry. Also, flat eyeliner brushes can be found.

Eye Shadow or Fluff Brush: There are many different sizes and shapes of a shadow brush. The brushes are used to apply eye shadow colors. The bristles are usually soft, with a rounded shape at the top.

Face or Foundation Brushes: These brushes are usually larger, flatter, with a rounded or oval bristle shape. Bristles can be made in a variety of hair, including synthetic to sable. Foundation brushes can cover wide areas of the face and body, and work well with liquids and creams.

Fan Brush: Shaped like a fan and come in a variety of sizes. Fan brushes disperse powdered makeup and add color with a sheer application. They can be used for applying mascara, as a powder or blush brush, a stipple brush, or as a blending brush.

Kabuki Brushes: Brushes that are often used with mineral-type powder makeup. They come in a variety of sizes and shapes. The most common shape is a fan or dome.

Lash Combs: Lash combs lash are made to separate the lashes after applying mascara.

Lip Brush: There are many choices of lip brushes, from shapes of the bristles to what the bristles are made of. Lip brushes are used to apply lip treatments and lip colors.

Paddle Brushes: These brushes are shaped like a small paddle with a lamb's wool covering on one side. They are used for blending blush or makeup colors.

Powder Brush: Larger brushes with rounded, softer bristles, often made with goat, sable, or badger hair. They are good for dusting large areas of the face with loose color, or with powder makeup to dust off any excess powder.

Puffs: These are found in so many different brands, shapes, and materials, but all used in basically the same way for makeup and powder application, setting the makeup, and touch-ups on-set.

Pump Brush: Brushes made with the product inside the stem of the handle. When the brush is pumped, the product disperses into the bristles.

Retractable: Brushes that can retract back into the handle of the brush. Some lip brushes and blush brushes are made retractable.

Smudger: Any brush that is used to blend and smudge the makeup.

Sponges: Are used for just about anything you can think of. They come uncut in squares or precut and as a brush form. Good sponges are gentle on the face, do not soak up your liquid or cream makeup, and aid in blending. Different brands of sponges are made from different materials.

Stipple: Several blends of bristles in the brush, plus the shape of the brush works to create textures or as a blender.

Wet and Dry Brush: Brushes that are made with several different kinds of bristles that can be used effectively wet or dry.

INDUSTRY STANDARDS

Antishines

There are many products out there. Antishine creates a matte look to wherever you apply product. We all have our favorite. One that's been around for a while is Make-up International's Face to Face Supermatte. It works well for large crowd scenes.

Adhesives

Beta Bond Plus by Premiere Products, Inc.: Acrylic adhesive for prosthetics.

K.D. 151 Ultra Matte Lace Adhesive: Strong adhesive hold for action-packed situations.

KRYOLAN Water Soluble Spirit Gum: Removes with soap and water.

Pros-Aide: Acrylic based, waterproof, strong hold, used mostly for appliances.

Telesis 5 Adhesive by Premiere Products, Inc.: Silicone-based adhesive.

Very Flat matt Matt Gum by Naimies: Used in the industry for lace fronts, facial hair, or wherever you don't want to have shine.

Xtra Hold Spirit Gum and Extra Hold Plastic Spirit Gum by W.M. Creations, Inc.: Two of the most popular spirit gums in the industry. Used for fine lace fronts, foam, gelatin, and silicone appliances.

Brush Cleaners

Cinema Secrets: Fast drying.

Naimies: Fast drying.

Effects Products

AM.E.K. Liquid Plastic by W.M. Creations, Inc.: Use in stone or silicone molds for wounds.

Gelatin in Bulk: Burman Industries carries gelatin products.

Latex Products in Bulk: Burman Industries carries a wide range of latex products.

Old-Age Stipple

Old Age Stipple A, B, C, Crusty by W.M. Creations, Inc.

Green Marble SeLr by Premiere Products, Inc.: Developed by RSD Inc. and CMI. Seals makeup, very durable, safe for sensitive skins, and also works as an aging product.

RCMA Old Age Stipple

Pax Paint
Tom Surprenant Pax Paints

Pax Paint by GM Foam: Premixed Pax Paint colors that match up to RCMA.

Foundation Colors
Plastic Sealers A, B, Soft, Extra Soft, Shiny by W.M. Creations, Inc.

Scab Materials Light, Medium, Dark, and Brown by W.M. Creations, Inc.: Pigmented, silicone-based liquid that is used for building up three-dimensional scabs.

Scar Material by W.M. Creations, Inc.: Acetone-based plastic material used to build things such as keloid scars and blisters.

Silicon Product in Bulk
Smooth-On Inc.: Easton, Pennsylvania-based manufacturer of Silicon Products. Their website sells direct.

Burman Industries: Carries a good inventory of silicone-related products. Based in Van Nuys, California.

Tattoo Ink Type Products: All of the products mentioned are Industry Standards. It's hard to remember what it was like before these products existed.

Reel Creations Palettes by Reel Creations.

Reel Creations Liquids by Reel Creations.

Skin Illustrator Palettes by Premiere Products, Inc.: Created by Kenny Myers/CMI.

Skin Illustrator Liquids by Premiere Products, Inc.: Created by Kenny Myers/CMI.

Stacolor Palettes by W.M. Creations, Inc.

Stacolor Liquids by W.M. Creations, Inc.

Tear Products
Burman Industries Menthol Blower and Crystals: A must for any makeup kit.

KRYOLAN Tear Stick

Makeup Products
Foundation or Correction Makeup
Ben Nye Mellow Orange: Neutralizes blue and green.

Ben Nye Mellow Yellow: Red neutralizer.

KRYOLAN Dermacolor Mini Palette: This makeup covers well, has a large selection of colors, and is easy for doing quick makeup or touch-ups on-set.

IMAN: Excellent makeup line for a range of skin tones from light to dark, including yellow. Great pigment in their shadows, blushers and lipsticks.

RCMA: Without question, a makeup line we could not do without. Foundation colors come in every possible range for any beauty or character makeup. One of the few makeup lines that understands skin tones.

Visiora: A sheer makeup that has a good coverage. Colors have been formulated to match our industry lights and different media. Visiora is also a wonderful makeup to use on men.

Water-Activated Makeup

Ben Nye: Good for theatrical use.

Mehron: Good for theatrical use.

Studio Fix by MAC: Good for flesh tones, editorials, and stylized beauty makeup.

Makeup Palettes

Viseart Palette of Neutrals: A simple palette of neutral colors. This palette is perfect for your set bag.

Powders

Kett No Color: Pressed powder

No Color Powder by RCMA.

Removers

It's always a safe bet to buy the same remover and adhesive that belong together.

Adklen Cleanser by RCMA: No travel-safety issues.

Beta Solv Remover: Works to remove Pax Beta Bond by Tom Surprenant.

Ben Nye Bond Off: Removes spirit gum, medical adhesive, and Pros-Aide.

Delasco Detachol: Removes Pros-Aide. Is mild and hypoallergenic.

Pax Remover by GM Foam: Removes Pax Paint.

RJS Adhesive Remover: No travel-safety issues.

Super Solv by Premiere Products, Inc.: Non-oily. Extra strength but safe for sensitive skin. Gentle enough for lace fronts.

Sealers, Primers, and Fixers

Sealers protect your work, act as a stronger bond for adhesives, and act like a shield between the skin and a product.

Green Marble SeLr Spray: Also can be used as an aging product.

RCMA Matte Plastic Sealer

Soft Sealer by W.M. Creations, Inc.: Also can be used as an aging product. Can be sprayed or stippled over makeup.

Top Guard by Premiere Products, Inc.

REFERENCES

Internet Resources

www.dickblick.com

www.danielamakeup.com

www.indeutsch.com

www.makeupartistschoice.com

www.makeupcreations.com

www.naimies.com

www.psdaimaandsons.com

www.sephora.com

www.solomakeup.com

UNITED STATES

California

Air Craft Cosmetics
www.aircraftcosmetics.com
1800 900 2400

Cinema Secrets, Inc.
4400 Riverside Dr.
Burbank, CA 91505
www.cinemasecrets.com
818 846 0579

Don Jusko Color Wheels
Frends Beauty Supply
5270 Laurel Canyon Blvd.
North Hollywood, CA 91607
www.realcolorwheel.com
818 769 3834

GM Foam, Inc.
Van Nuys, CA 14956 Delano St.
Van Nuys CA 91411
www.gmfoam.com
818 908 1087

Krembs, Inc.
420 East Easy St., Suite 1
Simi Valley, CA 93065
www.krembs.com
800 835 8267

Kryolan Corp.
132 Ninth St.
San Francisco, CA 94103
Email: Info-usa@kryolan.com
www.kryolan.com
415 863 9684

Mark Trainer Facial Lifts
Motion Picture F/X Company
123 South Victory Blvd.
Burbank, CA 91502
www.monsterclub.com
818 563 2366

Naimies Beauty Center
12640 Riverside Dr.
Valley Village, CA 91607
www.naimies.com
818 655 9933

Premiere Products, Inc.
10312 Norris Ave., Suite C
Pacoima, CA 91331
www.ppi.cc
800 346 4774
818 897 2440

Professional Vision Care Associates
14607 Ventura Blvd.
Sherman Oaks, CA 91403
www.fx4eyes.com
818 789 3311

Reel Creations, Inc.
7831 Alabama Ave
Ste. 21, Canoga Park, CA 91304
www.reelcreations.com
Email: Tblau@reelcreations.com
818 346 7335

247

Silpak
10611 Burbank Blvd
North Hollywood, CA 91601
www.silpak.com
818 985 8850

TriEss
Burbank, CA
www.tri-esssciences.com
818 848 7838

Tinsley Transfers, Inc.
PO Box 10011
Burbank, CA 91510
Email: info@tinsleytransfers.com
www.tinsleytransfers.com

W.M. Creation, Inc.
5755 Tujunga Ave.
North Hollywood, CA 91601
Email: Mmungle@nu-products.com
www.matthewwmungle.com/wmcreations
1800 454 8339

Florida
FX Warehouse, Inc.
1575 Aviation Ctr. Pkwy., Suite 414
Daytona Beach, FL 32114
Email: order@fxwarehouse.info
www.fxwarehouse.info
386 322 5272

New York
Alcone Company, Inc. (store location)
322 West 49th St.
New York, NY 10019
www.alconeco.com
212 757 3734

Alcone Company, Inc. (headquarters and warehouse)
5–45 49th Ave.
Long Island City, NY 11101
718 361 8373

Manhattan Wardrobe Supply (some makeup supplies; great bags and accessories)
245 West 29th Street, 8th floor
New York, NY 10001
www.manhattanwardrobesupply.com
212 268 9993

Make-Up Designory (New York and Los Angeles school and store)
375 W. Broadway, #202
New York, NY 10012
www.mud.edu
212 925 9250
129 South San Femando Blvd
Burbank, CA 91502
818 557 7619

Pennsylvania
Smooth-On, Inc.
2000 Saint John St.
Easton, PA 18042
www.smooth-on.com
800 762 0744
610 2525800

AUSTRALIA

Barnes Products Pty, Ltd.
53 King Street
Newton NSW 2042
Australia
www.barnes.com.au
+61 (02) 9557 9056
sales@barnesonline.com.au

Kryolan Australia Pty, Ltd.
147 Little Collins St.
Melbourne, VIC 3000
Australia
sales@kryolan.com.au
www.kryolan.com.au
+61 3 96544147

JMB FX Studio
Unit 3 13–15 Ereton Dr.
Labrador, QLD 4215
Australia
www.jmbfxstudio.com.au
+61 (0) 7 5528 8500
Jason@jmbfxstudio.com.au

CANADA

Complections International
85 Saint Nicholas St.
Toronto, ON M4Y IW8
Canada
info@complectionsmake-up.com
www.complectionsmake-up.com
416 968 6739

3D Plastics
12304 Garibaldi St.
Maple Ridge, BC V2W 1N2
Canada
Email: 3Dplastics@intergate.ca
www.3dplastics.net
604 462 7755
604 465 6569

R. Hiscott Beauty and Theatrical Supplies
435 Yonge St.
Toronto, ON M5B 1T3
Canada
416 977 5247

Silithane
14855 Du Froment St.
Quebec, QC J7N 2J7
Canada
Email: Silithane@supernet.ca
514 8241 587

Takara PBG Group (highest-quality handmade Japanese brushes)
244 Elson St.
Markham, ON L3S 3B9 Canada
Email: Info@takaracanada.com
www.takaracanada.com
905 472 6105

FRANCE

Paris Berlin
56 Boulevard Richard Lenoir
75011 Paris
France
www.parisberlin.com
info@parisberlin.com
+33 (0) 1 433393590

GERMANY

Bela Kosmetik
Birnauerstrasse 12
D-80809 Munchen
Germany
www.bela-kosmetik.de
+49 (0) 89 35652223

Kryolan GmbH
Papierstr.10
13409 Berlin
Germany
Email: Info@kryolan.de
www.kryolan.de
+49 30 499 8920

GREECE

Beautyworks
Kolokotroni 8
Kifitssia
Athens, 145 62
Greece
+30 210 8089070

HONG KONG

May's Co./Gala Gold Ltd.
Unit G 19, Tung Ying Building
100, Nathan Rd.
TST Kowloon
Hong Kong
Email: galagold@netvigator.com
+852 2367 5332

IRELAND

Nue Blue
7 South William Eriu St.
Dublin, 2
Ireland
www.nueblueriu.com
dublin@nueblueriu.com
+353 (0)1 672 5776

ITALY

Kiehl's Milan Store
Corso Di Porta Ticinese, 40
Milano, 20123
Italy
www.kiehls.com
+39 (0)2 832 41084

KOREA

Kryolan Korea
1F, Sungdo Bldg.
336-1, Seogyo-Dong
Seoul
Korea
Email: Kryolan@kryolan.co.kr
www.kryolan.co.kr
+82 (0)2 3143 2732

MEXICO

Kiehl's Mexico City
Centro Comercial Perisur
Periférico Sur #4690 Local 179 PB
Col Ampliacion Jardines del Pedregal
Mexico City, DF
www.kiehls.com
+52 55 5171 4505

NEW ZEALAND

Gelita NZ Ltd. (gelatin and related
products) 135-145 Connal Street
Christchurch 2
New Zealand
www.gelita.com
+64 3384 3093

ROMANIA

Beauty Shop Bucuresti
55-59 Calea Vitan
Bucuresti
Romania
+40 21 327 7532

SWEDEN

Goteborgs Perukmakeri

Stora Nygatan 11

5-411 08 Goteborg

Sweden

Email: Info@perukmakeri.se

www.perukmakeri.se

+46 (0)31 15 7881

Mapont & Co.

Odelbergs vag 9B

134 40 Gustavsberg

Sweden

Email: Info@Mapont.se

www.mapont.se

+46 (0)70 3523109

MB Sveda (glycerin and sorbitol)

TAIWAN

Kiehl's Taipei Store

No. 97 Fu Shin Road

Taipei, 105

Taiwan

+88 6227125005

UNITED KINGDOM

Charles H. Fox Ltd.

22 Tavistock St., Covent Garden

London WC2E 7PY

United Kingdom

Email: Makeup@charlesfox.co.uk

www.charlesfox.co.uk

+44 (0)20 7240 3111

Creature Effects

Unit 2, 549 Eskdale Rd.

Uxbridge Middlesex UB8 2RT

United Kingdom

Email: Creatfx@dircon.co.uk

+44 (0) 1895 251107

Mouldlife

Tollgate Workshop

Bury Road

Kentford

Suffolk

CB8, 7PY

United Kingdom

Email: Justin@mouldlife.co.uk

www.mouldlife.co.uk

+44 (0) 1638 750679

Screen Face

20 Powis Terrace

Westbourne Park Rd.

Notting Hill, London W11 1JH

United Kingdom

Email: Info@screenface.co.uk

www.screenface.com

+44 (0)20 7221 8289

The Makeup Shop

www.themakeupshop.co.uk

California

Cimuha, Inc.

Erwin H. Kupitz Wig Maker

Hair Goods by Teresa

Teresa Valenzuela

7618 Woodman Ave., Unit 1

Panorama City, CA 91402

WIGS

Germany

Fischbach-miller (wig-making supplies)
Email: Info@fischbach-miller.de
www.fischbach-miller.de

E&G Hair Goods
Gerhard A. Zeiss
Erwin H. Kupitz
Cologne
Germany
Email: gerdizwiss@aol.com (Gerhard)
Email: E&G@cimuha.com (Erwin)

WHO'S WHO

Makeup Artists: (Definition provided by the IASTE, Local 706)

Makeup Artists perform the art of makeup, which includes:

- Application of all moustaches, chin pieces, side burns, beards, false eyebrows and lashes.
- Application of any facial or body appliances, masks, etc., used in the art of makeup whether made of rubber, plastic, or any other material.
- All body makeup. (Except on Network Broadcasting productions, i.e. NBC, CBS, etc.)
- May apply wigs or toupees, or cut the hair on male performers.
- May also do hairstyling on Legitimate Theater and Opera productions.

Assistant Director (AD): An AD is a person who helps the Director in the making of a movie. The duties of an AD include setting the shooting schedule, tracking daily progress against the filming production schedule, logistics, preparing daily call sheets, checking the arrival of cast and crew, maintaining order on the set, rehearsing cast, and directing extras

First Assistant Director (First AD): The first AD is directly responsible to the Producer and "runs" the floor or set.

Second Assistant Director (Second AD): The Second AD creates the daily call sheets from the production schedule, in cooperation with the Production Coordinator. The Second AD also serves as the "backstage manager," liaising with actors and putting cast through Makeup and Wardrobe, which relieves the First AD of these duties. They supervise the Second Second Assistant Director, Third Assistant Director (Third AD), Assistant Director Trainees; the setting of Background (extras) are parts of the Second AD's duties.

Second Second Assistant Director (Second Second AD): The Second Second AD deals with the increased workload of a large or complicated production. For example, a production with a large number of cast may require the division of the aspects of "backstage manager" and the call sheet production work to two separate people.

Third Assistant Director (Third AD): The Third AD works on-set with the First AD, and may liaise with the Second AD to move actors from "base camp" (the area containing the Production, Cast, and Hair and Makeup trailers), organize crowd scenes, and supervise one or more Production Assistants (PAs).

Key Production Assistant (Key PA): The Key PA may have a number of duties assigned to them by the AD staff. A PA is the lowest on the crew's hierarchy in terms of salary and authority. They perform various duties required by the ADs. The subroles of Assistant Directors differ among nations. For example, the distinction between Second Second and Third AD is more common in North America. British and Australian productions, rather than having a Second Second AD, will hire an additional Second AD to fulfill the same duties. In Britain and Australia, Third ADs have different duties from a Second Second AD, and the terms are not synonymous.

TERMS

Calling the Roll: One of the First AD's responsibilities is to "call the roll"—when all of the relevant heads of department (HODs) and above-the-line people seem ready to perform, the First AD initiates the take. Over the years, special procedures have been developed for this task in order to achieve maximum efficiency during shooting, which is usually some variant on the following dialogue:

1. **"Waiting on . . ."** First ADs are constantly calling out which department is responsible for any delays. If the lights need to be adjusted, the First AD calls out, "Waiting on Gaffers." If the actors are still in their trailer, the First AD calls out, "Waiting on Talent." If a mascara smear needs attention, the First AD calls out, "Waiting on Makeup."

2. **"Last looks, please."** Once everyone is in place, and rehearsals and blocking have finished, the First AD calls out, "Last looks." This allows for last-minute finishing touches—whether to the Set,

to Hair and Makeup, to Lights, or anything else.

3. **"Quiet on the set."** The First AD calls out, "Quiet on the set" to alert everyone that the take is ready to be filmed.

4. **"Roll sound."** The First AD waits for complete quiet, then signals the Production Sound Mixer to "Roll sound," after which the Mixer rolls his sound gear, verifies its status, and replies, "Rolling" or "Speed."

5a. **"Roll camera."** The First AD then signals the camera department to "Roll camera." The camera assistant starts the camera, verifies its status by watching the timecode for three seconds, and replies, "Rolling" or "Speed."

5b. **"Lock it down."** Sometimes the First AD will also call out, "Lock it down" to ensure that all objects on the set are "locked down" and will not drop during the take. At this point, everyone must be totally quiet and move out of frame. This can also called when the camera is locked down. In some filming situations the camera body needs to be "locked down," not touched and no movement around the camera because the focus is critical or the stunt is dangerous so the camera is unmanned.

6. **"Marker."** The First AD signals the Clapper Loader, or Assistant Camera (Second AC), by saying, "Marker" or "Slate it." The Second AC marks the shot by clapping the clapper board, or slate, and announces the scene for editing purposes ("Scene 67, Take 4").

7. **"Action."** The Director says, "Action," although a First AD might perform this function if the Director prefers it. Only the Director is allowed to say, "Cut."

The Low-Budget First AD's Eternal Dilemma: On low-budget productions, the means are often not enough to realize the Director's vision. It is for the First AD to work between the Director and heads of department (HODs) to call the necessary compromises when they need to be made, without jeopardizing the integrity of the Director's vision. This process can begin as early as the scriptwriting phase, with the AD suggesting such practical compromises as combining sets or reducing the number of story days. The process may progress through to the actual shooting of a scene, at which time the AD may call for the Director and DP to refine the blocking of a scene in such a way that it can be adequately shot within the time available. This can be the most indirectly creative an AD gets, and may gain great understanding of the conflict between resources and vision. This can prove a useful skill to ADs who move on to Produce.

Script Supervisor, or Continuity: A Script Supervisor, or Continuity, is a member of a film crew responsible for maintaining the film's internal continuity and for marking the Production unit's daily progress in shooting the film's screenplay. In preproduction, the Script Supervisor creates a number of reports based on the script, including a one-line continuity synopsis providing basic continuity information on each scene. These reports are used by all departments in order to determine the most advantageous shot order and quantities of supplies, materials or

crew surport needed. Example: A character that wears a particular shirt that (in different scenes) progresses from clean to dirty to dirty and torn may require at least three sets of that shirt in order to ensure that continuity can be properly managed.

During production, the Script Supervisor acts as a central point for all production information on a film shoot, and has several responsibilities.

Script: The working text of the project. The Script Supervisor is responsible for ensuring that everyone involved has the most current copy of the script. Once the script is finalized, changes are made on a different color of paper. The Script Supervisor is given any changes, and ensures that they are printed on the correct color paper and distributed to all necessary parties. This will on many productions lead to a multicolor working script. The actual progression of colors can vary. One such progression is (starting with the original script) white, blue, pink, yellow, green, goldenrod, buff, salmon, cherry, tan, gray, and ivory.

Continuity: The Script Supervisor takes notes on all the details required to re-create the continuity of a particular scene, location, or action. The Supervisor is responsible for making sure that continuity errors do not happen. For every take, the Script Supervisor will note the duration of the take (usually with a stopwatch), and meticulously log off information about the action of the take—including position of the main actor(s), screen direction of their movement, important actions performed during the shot, type of lens used, and additional information

that may vary from case to
case. When multiple cameras are in use, the
Script Supervisor keeps separate notes on
each. The Script Supervisor will also keep
track of dialogue as it is spoken, and ensure
that if it varies from the screenplay, any
variation made is known to the Director and
noted.

Slating: The Script Supervisor interacts with
the Second Assistant Camera (Second AC, or
Clapper Loader) and the Production Sound
Mixer to make sure that each take of exposed
film has a consistent and meaningful slate,
that the sound and picture slates match. The
Script Supervisor also notes the sound roll
of each sync take, and the state of all MOS
takes (a film take without sound recording:
Metz out sound).

Lined Script: The Script Supervisor is
responsible for keeping the most current
version of the shooting script, and for
keeping a copy of it as the lined script for the
shoot. A lined script is a copy of the script
with vertical lines drawn down the pages,

indicating which takes cover which parts of
the script.

Production Reports: The Script Supervisor
is responsible for preparing daily reports for
the Production team. These reports vary in
form depending on the studio or production
company; however, they generally include a
continuity log; a log of the actual times that
shooting and breaks started and stopped;
and a breakdown of the pages, scenes, and
minutes that were shot that day—as well as
the same information for the previous day,
the total script, and the amounts remaining
to be done. Also included are the number
of scenes covered (completely shot), the
number of retakes (when a scene has to
be reshot), and the number of wild tracks
(tracks with sound recorded separately). The
AD staff also is responsible for preparing
daily productions reports regarding
scheduling and the crew, noting delays in
filming, scenes shot, and payroll (call times
and out times), as well as accident reports,
and actors times.

ANATOMY

Studies in anatomy are a complex field, but we'll concentrate on the areas Makeup Artists most likely will use as reference. The following terms outline only a few of the examples found in the skeletal, muscular and circulatory systems.

The Skeletal System: The skeleton is divided into two different areas. The axial makes up the skull, vertebral column, sternum, and ribs. The appendicular skeleton is made up of the upper and lower extremities. The skull is divided into cranial bones. These bones form the cranial cavity. The cranial cavity houses the brain and facial bones, which in turn form the face.

THE SKULL

Frontal Bone: Bone located at the forehead that helps define the orbits of the eye.

Mandible: Bone that forms the lower jawbone.

Maxilla: The upper jawbone.

Nasal Bones: There are two nasal bones. The vomer bone separates the nasal cavities.

Occipital Bone: Large bone that makes up the base of the cranium.

Zygomatic Arch: Bone that defines the cheekbone.

The Spinal Column: The spinal column is made up of 26 bones. The bones protect the spinal cord. The spinal cord is strong and flexible, allowing movement, supporting the head, and serving as the attachment for the ribs and muscles.

UPPER BODY

Carpal Bones: Wrist bones.

Clavicle: Collarbone.

Humerus: Upper arm bone.

Metacarpals: Hand bones.

Phalanges: Finger bones.

Radius: One of two lower arm bones. The radius is narrow at the end that connects with the humerus, and wider at the joints it forms with the wrist bones.

Ribs: Curved bones connected to the thoracic vertebrae.

Scapula: Helps to form the shoulder joint with the humerus.

Sternum: Breastbone.

Ulna: One of two lower arm bones opposite in shape to the radius.

LOWER BODY

Femur: Thighbone; it is the strongest bone in the body.

Fibula: One of two bones that form the lower leg bone. The fibula is smaller of the two.

Joints: When two or more bones come together to either aid movement and/or to keep the skeleton together.

Metatarsals: Foot bones.

Patella: Kneecap

Pelvic Bone: Attaches the lower body to the axial skeleton.

Phalanges: Toes.

Tarsals: Anklebones.

Tibia: One of two bones that form the lower leg bone. The tibia is the larger of the two.

The Muscular System: Muscles are described by size, shape, origin, and function. There are over 700 known muscles in the body.

FACIAL MUSCLES
JAW MUSCLES

Masseter Muscle: Raises the jaw and clenches the teeth.

Temporalis Muscle: Helps the masseter muscle to raise the jaw and clench the teeth.

MOUTH MUSCLES

Buccinator: Draws the corners of the mouth backward, flattens and tightens lips.

Caninus: Raises the corner of the mouth.

Mentalis: Raises and tightens the chin, thrusts lower lip up and outward.

Orbicularis Oris: Circles the mouth and purses the lips.

Risorius: Pulls the corner of the mouth sideward and outward.

Triangularis: Pulls the corner of the mouth downward.

Zygomaticus Major and Minor: Raises the mouth upward and outward.

EYE MUSCLES

Corrugator: Assists the orbicularis in compressing skin between the eyebrows. Vertical wrinkles form.

Orbicularis Oculi: Closes the eyelids and compresses the opening of the eye from above and below the eyes.

Procerus: Tightens the inner eye by wrinkling the skin on the nose.

FACE MUSCLES

Frontalis Frontal Part: Draws the scalp to the front, wrinkles the forehead, and pulls the eyebrows upward.

Platysma: Muscles on the neck that draw the lower lip downward and upward.

MUSCLES OF THE BACK AND ABDOMEN

Circulatory System and Veins: The circulatory system is made up of two different systems: the pulmonary (the right side of the heart receives deoxygenated blood from the body and pumps it to the lungs) and the systemic (the left side of the heart receives oxygenated blood from the lungs and sends it to the body; arteries carry blood from the heart to the tissues and organs; veins return the blood to the heart).

ARTERIES

Aorta: Largest artery in the body.

Brachiocephalic Trunk, Right Carotid, and Right Subclavian Arteries: Provide blood to the neck, head, and upper limbs.

Celiac Trunk, Superior Mesenteric Artery, and Inferior Mesenteric Artery: Supply blood to the abdominal internal organs.

Coronary Arteries: Supply blood to the heart.

Left and Right Common Iliac Arteries: Abdominal aorta divides into left and right common Iliac arteries.

Left Carotid, Left Subclavian Arteries: Provide blood to the left side of the head, neck, and upper limbs.

Renal, Suprarenal, and Gonadal Arteries: Provide blood to internal organs at the back of the abdominal wall.

THE VEINS

Brachiocephalic: One of two veins that form the superior vena cava.

Hepatic Portal Vein: Vein that leads from intestinal veins to the liver.

Inferior Vena Cava: Receives blood from the pelvis, abdomen, and lower limbs.

Internal Jugular: Receives blood from the head and neck area, including the brain.

Portal System: A set of veins that deplete blood from the intestines and the supporting organs.

Splenic Vein: Vein leaving the spleen.

Subclavian: Empties blood from the shoulder area.

Superior Mesenteric: Blood returns to circulation by way of the small intestine.

Superior Vena Cava: Receives blood from the upper body by way of the internal jugular, subclavian, and brachiocephalic veins.

ADDITIONAL TERMS

AD: Assistant Director

Adding color: Mixing pigments to a product.

Additive Color: adding primary Colors to come to white light.

Additive Color Mixing: Color mixing with lights.

Airbrush: A small air operated tool that sprays various media.

Air Regulator: To adjust the air pressure.

Alginates: Seaweed based products used to take an impression of an object or person.

Analogous: Colors next to each other on the color wheel.

Background: Background artists (actors) or extras working in a scene.

Black: Absence of all colors.

Blank Out: To start with a blank canvas.

Blending: applying Makeup using tools to achieve a smooth seamless finish.

Bloom: The strength or rigidity of the brand of Gelatin.

Bondo: Cobosil that is mixed with Pros-Aide to form a thick paste.

Brightness: Percentage of Transmission of the full spectrum of energy.

Bull Pen: Working the Line with many other Makeup artists painting for the crowds with little time to do it.

Cast: Actors appearing in the scenes.

Casting: A product that is used in a mold.

Center of Gravity: The point of the body that dictates where the weight is distributed.

CFM: Measurement of airflow.

Characters: Names of the characters the actors will be playing.

Chavant NSP Clay: Sculpting clay.

Chiaroscuro: An Italian term meaning light Dark. The term Originated as a type of Renaissance drawing on colored paper.

Chief Makeup Artist: What a Department head is called in Europe.

Closed set: Means there are no visters.

Complementary: Any colors 180 degrees apart on a 360 degree wheel.

Complementary Colors for Light: Complementary Colors are also called secondary Colors.

Contour: Darker Colors that are applied to any area the Makeup Artist wants to set back.

Correction Filters: To Balance a given light source.

Crew Call: Time the crew is called into work.

Cure: Chemical reaction between two ingredients when done Dark and Halftones: Halftones divided into light and dark.

De-mold: Taking the product out of the mold.

Digital Cinematography: When film is being substituted for Digital.

Digital Motion Pictures: Images that are captured on digital Formats. In this case Motion Pictures

Digital Photography: Images that are captured with electronic devices that record the images.

Digital Television: Pictures and sound are received by digital signals.

D/N: Means Day or Night on a call sheet.

Dominate Wavelength: Apparent Color of the Light

Dot Method: placing dots instead of straight lines in Makeup application. For example to create a stronger lash line.

DP: Director of Photography

Dual Tone: A pigment that changes hue from mass tone to top tone.

Extra: Back ground actor or Back ground artist.

Foundation Primers: Even out the texture of the skin.

Gaffer: Lighting Designer

Gel Filters: Filters are used in front of a light source to change what the light is putting out.

Gelatin: A colorless protein formed by boiling the skin, bones, and connective tissue of animals used by Makeup artists for a variety of reasons such as Casting in a mold.

Green Marble: A Makeup sealer.

Half tones: All of the Value variations

High-Definition Television or HDTV: Television broadcast using higher resolution formats.

Highlight: Lighter Colors that are applied to any area the Makeup artist wants to stand out.

Holding and Catering: Where the extras are being held and where the food is.

Hue: Any Color

Imaginary axis: An imaginary axis used by artists to determine where the weight of the body changes.

Licensed Aestheticians: Someone learned in the study of Skin Care.

Makeup Department Head: In charge of designing and running the department.

Mass Tone: Color right out of the tube or pure powder pigment.

Mattifying Products: Products that are made to take down shine.

Moisture Filter: Removing water from air.

Monochromatic: Any color mixed with white.

Oil Filter: Removing oil from air.

Opaque: Dense like a rock

On The Clock: Official time of payment.

Primary Color: Three Primary colors that can be mixed together to make all other colors.

Pros-Aide: A prosthetic adhesive.

PSI: Measurement of air pressure, pounds per inch.

Purity: The Purity of color is similar to chroma.

Rays: Ultra Violet Rays of UV.

RCW Color Wheel: Don Jusko Color wheel is one in which every color has an opposite color to be mixing neutral darks.

Reflected Light: light source that bounces off the surrounding environment.

Releases: Products that help to release a product from a mold.

Removers: Products that come in many different formulas used to remove adhesives, eye Makeup, or a variety of Makeup applications.

SC: Scene numbers in the script.

Secondary Colors: Colors made by mixing together two primary colors.

Secondary Colors in Light: Combination of two primary Colors.

Set Call: The time stand in's and background actors report to the set.

Shadow: When a form turns away from the light source, half tones become darker until the light completely goes away.

SPF: Sun Protection Factor.

Spot Paint: Technique to balance out the skin tone.

Stippling: To use an up and downward motion while applying makeup with a brush, sponge, or textured sponge.

Stipple sponges: Textured sponges used for different stippling effects.

Superior Mesenteric: Blood returns to circulation by way of the small intestine.

Swinging: caused by the center of gravity being shifted from one leg to another.

Textures: the surface properties of a color.

Thinners: Thinners are products made to thin adhesive products.

Tints: Adding white to any hue.

Top Tone: adding white to a color.

Translucent: Milk is translucent. Milk can never be transparent by adding a clear medium.

Transparent: Dye that are clear.

Triadic: Any three colors that are 120 degrees apart on the wheel.

Undertone: Adding clear media.

UVA Rays: Penetrates the surface of the skin and damages the connective tissue.

UVB Rays: Causes damage to the surface of the skin such as burning.

Vertical axes: The centerline that correctly defines proportions of the facial features when the head is moved in different angles.

Value: Means Tonal Value for an object

White: The presence of all colors in the light.

Working out of your Kit: term used by Makeup artists to describe what products will be used from their own Makeup Kit.

Wrap: Term called by the Assistant director at the completion of the days filming.

RECOMMENDED BOOKS AND TRADE JOURNALS

Books

Art of Makeup, The, by Kevyn Aucoin

Atlas of Clinical Dermatology, by Anthony du Vivier

Atlas of Clinical Gross Anatomy, by Kenneth P. Moses, John C. Banks, Pedro B. Nava, and Darrell Peterson

Atlas of Pathophysiology, by Lippincott Williams and Wilkins

Beauty of Color, The, by Iman

Bloom Book, by Li Edelkoort and Lisa White

Body Painting: Masterpieces, by Joanne Gair and Heidi Klum

Brown Skin, by Susan C. Taylor

Clinical Dermatology, by Thomas P. Habif

Color Atlas of Forensic Pathology, by Jay Dix

Costuming for Film: The Art and The Craft, by Holly Cole and Kristin Burke

Crew Freelancing 101: A Guide to Building a Career in Film and TV Production, by Gena Seif

Cyclopedia Anatomicae, by György Fehrér and András Szunyoghy

Digital Cinematography, by Paul Wheeler

Don't Go To The Cosmetics Counter Without Me, 6th ed. by Paula Begoun

Face Forward, by Kevyn Aucoin

Fine Beauty, by Sam Fine

Forensic Pathology, by David J. Williams, Anthony J. Ansford, David S. Priday, and Alex S. Forrest

Milady's Skin Care and Cosmetics Ingredients Dictionary, by Natalia Michalun and M. Varinia Michalun

Milady's Standard: Fundamentals for Estheticians, by Joel Gerson, Shelley Lotz and Janet D'Angelo

Skin Care Beyond the Basics, by Mark Lees

Vintage Face, by Angela Bjork and Daniela Turudich

Magazines

Make-Up Artist Magazine, www.makeupmag. com

Make-Up Artist International, www. makeupinternational.eu

Web Sites

www.airbrushmakeup.com

www.anatomical.com

www.badgerairbrush.com

www.beautyhabit.com

www.benefitcosmetics.com

www.bennye.com

www.blincinc.com (lash primer)

www.bluescreen.com

www.bobbibrowncosmetics.com

www.Brushupwithbarbara.com

www.burmanfoam.com

www.cinemasecrets.com

www.clinique.com

www.cosmeticmall.com

www.creativeartistryfx.com

www.dangheno.net

www.Danielamakeup.com

www.dhccare.com

263

www.dickblick.com

www.dow.com (product information)

www.eefx.com

www.eeyelash.com

www.flaxart.com

www.folica.com (brushes, tools, etc.)

www.fxwarehouse.com (products)

www.gerdaspillmann.com

www.getspfx.com (adhesive information)

www.hollynorth.com

www.imancosmetics.com

www.imdb.com (professional film site for
production information, résumés)

www.immune.com (chemical reaction
information)

www.indeutsch.com (brushes)

www.joeblasco.com

www.kanebo.com

www.kd151.com (blood products, effects)

www.kettcosmetics.com

www.kiehls.com

www.lancome-usa.com

www.lauramercier.com

www.loraccosmetics.com

www.maccosmetics.com

www.makeupartistschoice.com (brushes)

www.makeupcreations.com (brushes)

www.makeupforever.com

www.makeupmania.com

www.mallatts.com (products)

www.marshallelectronics.com

www.mehron.com

www.monstermakers.com

www.occmakeup.com

www.oshunsupply.com (oils, chemicals,
clays, salts, botanicals, etc.)

www.paascheairbrush.com

www.paintandpowderstore.com

www.pauladorf.com

www.paulwheelerbsc.com (HD cameras,
crews, technical information)

www.ppi.cc

www.psdaimaandsons.com (brushes)

www.realcolorwheel.com

www.rickysnyc.com (beauty supply,
NYC)

www.ronjo.com (products)

www.screamteam.com (masks)

www.screenface.com

www.sculpt.com

www.sephora.com

www.shopofhorrors.com (effects)

www.smooth-on.com

www.solomakeup.com (brushes)

www.temptu.com

www.vwr.com (international chemical
supplies)

www.worldwidebeautystore.com

DARLA ALBRIGHT

Emmy Award winner and Makeup Artist Darla Albright has worked on numerous TV, film, and music industry events. Her credits include the Academy and Emmy Awards, department heading, and working on the hit TV series *Scrubs, Justice, That '70s Show, General Hospital, Ghost Whisperer,* and *The Riches.* Her film work includes *The Good Girl,* starring Jake Gyllenhaal; *Dr. Dolittle 2;* and working with Tyra Banks on *Coyote Ugly.* Darla has also toured the world with her personal client Neil Diamond for all of his stage, TV, and personal appearances. Currently, Darla is also working as a collaborator for Air Craft with Kris Evans.

CRISTINA PATTERSON CERET

Born in Madrid, Spain, Cristina Patterson Ceret came to Los Angeles at the age of 1. Cristina was introduced to the film industry by her mother, Raffaelle Butler, a Hollywood Makeup Artist. Following her mother's example, Cristina dived into makeup for motion pictures. In 1995, she joined Professional Vision Care Associates as a Contact Lens Technician. In 2002, Cristina was promoted to Special Effects Coordinator. She is now designing and painting contact lenses for film and television, and prosthetic lenses for patients. Cristina is an accomplished, self-taught painter in fine arts. She is always working to find new ways to paint contact lenses.

RICHARD DEAN

Richard Dean has painted some of the most unforgettable faces in the world—including Nicole Kidman, Uma Thurman, Madonna, Eva Mendes, Amber Valletta, Demi Moore, Glenn Close, Diane Lane, Tom Cruise, Michael Douglas, and Bruce Willis. Richard has collaborated with Julia Roberts on 16 movies—from *Sleeping With the Enemy* and *My Best Friend's Wedding* through *Erin Brockovich, Closer,* and, most recently, *Charlie Wilson's War.* Richard's first movie experience was on the tiny independent film *Union City,* starring Deborah Harry. Currently, he is shooting *Baby Mama* with Tina Fey in New York. With a master's degree from the University of Michigan focused on theatrical design, Richard began doing makeup in the fashion and print arena before moving on to television, then 50-some features—among them *Desperately Seeking Susan, The Cotton Club, Something Wild, Fatal Attraction, Mona Lisa Smile,* and *Hitch.*

KENNETH DIAZ

When Kenny Diaz was young, his father would go all out for Halloween. He would make Kenny and his younger brothers very elaborate costumes. That paved the way for Kenny to make his own costumes for kids in the neighborhood, even winning an award for his efforts. Who knew that would lead to an exciting career working extensively as one of the top Makeup Artists in the motion

265

picture industry today? Kenny has two Academy Award nominations and is a two-time Emmy Award winner. He is Founder of K.D. 151 Blood Products, which is an Industry Standard. Kenny had a special interest in pyrotechnics after watching a television special on the subject. He inquired about pyrotechnics classes at schools located in the Los Angeles area. He enrolled in a makeup school, finding no other avenues that could help him. This included classes in Salon Makeup! By the end of the one-year course, Kenny knew he would become a Makeup Artist for the entertainment industry. He continued his career working for student and independent films such as *Roar,* starring Tippi Hedren and her daughter Melanie Griffith. After the film completed, Diaz became an instructor, developing the skills and confidence that have contributed to his success today.

DANIELA ESCHBACHER

Daniela Eschbacher is one of today's newest Makeup Artists. She lives in Paris, and works for international magazines and commercials in places such as Switzerland, Germany, Sweden, Holland, England, Austria, and Japan. She started out assisting various artists before branching out on her own projects with Photographers, Stylists, and independent movies. Daniela has always been fascinated by photography, fashion, and the creation of illusion. After graduating from Economy High School, she went to Vienna to become learned in Hairdressing and acquire a degree. At the age of 20, Daniela moved to Paris and attended an international artist's school. By this time, she

had already started to work with established Makeup Artists and Hairstylists. Daniela's work has been featured by such publications as *Make-Up Artist Magazine.*

KRIS EVANS

For over 20 years, Kris Evans has created unique makeup designs in the world of entertainment. Kris has worked on everything from *Saturday Night Live* to large production films, creating characters in such movies as *X-Men: The Last Stand* and *National Treasure.* She has also used her skills on Broadway in *The Phantom of the Opera.* Kris is used to traveling worldwide in the NBC Olympic broadcast team or for couture runway shows and fashion shoots. Evans is Founder of Air Craft Cosmetics with partner Darla Albright.

KIM FELIX-BURKE

Kim Felix-Burke grew up in the film business. She wanted to be a fashion illustrator but her stepfather, Ed Levy, a successful film producer, suggested that Kim try makeup instead, reasoning that "Painting a face is just another form of a canvas." This sent Kim off to basic training at the Joe Blasco School in Los Angeles. Kim was fortunate to continue her education in makeup by working for some of the great "old timers" in Hollywood. Twenty years later she still loves "slinging dirt" and "primping pretty faces." Kim lives in the Los Angeles area with her family.

DAN GHENO

Dan Gheno teaches and lives in New York City. Professor Emeritus at the Lyme

Academy College of Fine Arts in Old Lyme, Connecticut, he lectures and teaches at The Art Student League and the National Academy School in New York City. Dan has been featured in numerous national and international publications, including *American Artist, Drawing,* and *Drawing Highlights.* Dan Gheno studied at Santa Barbara Art Institute, Art Students League, and National Academy of Design. His work is featured in exhibits nationally and in the collections of several museums.

STEVEN HORAK

Steven Horak graduated with degrees in Vocal Performance from Washington State University and the Cincinnati College-Conservatory of Music, intending a career as an opera singer, but always having an interest in and an affinity for the field of theatrical makeup and wigs. Steven began singing for Detroit's Michigan Opera Theatre in the old-man roles often assigned to young bass-baritones, "doing my own makeup in all cases, as no real makeup department existed." Observing that he appeared to have some talent in this area, the company offered to pay a large portion of his tuition to the San Francisco Opera Wig and Makeup Training Program, on the condition that he return to MOT and establish a department for them. After receiving his certificate from the program, which was led by SFO's Wigmaster, Richard Stead, he fulfilled my commitment to MOT and returned to Detroit to accept the staff position, which he held for 12 seasons. During the off-season, he represented several wig and makeup companies (Theatrical Hairgoods Co., Bruce Geller Associates, and Tom Watson Associates) at opera companies across the nation, including the Greater Miami Opera, Opera Co. of Philadelphia, and Opera Theatre of St. Louis, among many others. He also began building his own wig stock and client list, which included Chicago Opera Theatre. In 1994, a staff position in the Makeup Department at the Metropolitan Opera was offered. He continues to do wig rentals and wig building, most notably for Studio EIS, a company in Brooklyn which fabricates realistic human figures to museums across the U.S., including the recent, extensive exhibit illustrating the life of George Washington at Mount Vernon, Virginia. He also takes one summer opera job in the NYC area each year, where he hones his skills at cranking out full makeups, including wig application, in 10 to 15 minutes, recalling his early days "on the line" at SFO.

DON JUSKO

Don Jusko was an artist before art college. After college in 1962, during the Cuban Crisis, Don was a part of Naval Photo Squadron VFP-62, based in Jacksonville, Florida. After four years in the navy, he worked as the Art Director for an advertising agency in Jacksonville. He then opened his own agency in San Francisco. For the past 30 years, he has been painting Maui scenes on location, capturing the island's history. Don's work continues to be admired by all. While painting on location with his own choice of transparent primary pigments, the Real Color Wheel was born. By 1996, a printed copy was being sold on the internet. Today, his color site garners 1.7 million hits a month, with free printable downloads of his color wheel. This color wheel has given artists the ability to paint natural-looking dark shadow colors by mixing real color oppositions together and not using black pigment.

ERWIN H. KUPITZ

Erwin Kupitz is a professional Hairstylist, Wig Maker, and Makeup Artist, with more than 25 years of experience in the fields of opera, theater, film, media, and management. He has been the owner of the wig-making business Custom Made Hair Goods for the past 12 years. Erwin is the President and Founder of Cimuha, Inc., which has been in operation for the past three years. He is also the Designer of Hair Replacement, EHK, for the hair-replacement company J.A. Alternatives, Inc., located in New York and New Jersey. Erwin completed his education and corresponding apprenticeships in Germany. In addition, he has expanded his professional training by attending workshops and seminars at various institutions in the following fields: Special Effects Makeup, Hair Coloring, and Modern Hair Cutting techniques. Erwin's professional affiliations include membership in the Chamber of Handcrafts, Germany, and the IATSE Local Makeup Artists of Hollywood. Erwin embarked on his career in Europe, and from 1982 to 1992 held the positions of Makeup Artist, Principal Makeup Artist, Wigmaster, Vice Department Head, and Department Head in performing-arts productions ranging from the Bavarian State Opera and Theatre in Munich, Germany, and the Royal Opera in Belgium to the Salzburg

Festival in Austria. From the onset of his professional work in the United States in 1992 to the present, Erwin has had a prolific career that has encompassed the following: 59 major motion pictures (including Academy Award–winning films *Forrest Gump*, *Titanic*, and *Dreamgirls*), 22 television shows, and eight stage productions. Erwin received Emmy nominations in 1994–95 for Outstanding Achievement in Hairstyles for a Mini Series (*In Search of Dr. Seuss*, TNT), and in 1998–99 for Outstanding Achievement in Makeup for a Television Series (*Buffy The Vampire Slayer*, FOX TV). The list of accomplished actors that Erwin has worked with include Academy Award winners, screen legends, and contemporaries such as Jack Nicholson, Shirley MacLaine, Warren Beatty, Sir Anthony Hopkins, Angelina Jolie, Anthony Quinn, Diane Lane, Michael Caine, Patrick Stewart, Gene Hackman, Diahann Carroll, Edward Norton, Plácido Domingo, Jane Seymour, Hugh Jackman, Andy Garcia, James Woods . . . and the list goes on and on. Erwin's body of work reflects his flexibility to traverse the diverse media of the performing arts with a degree of technical expertise and professional experience that future Makeup Artists and Hairstylists can respect and aspire to in their own careers.

BRADLEY M. LOOK

Emmy-winning for *Star Trek: Voyager* ("Threshold" episode) and eight times nominated, Makeup Artist Bradley Look has written numerous articles on makeup, including co-writing the book *Star Trek Aliens & Artifacts*. Born in Peoria, Illinois,

Brad now lives in Southern California, where he works in the entertainment industry. Besides teaching The Art of Film and Television Makeup at national and international universities, Brad has worked on productions such as *Pirates of the Caribbean: At World's End, The Santa Claus 3: The Escape Clause, Boston Legal, Poseidon, Star Trek: Deep Space Nine, Star Trek: Voyager,* and *Star Trek*—just to name a few.

GIL MOSKO

Gil Mosko, President of GM Foam, Inc., created GM Foam in 1987 to meet the needs of the Makeup Artist for a more-user-friendly foam latex. Gil Mosko has numerous awards, including 10 Emmy nominations, and five Emmy Awards for Outstanding Achievement in Makeup for a Series. He was also Director of the Star Trek Makeup Lab. Mosko has developed foam latex, which has become the standard of the industry. He started his career with a major in Environmental Biology and a minor in Chemistry at the University of Colorado. From there, he worked at Mattel Toymakers for two years as a designer in the Preliminary Design Department. For the next 15 years, Gil owned and operated Gil Mosko Pottery and worked as Director at R&D Nearly Me Corp., holding patents for revolutionary designs for prostheses for mastectomy patients.

MATTHEW MUNGLE

Academy Award and Emmy Award winner Matthew W. Mungle is regarded as one of Hollywood's premier Makeup Special Effects Artists. With over 100 film and television projects to his credit, Matthew has earned accolades and recognition as one of the industry's top masters of makeup illusion. Born in Durant, Oklahoma in 1956, Matthew was one of five children. As a boy, he was fascinated by makeup. Matthew credits the film *7 Faces of Dr. Lao* as a factor in him deciding to become a Makeup Effects Artist. In 1978, Matthew applied to and was accepted into Joe Blasco's Makeup Center, the premier academy responsible for training many of the film and television industries' elite Makeup Artists. Matthew's impressive list of film, television, and theater credits include the box office hits *The Perfect Storm, Bedazzled, The Polar Express, The Omen, X-Men, The X Files, CSI: Miami, Six Feet Under, The Fast and the Furious,* and the Broadway hit *Wicked*—just to name a few. Matthew, Founder of W.M. Creations, Inc. along with John E. Jackson, has developed products for the Makeup Artist that no one should be without. Matthew wanted to give the working Makeup Artist a chance to create and buy products he would use himself. Matthew continues to educate and influence new Makeup Artists today worldwide.

KENNY MYERS

Nominated twice for Emmy Awards and Department Head on the Academy Award–nominated picture *Star Trek VI: The Undiscovered Country*, Kenny Myers has mastered many projects and has had many successes over the years. Kenny graduated from William Paterson College in 1976 with a master's degree in Communication Arts-Theatrical Design. In 1976, Kenny moved to Los Angeles and began to work as an apprentice to Chris Walas. During the past 20 years, Kenny has been involved with many pictures, including: *The Prestige, X-Men: The Last Stand, War of the Worlds, Collateral, The Last Samurai, Home Alone, Star Trek, Back to the Future Part III, The Return of the Living Dead,* and *Austin Powers: The Spy Who Shagged Me.* In 1999, Kenny, in conjunction with his company Cine Makeup, Inc., created an effects makeup line of highly pigmented flesh tone inks called Skin Illustrator. Shortly after, Kenny teamed with industry manufacturer Premiere Products, Inc., and is continually expanding the product line. Kenny was truly honored when asked to become a member of the Academy of Motion Picture Arts and Sciences.

DINA OUSLEY

Over the past 15 years, Dina Ousley, President and Founder of Dinair Airbrush Makeup Systems, Inc., has guided and directed the development of a sprayable glamour makeup and glamour makeup application system. Of even more significance, during that time, she pioneered "the new art of airbrush makeup." The artistic makeup techniques she has developed go far beyond the boundaries of traditional application, and more fluently and vividly express the Makeup Artist vision. The new art of micropointillism makeup is a futuristic version of pointillism where one dot of color at a time is applied to depict images. The 15-year proving ground of the makeup and techniques have occured during her work as a Hollywood Makeup Artist. Over the past 20 years she has worked on

feature films, TV specials, national and regional commercials, music videos, and star still-photo shoots. Her Makeup Artist career followed her earlier career as a film and television actress.

CHRISTIEN TINSLEY

Christien Tinsley is an Academy Award–nominated Makeup Artist who grew up in Auburn, Washington. At the age of 21, Tinsley moved to Los Angeles after receiving his first job as an Effects Artist. Working at Steve Johnson's FX Shop, Christien developed a range of materials and was soon overseeing and supervising effects for several films. Tinsley's first union job was applying prosthetics to Clint Howard in *How the Grinch Stole Christmas.* Tinsley continued on to his next film, *Pearl Harbor,* which ultimately launched his signature product, Tinsley Transfers. Christien developed "prosthetic transfers" when creating the look for Jesus in *The Passion of the Christ.* Today, Tinsley Transfers, Inc. has emerged into a leading provider of tattoos and prosthetic transfers effects for some of Hollywood's biggest stars, including Brad Pitt, George Clooney, Vin Diesel, and Justin Timberlake. Tinsley accredits his influences to such individuals as Rick Baker, Greg Cannom, Steve Johnson, Rob Bottin, and Dick Smith.

JOSEPH N. TAWIL

Joseph N. Tawil is Founder and President of GAM Products, Inc., the Los Angeles–based theatrical lighting and special-effects company. He is a graduate of Carnegie

Mellon University, a fellow of the United States Institute of Theater Technology, and an associate member of the American Society of Cinematographers. Tawil has authored a dozen articles on lighting that have been published in industry trade journals. He often guest lectures at universities on the subject of color, and is a frequent speaker for the International Photographers Guild about color measurement. Tawil holds more than a dozen patents in the lighting field, and has created many special-effects and projection devices (including the patented Film/FX and SX4 film loop) that have become standard production tools for the entertainment industry. They include the first deep-dyed polyester color filter, the first off-the-shelf stainless-steel pattern, and Black Wrap, the original, for which he received an Academy of Television Arts & Sciences Award.

NANCY TOZIER

Nancy-Tozier went to Salem State University, majoring in Psychology. She attended cosmetology school in Massachusetts. In the 1980s, she owned her own spa and managed another spa with 22 styling chairs, heading the Makeup and Skin Care Department. Nancy graduated from the Catherine Hinds Institute in Woburn, Massachusetts, in 1989, valedictorian and winner of the Marietta Hinds Award. She has studied the art of skin tones, color theory, and skin care with mentors such as Glen Lockhart of Bion Research Skin Care, James Vincent, and Nancy Feliciano. Tozier is a respected educator and innovator.

PAUL WHEELER

Renowned Cinematographer, Director of Photography, and writer are only just the start of a list of titles that outline Paul Wheeler's career. He was twice nominated by BAFTA for a Best Cinematography Award, and has twice been the winner of the Indie Award for Best Digital Cinematography. Paul is the author of several popular books on cinematography. He also lectures at establishments such as The London International Film School and the Royal College of the Arts. He is a member of the Guild of British Camera Technicians, a Fellow of the British Kinematograph, Sound and Television Society, and a Member of the British Society of Cinematographers.

PATTY YORK

Patty York wanted to be involved in movie making since she was a little girl. Being a big dreamer, movies activated her imagination; she was a natural at creatively expressing herself. Patty worked as a commercial artist in her early years, moving to New York City working with fashion designers, all the while stimulating her lifelong obsession with the beauty industry. A need to generate more income in New York City sent Patty back to school to earn a degree in business. Patty became a "suit." The stagnation was killing her spirit and she craved and missed being creative; she woke up one day to realize this was not her! Time to put her brush strokes to a living breathing canvas. She apprenticed with several professional makeup artists in New York City, learning everything she could from them. She worked as a Print Makeup Artist before moving to Hollywood to pursue her dream. With additional training in the film industry to fine tune her instincts as an artist, she learned film techniques and set protocol. Today, Patty still lives in Los Angeles, and enjoys a successful career as a Makeup Department Head and Personal Makeup Artist to the stars!

International Alliance of Theatrical and Stage Employees (IATSE): Theatrical Stage Employees, Moving Picture Technicians, Artists, and Allied Crafts of the United States, its Territories, and Canada, AFL-CIO.

The IATSE is the labor union representing technicians, artisans and craftspeople in the entertainment industry, including live theater, motion picture and television production, and trade shows.

LOCAL 706: Makeup Artists and Hair Stylists
828 N. Hollywood Way
Burbank, CA 91505
Tel: 818-295-3933
Email: info@ialocal706.org
Web site: www.local706.org

LOCAL 798: Make-Up Artists and Hair Stylists
152 West 24th St.
New York, New York 10011
Tel: 212-627-0660

Abrasion wound, 207
AD, *see* Assistant director
Additive color mixing, 50
Adhesives
   facial hair, 151–152
   products, 243
   prosthetic makeup, 214–215
Aging
   Green Marble S e L r technique, 121–123
   overview, 120
   removal, 125
   repairs, 125
   stipple products, 243–244
   stretch and stipple, 121, 125
   stretching areas, 123–124
Airbrush
   all-in-one systems, 161
   beauty makeup, 165–167
   blusher, 170
   body makeup
      applying, 175–176
      cleaning of airbrush, 176
      preparation, 173–175
      removal, 176
      supplies, 174
      testing, 174
      touch-ups, 176
   characteristics, 156
   compressors, 159–160
   definition, 156
   eyebrows, 170
   eyeshadow, 168–169
   eyeliner, 170
   feeds, 157
   foundation, 168
   lips, 170
   makeup products, 162–164
   safety, 161–162, 176–177
   stencils
      applications, 167–168
      cleaning, 171–173
   tips, 164–165
   triggers, 156
   types, 157–158
Albright, Darla, 165, 263
Alginates, definition, 185
Allergy, 25
Analogous colors, definition, 39

Angled brush, 241
Animal bites, 207
Anthrax, 26
Antishine, products, 243
Arteries, 30, 255
Artist color wheel, 69
Assistant director (AD), definition and functions,
      251

Background
   checking, 232
   terminology, 231–232
   working with, 232
Badger bristle, 241
Balanced eyes, 12
Bald caps, 130–131
Beard, *see* Facial hair
Beauty makeup
   airbrush lesson, 165–167
   example of shoot experience
      design, 238
      kit, 238
      luxury hotel shoot, 239
      Madonna theme shoot, 239–240
      preparation, 237–238
      prepping of model, 238
      tips, 240
   overview, 95
   tips, 95–96
Black
   light, 49
   mixing, 44, 233
Black-and-white photography, *see* Photography
Blending, foundation, 78–79
Blood
   continuity considerations, 210–211
   lighting considerations, 208
   mouth blood products, 209–210
   physiology, 206
   simulation, 205–207
   viscosity, 208–209
Blue, mixing, 38, 43, 233
Bluescreen, 62
Blush
   airbrushing, 170
   brush, 241
   types and functions, 80
Boar bristle, 241

Body makeup
  airbrushing
    applying, 175–176
    cleaning of airbrush, 176
    preparation, 173–175
    removal, 176
    supplies, 174
    testing, 174
    touch-ups, 176
  overview, 101–102
Body
  center of gravity, 7–8
  drawing in motion
    angles, 8
    line of action, 9–10
    positive and negative space, 9
  proportions, 5–6
  torso triangle, 6–7
Box rental, *see* Kit fee
Brightness, 49
Bring it back to life, 91–92
Bristles, types, 241
Brow, *see* Eyebrow
Brow brush, 241
Brushes
  bristle types, 241
  cleaners, 243
  types, 241–243
Buccinator muscle, 29
Burn, types, 207–208

Cake makeup, types and functions, 75
Call sheet, interpretation, 219–223
Calling the roll, 252–253
Camera filters, types, 53–54
Caninus muscle, 29
Canned spray water, 88–89
Casting, definition, 185
Cathode ray tube monitor, 63
Ceret, Christina Patterson, 263
Chavant NSP clay, definition, 185
Cheek, aging makeup, 124
Chicken pox, 29
Children, makeup tips, 101
Chin, aging makeup, 124
Color compensating filter, 53
Color correction filter, 53
Color wheels, *see* Artist color wheel; Real Color Wheel
Complementary colors
  definition, 39
  types and use, 40–42, 44
Compound fracture, 207
Concealers
  brushes, 241–242

color theory, 89
  types and functions, 75, 77, 90
Conjunctivitis, 27
Contact lens
  costs, 127
  examples, 125–126
  fitting, 126–128
  irritants, 126–127
  ordering, 126
  scleral lenses, 127
  soft versus rigid, 127
  timing of placement, 127
Continuity
  blood considerations, 210–211
  makeup, 116
  script supervisor, 253–254
Contour brush, 242
Contours, foundation, 78
Core shadow, definition, 3
Correction filter, 50–51
Corrugator muscle, 29
Cream foundations, types and functions, 74–75
Cream to powder foundations, types and
        functions, 75
Crease brush, 242
Crow's feet, aging makeup, 123
Crowds, *see* Background
Cure, definition, 185
Cure inhibition, definition, 185

Dark halftone, 2–3
Day checking
  call sheet reading, 219–223
  commercials, 223, 228–229
  films, 218, 221, 228–229
  kit fee, 229–231
  makeup kits
    film set, 226–228
    overview, 223–224
    set bag, 225–227
    treatment products, 224–225
    working out of, 232–233
  overview, 218
  set chair, 228
  time card, 229
Dean, Richard, 64, 95, 112, 115, 263
Deep-set eyes, 12
Demolding, definition, 185
Design
  character design, 115–117
  development, 114
  inspiration, 113
  relationships with production members, 112–115
  script, 113

Diamond face, 11
Diaz, Kenny, 263–264
Digital video
    motion pictures, 61
    resolution, 61
    television, 61
Disinfection, workstation, 88, 108
Dominant wavelength (DWL), 48
Double fog filter, 54
Drawing
    body in motion
        angles, 8
        line of action, 9–10
        positive and negative space, 9
    lessons
        contour drawing, 14–15
        shadows, 15
Drug addict, makeup tips, 234
Dual tone, definition, 39
DWL, *see* Dominant wavelength

Elderly, *see* Aging
Emotion, *see* Facial expression
Enhancing filter, 54
Eschbacher, Daniela, 237, 264
Ethmoid bone, 19
Evans, Kris, 165, 264
Extras, *see* Background
Eyebrow
    airbrushing, 170
    blocking
        adhesive block, 117–118
        appliance block, 119
        waxing out, 118–119
    makeup types and functions, 81
    shaping, 97–98
Eye injury, 207
Eyelash comb, 242
Eyelids, aging makeup, 123
Eyeliner
    airbrushing, 170
    brush, 242
    types and functions, 79–80
Eyeshadow
    airbrushing, 168–169
    brush, 242
    types and functions, 79
Eye shapes
    balanced eyes, 12
    deep-set eyes, 12
    large eyes, 12
    round eyes, 12
    small eyes, 13
    wide-set eyes, 12

Face Chart, 116–117
Face shapes
    diamond face, 11
    heart face, 11
    oval face, 11
    round face, 11
    square face, 11
Face triangle, 5
Facial expression
    anger, 23
    disgust, 23–24
    enjoyment, 23
    fear, 23
    muscular control, 19, 23, 29–31, 256
    sadness, 24
    surprise, 23
Facial hair
    adhesives, 151–152
    beard stubble
        approaches, 149
        brush application, 151
        sample application, 147–149
    five o'clock shadow simulation,
        104–107
    hair ball method, 149–150
    lace cleaning after removal, 152–153
    Makeup Artist experience, 134–135
    masking tape technique, 139–142
    net lace method, 150–151
    template creation for full beard, 135–139
    texturizing, 153
    ventilated beard construction
        base, 142–143
        cutting, 143–147
        hair preparation, 143
        overview, 142
        ventilating, 143
Facial muscles, 19, 23, 29–31, 256
False eyelashes, 100–101
Fan brush, 242
Felix-Burke, Kin, 264
Fillers, types and functions, 75
First assistant director, definition and functions,
        251–253
Five o'clock shadow, simulation, 104–107
Flat brush, 241–242
Flesh tones, mixing, 42–44
Fluff brush, 242
Fluorescent light, 51
Fluorescent light correction filter, 54
Foam latex mold
    curing, 203
    demolding, 203
    making, 199, 201

overview, 197
painting, 203–204
safety, 201–202
Fog filter, 54
Foundation
airbrushing, 168
artist color wheel, 69
blending, 78–79
brushes, 242
color theory, 70–71
concealers, 75, 77
contours, 78
functions, 72–73
highlights, 77–78
mixing tips, 71–72
primers, 73–74
product comparisons, 76, 244
special needs, 72
types, 74–75
Frontal bone, 18, 28
Frontalis muscle, 39
Frostbite, 28
Furrow lines, aging makeup, 123

Gel filters
color wheel, 52
lesson, 57
types, 52–53
Gelatin mold
applying, 195–196
making
heating, 193–194
molding, 194
overview, 192–193
prepping, 194–195
material, 181, 192
painting, 196–197
Gheno, Dan, 2, 8, 264–265
Glamour makeup, 99–100
Goat bristle, 241
Graduated filter, 53
Gray, mixing, 233
Green, mixing, 39, 43, 233
Green Marble S e L r
aging technique, 121–123
definition, 185
Greenscreen, 62
Grooming equipment, 89
Gunshot wound, 208
Gypsum mold
making, 197–199
material, 197
prepping, 202–203

Hair, see Facial hair
Halftone
dark halftone, 2–3
definition, 2
light halftone, 2–3
HD, see High definition
Head
cranial bones, 18–19, 28
face triangle, 5
facial bones, 19
movement axes, 3–4
muscles, 19, 23
proportions, 4–5
Heart face, 11
Heat exhaustion, 28
Heatstroke, 28
Herpes zoster, 27
High definition (HD)
features, 60
makeup considerations, 60–61
monitors, 63–64
television, 61
Highlights, foundation, 77–78
HIV, see Human immunodeficiency virus
Homeless, makeup tips, 233–234
Horak, Steven, 91, 98, 265–266
Hue, definition, 38
Human immunodeficiency virus (HIV), 27

Illness, makeup tips, 234

Jaw fracture, 207
Jusko, Don, 4, 36, 42, 265

Kabuki brush, 242
Key production assistant, definition and functions, 251–252
Kit fee, 229–231
KRYOLAN Crystal Clear, definition, 185
Kupitz, Erwin H., 135, 149, 266

Lacrimal bone, 19
Large eyes, 12
Lash comb, 242
Latex, mold making, 180
LCD monitor, see Liquid crystal display monitor
Leukemia, 27
Lift, age reversal, 119–120
Light halftone, 2–3
Lighting
black-and-white photography, 54–56
camera filters, 52–53
color description terms, 48–49

color mixing, 49–51
gel filters, 51–52
lessons, 56–57
research by Makeup Artist, 48
Lips
aging makeup, 124
airbrushing, 170
brushes, 242
shapes, 13–14
Lipstick, types and functions, 81
Liquid crystal display (LCD) monitor, 64
Liquid foundations, types and functions, 74
Look, Bradley M., 26, 161, 171, 173, 176, 266–267
Low contrast filter, 54

Makeup Artist, definition and functions, 134, 251
Makeup Chart, 116–117
Mandible, 19, 28
Mascara, types and functions, 80
Mass tone, definition, 39
Masseter muscle, 29
Maxillae, 19, 28
McNeill, Daniel, 23
Melanin, 68
Men, see also Facial hair
Mentalis muscle, 29
Men
five o'clock shadow simulation, 104–107
makeup tips, 101
Mineral foundations, types and functions, 74
Mix ratio, definition, 185
Mold making
foam latex mold, 199, 201
gelatin mold
heating, 193–194
molding, 194
overview, 192–193
prepping, 194–195
general steps, 181–184
gypsum mold, 197–199
materials, 180–181
problems, 181
safety, 181
silicone mold
making, 186
painting, 188–189
terminology, 185–186
Monochromatic, definition, 39
Mosko, Gil, 197, 203, 267
Mumps, 27
Mungle, Matthew, 150, 267
Muscular system, 19, 21
Mustache, see Facial hair

Myers, Kenny, 121, 192, 196, 267–268
Myristate, definition, 185

Nail care equipment, 89
Nasal bone, 19, 28
Natural makeup, tips, 90–91
Neck, aging makeup, 124
Net filter, 54
Neutral density filter, 54
News anchors and reporters, makeup tips, 235
Nose fracture, 207

Occipital bone, 18, 28
Old age, see Aging
Opaque, definition, 39
Opposition colors, types and use, 40–42, 44
Orange, mixing, 43
Orbicularis ocul, 30
Orbicularis oris, 29
Ousley, Dina, 167, 268
Oval face, 11

Paddle brush, 242
Palettes, products, 245
Parietal bone, 18
Pax Paint, mixing, 36
Period makeup
1950s, 235
1960s, 235
1970s, 236
1980s, 236–237
Photography
black-and-white photography
filters, 54–56
makeup tips, 240–241
film types, 62
lighting, 51
Makeup Artist collaboration, 112–113
Pink, mixing, 43–44
Plasma screen, 64
Plastics, definition, 185
Platinum cure silicone rubber, definition, 185–186
Platysma muscle, 39
Pneumonia, 27
Polar screen, 54
Police officer, makeup tips, 234–235
Pony bristle, 241
Port-wine stain, features and camouflage, 26, 90
Pot life, definition, 185
Powder brush, 242
Powder foundations, types and functions, 75
Powder, products, 245
Primary color, definition, 38

Primers
    prosthetic makeup, 215
    types and functions, 73–74
Pro mist filter, 54
Procerus muscle, 39
Production report, script supervisor role, 254
Pros-Aide Bondo, definition, 185
Pros-Aide, definition, 185
Prosthetic makeup
    adhesives, 214–215
    molds, see Foam latex mold; Gelatin mold; Gypsum
        mold; Mold making; Silicone rubber mold
    painting
        foam latex mold, 203–204
        gelatin mold, 196–197
        silicone rubber mold, 188–189
    removers, 215
    skin primers, 215
    thinners, 215
    transfer of prosthetics
        applying, 190
        materials, 189
        on-set, 190–191
        prosthetic preparation, 189–190
        removal, 191–192
        skin prepping, 189
Psoriasis, features and camouflage, 26
Puff, 242
Pump brush, 242
Purity, color, 49
Purple, mixing, 233

Raccoon bristle, 241
RCW, see Real Color Wheel
Real Color Wheel (RCW), 36–37, 44, 69
Red, mixing, 38, 43, 233
Reflected light, definition, 3
Release agent, definition, 186
Removers
    products, 245
    prosthetic makeup, 215
    take down tips, 240
Reporter, makeup tips, 235
Retractable brush, 243
Rigid gypsum mold, definition, 186
Risorius muscle, 29
Rosacea, features and camouflage, 26
Round eyes, 12
Round face, 11
Rubella, 27

Sable bristle, 241
Safety, sanitation, 108
Scars, features and camouflage, 26–27

Schedule, Makeup Artist day, 85–86
Script
    breakdown, 64–65
    makeup design, 113
    supervisor functions, 253–254
Sealers, products, 245
Second assistant director, definition and functions, 251
Second second assistant director, definition and
        functions, 251
Secondary colors, definition, 38, 49
Setup, workstation, 87–89
Shadow
    definition, 3
    drawing, 15
Shock, 24
Sideburns, see Facial hair
Silicone rubber mold
    applying, 186–188
    making, 186
    material, 180–181
    painting, 188–189
    products, 244
Skeletal system
    chart, 20
    cranial bones, 18–19, 28, 255
    facial bones, 19
    lessons, 31
    lower body, 29, 255–256
    spinal column, 28
    upper body, 28–29, 255
Skin
    anatomy, 24, 25
    disorders, 26–28
    wound lesson, 31–32
Skin care
    Makeup Artist role, 86–87
    sun protection, 107–108
Skin tone warmer filter, 53
Slating, script supervisor role, 254
Slush casting, definition, 186
Small eyes, 13
Smallpox, 28
Smudger, 243
Snell, Richard, 121
Soft Sealer, definition, 186
Sphenoid bone, 19
Sponge, 243
Spot painting
    overview, 93–94
    steps, 94–95
Square face, 11
Squirrel bristle, 241
Stab wound, 207
Stage lighting, 51

Stencils, airbrushing
    applications, 167–168
    cleaning, 171–173
Stipple sponge
    five o'clock shadow simulation, 104–107
    preparation, 107
Stipple
    definition, 243
    old-age stipple products, 243–244
Subtractive color mixing, 49–50
Sun protection, 107–108
Synthetic bristle, 241

Take down, tips, 240
Tattoo
    cover-up
        quick and easy, 102
        steps, 103–104
    temporary tattoos
        applying
            colors, 213–214
            sealer, 213
            tattoo, 212–213
        maintenance, 214
        overview, 211
        removals, 214
        skin prepping, 211–212
Tawil, Joseph N., 48, 268–269
Tear products, 244
Teeth
    touch-ups, 130
    transformation, 128–130
    veneer care, 130
Temporal bone, 19
Temporalis muscle, 29
Tetanus, 27
Thinners, prosthetic makeup, 215
Third assistant director, definition and functions,
        251
Time card, 229
Tinsley, Christien, 103, 189, 211, 268
Tint, definition, 39
Tinted moisturizers, types and functions, 74
Top tone, definition, 39
Torso triangle, 6–7
Tozier, Nancy, 68, 70, 269

Translucent, definition, 39
Transparent, definition, 39
Traynor lift, 119–120
Triadic colors, definition, 39
Triangularis muscle, 29
Tuberculosis, 27

Ultra contrast filter, 54
Undertone, definition, 39
Unions, contacts, 271

Value, definition, 2
Vascular system, 19, 22, 30, 256
Veins, 30, 255
Vendors
    Asia, 249–250
    Australia, 248
    Canada, 248
    Europe, 249–250
    Mexico, 249
    New Zealand, 249
    United States, 247–248
Veneers
    care, 130
    fabrication, 129–130
    touch-ups, 130
Video lights, 51
Violet, mixing, 43
Vitiligo, features and camouflage, 27

Water-activated makeup, products, 245
Wet and dry brush, 243
Wheeler, Paul, 53, 60, 269
Whitescreen, 63
White
    light, 49
    mixing, 44, 233
Wide-set eyes, 12
Wigs, vendors, 250
Workstation, setup, 87–89

Yellow, mixing, 43
York, Patty, 116, 269–270

Zygomatic arch, 19, 28
Zygomaticus muscles, 29